BETRAYING
THE
NOBEL

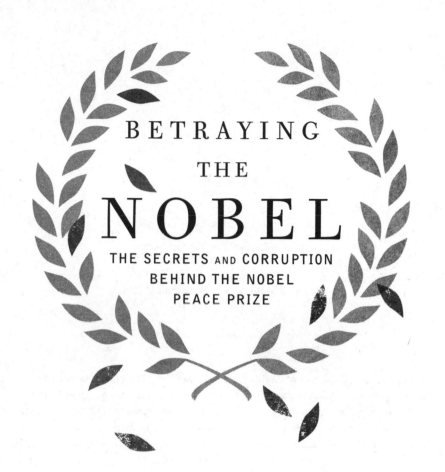

BETRAYING
THE
NOBEL

THE SECRETS AND CORRUPTION
BEHIND THE NOBEL
PEACE PRIZE

UNNI TURRETTINI

FOREWORD BY
MICHAEL NOBEL

PEGASUS BOOKS
NEW YORK LONDON

BETRAYING THE NOBEL

Pegasus Books, Ltd.
148 W. 37th Street, 13th Floor
New York, NY 10018

First Pegasus Books edition November 2020

Interior design by Maria Torres

Library of Congress Cataloging-in-Publication Data is available.
ISBN: 978-1-64313-564-9
10 9 8 7 6 5 4 3 2 1

Printed in the United States of America
Distributed by Simon & Schuster
www.pegasusbooks.com

FOR
AXEL AND ELLA

May your generation grow up to become the leaders our world needs.

CONTENTS

FOREWORD
BY MICHAEL NOBEL · ix

INTRODUCTION
PRIZE AND PARADOX · xiii

1 | ALFRED AND BERTHA   1

2 | COMMITTEE OF SECRECY   17

3 | NORWEGIAN EXCEPTIONALISM   37

4 | PEACE PRIZE IN A WORLD OF WAR   51

5 | INCONSISTENT CHOICES   67

6 | PISTOLS AMONG THE OLIVE BRANCHES   79

7 | DEVALUING WOMEN   97

8 | UNITED NATIONS: A LOVE AFFAIR   115

9 | POLITICAL CURRENCY   133

10 | ET SPARK I LEGGEN   145

11 | BANKER TO THE POOR   161

12 | GANDHI: OVERLOOKED AND DISREGARDED   177

13 | OVERLOOKED PEACE CHAMPIONS   193

14 | THE FASCIST, THE DICTATOR, THE ASSASSIN,
     & THE HEIR APPARENT   211

15 | LIFE AFTER THE PRIZE   231

16 | THE OTHER SIDE OF THE MEDAL   241

APPENDIX I
LIST OF NOBEL PEACE PRIZE LAUREATES • 255

APPENDIX II
ALFRED NOBEL'S LAST WILL • 259

ACKNOWLEDGMENTS • 263
NOTES • 265
INDEX • 277

FOREWORD
BY PROFESSOR MICHAEL NOBEL, PhD

—∽—

AS VICE CHAIRMAN and chairman for fifteen years of the Nobel Family Society and thus, in that position, the informal representative of the family, I had frequent and friendly relations with the former Executor Director of the Nobel Foundation, Michael Sohlman. We both shared the worldwide interest in the Nobel Prizes, of which the Nobel Peace Prize is the best-known and is recognized internationally by the general population as the one the world refers to when they attempt to define what the Nobel Prizes are.

In reality, there were five prizes described in Alfred Nobel's will: peace, medicine, physics, chemistry, and literature. The prizes are commonly regarded around the world as the highest accolade which can be bestowed upon an individual, whether he or she is a scientist, writer, or peace activist.

Among those, the award for peace is often identified as *THE NOBEL*. It is by far the best-known prize internationally but is also the most controversial. The science prizes—physics and chemistry—as well as the so-called "Nobel Memorial Prize in Economic Sciences," which is the Swedish Central Bank's award in Economic Sciences to the Memory of Alfred Nobel that was created in 1968 and thus cannot be considered a true Nobel Prize, are chosen by the Swedish Academy of Science, while the medicine award is decided upon by another Nobel committee in cooperation with the Nobel Assembly, whose members are professors at the Karolinska Institute, a Swedish medical university.

The subjects and discoveries in these fields are usually beyond the understanding or knowledge of the general public so the choices generally do not cause any controversy, except maybe among colleagues of those who are fortunate to receive these awards. But the Norwegian Nobel committee has often selected candidates for the Peace Prize who were well known to the general public and mass media and therefore liable to invite critical comments and reactions.

The Norwegian Nobel committee has also expanded the concept of peace to include categories, which to the critical observer, have little or nothing to do with the original conditions of Alfred Nobel's will and intentions, and they also apear to have done very sketchy investigations into the qualifications of some of the selected candidates.

Betraying the Nobel points out and describes in detail such fallacies in past selections, showing that the choices often appear based upon political and national considerations of Norway since all committee members (except one, recently appointed) continue to be selected among former representatives of the main political parties in Norway.

Prize laureates in the past such as Henry Kissinger, Yasser Arafat, Rigoberta Menchù, and Kim Dae-jung have evoked strong negative comments and criticisms. Also, the selection of more recent laureates such as Barack Obama, Al Gore, Malala Yousafzai, Liu Xiaobo, and Wangari Maathai have caused strong negative reactions from a wide range of critics around the world.

These processes are well described in Turrettini's book. The committee's expanded peace concept, involving as it does environmental challenges, human rights activities and measures, as well as the laws for the protection of minorities and sexes, is a far cry from the conditions of Alfred Nobel's testament. In it he stated that the award should go to "the person who shall have done the most or the best work for fraternity between nations, for the abolition or reduction of standing armies and for the holding and promotion of peace congresses." He did not mention human rights or global warming and, in many people's opinion, the committee in this way has abandoned the true reasons for what Alfred Nobel intended to accomplish by his last will.

Betraying the Nobel performs a useful task through its description of the peculiar manner in which these choices were made, and the sometimes hazardous process or personal interests that led up to an unjustified selection of candidates. Some people, notably the Norwegian lawyer Fredrik Heffermehl, regard this as an abandonment of the conditions established by Alfred Nobel in his will specifically regarding the conditions of the prize. The underlying reasons for these reactions are clearly presented and well explained.

The book follows up with a chapter on Nobel Peace Prize laureates who, later in their careers and lives, appear to no longer embrace the attitudes and values for which they worked and won the Peace Prize as a result—most notably Aung San Suu Kyi in Myanmar.

Betraying the Nobel ends with a description of candidates such as Adolf Hitler and Joseph Stalin—whose nominations have been claimed to have been made in jest—as well as recommendations of what needs to be done in order for the Nobel Peace Prize to continue to be regarded as the foremost of its kind.

Betraying the Nobel constitutes a much-needed report on the background and past history of some of the Nobel Peace Prize laureates who, for a number of reasons, appear to be unqualified and the sometimes badly or insufficiently researched decisions leading up to their selection. In summary, this is an excellent book of reference for the critically minded individual.

INTRODUCTION
PRIZE AND PARADOX

—⁓—

NO OTHER PRIZE holds more prestige than the Nobel. An aura of admiration surrounds it. As 1984 winner Desmond Tutu put it, "No sooner I had got the Nobel Peace Prize than I became an instant oracle. Virtually everything I had said before was now received with something like awe." No other award is followed by just about every country in the world and commented on by just about every newspaper and television network.

However, the Nobel Peace Prize as we know it is corrupt at its core.

"The prize," former secretary and director of the Nobel Institute, Geir Lundestad, said to the Norwegian state television station NRK in 2014, "has not become renowned because the committee rewards the Red Cross and Nelson Mandela, but rather because of its controversial choices."[1]

Controversial choices are fine as long as the committee, as executors of Alfred Nobel's last will, sticks to his instructions. Nobel wanted the Norwegian Nobel Peace Prize Committee to select peace champions to act as role models for the rest of us. Naming someone a peace champion, then, is a risky business. First, the committee's choice may not be everyone's cup of tea or have the most convenient political leanings. Second, the committee cannot predict how a Nobel laureate will behave in the aftermath of the prize. What if the winner doesn't turn out to be the beacon of hope and inspiration the committee had hoped for? Thus, the committee must show courage and conviction in their choices, because history will reflect back to them—and their choices—making it all the more vital that the committee research their candidates properly.

"The Norwegian Nobel Committee," Lundestad said, "must dare to speak when others don't."

No matter how honorable his statement is, many, including Michael Nobel—the great grandson of Ludvig Nobel, Alfred's brother—believe the committee has created its own prize. A prize not necessarily with peace in mind, nor one that selects winners in accordance with Alfred Nobel's last will.[2]

Selecting winners who are clearly not peace champions creates distrust. But the Nobel Peace Prize, as an institution, isn't alone in this. Today, trust in leadership is also at a historic low in governments and corporations. Facebook's Mark Zuckerberg has repeatedly put profit above his customers' privacy concerns, most infamously by sharing user data with the now-defunct Cambridge Analytica political firm. This facilitated the spread of misinformation and propaganda on Facebook during elections everywhere in the world, including in the 2016 US presidential election. Investigations by the US Congress have shown that Facebook's ad tools can easily be fine-tuned to discriminate, including ad-targeting options that allow realtors to "narrow" their ads to exclude African Americans, Hispanics, and Asian Americans from buying or renting property. And recent reports show that Facebook was used by the military in Myanmar to post false stories about violence perpetrated by the Muslim Rohingya minority upon Myanmar Buddhists, in an attempt to justify the genocide committed on Rohingya citizens by the government.

Amazon's Jeff Bezos is another example of greedy leadership. For years, Amazon's warehouse workers and delivery drivers have dealt with brutal working conditions, including insufficient bathroom breaks, frequent and serious on-the-job injuries, requirements to report to work during severe weather and hazardous driving conditions, and wages so low that many employees are on food stamps. Most recently, Amazon has been accused of fighting against employee efforts to unionize. Meanwhile, Bezos remains the richest man in the world, even after giving up 25 percent of his Amazon stock in his recent divorce.

An increasing rage is spreading worldwide as lower- and middle-class citizens feel ignored, taken advantage of, and abused. The Yellow Vest protests in France started in November 2018, when about 280,000 people took to the streets in cities across the country to push back against a proposed tax increase, which—according to protesters—is part of a scheme run by President Emmanuel Macron and his government to favor the wealthy to the detriment of the lower- and middle-class population. The protests were ongoing until March 2020 when social distancing rules due to the COVID-19 pandemic forced the movement to a halt. As of this writing in June 2020, the Yellow Vests are starting to organize again. So far, at least ten people have died and thousands more have been injured. Protestors have vandalized landmarks such as the Arc de Triomphe, looted and defaced stores, and started fires. The demonstrations that erupted at the 2019 World Economic Forum in Davos, Switzerland, over corporate power and economic inequality, reflect that same rage. Asia has also seen uprisings. A movement of protests began in Hong Kong in June 2019, over an extradition bill to mainland China, which was feared to threaten Hong Kong's judicial independence and endanger dissidents. Although the bill was withdrawn in September 2019, the demonstrations continue as of this writing in June 2020, despite COVID-19 social distancing rules, demanding full democracy and an inquiry into police actions. Meanwhile, the Covid-19 pandemic continues to cause people around the world to fall grievously ill.

SIMILARLY, THE NOBEL Peace Prize Committee is showing an example of leadership that is divisive instead of unifying. Instead of making the bold choices our world needs, it has fallen into the temptation of power and politics. It has been swayed by popularity and fame instead of standing up for the true values of the Nobel Peace Prize—Alfred Nobel's intentions of peace and unity. As a consequence, unworthy candidates have been chosen and other, more deserving ones, including Mahatma Gandhi, have been ignored.

The committee's betrayal may not always have been intentional. Since Alfred Nobel's death in 1896, our societies have changed and so has warfare.

This book will examine how the committee has widened the scope of Nobel's prize and the inconsistencies that have led to criticism.

Before people and organizations are put on pedestals, especially one as lofty as the Nobel, it is imperative to examine what those pedestals rest on. Only then will we know the true worth of a prize.

By shining light on today's dysfunctions and proposing a solution, my hope is that *Betraying the Nobel* can be a catalyst for change, not only in the Nobel Peace Prize Committee, but for the rest of us to step up and become the peace champions our local—and global—environment needs.

BETRAYING
THE
NOBEL

ALFRED AND BERTHA

*I am a misanthrope and yet utterly benevolent, have more
than one screw loose yet am a super-idealist who digests
philosophy more efficiently than food.*

—ALFRED NOBEL

WHAT COULD TURN the inventor of dynamite into an icon of peace?
Love, perhaps? This man who called war "the horror of horrors, the
greatest of all crimes," invented dynamite, the most dangerous industrial
explosive at that time, which would occasionally be used as a weapon.

In his memorial address, Professor Tore Frängsmyr, director of the Center
for History of Science at the Royal Swedish Academy of Sciences, said, "It
was the idealist in him that drove Nobel to bequeath his fortune to those
who had benefited humanity through science, literature, and efforts to
promote peace."[1]

Some, including Albert Einstein, a recipient himself, believed otherwise. Einstein, who won the physics prize in 1921, gave a speech in 1945, after the United States dropped atomic bombs on the Japanese cities of Hiroshima and Nagasaki.

"Alfred Nobel invented an explosive more powerful than any then known—an exceedingly effective means of destruction," he said. "To atone for this accomplishment and to relieve his conscience, he instituted his award for the promotion of peace." Others also believed Nobel established the peace prize out of guilt. Author and poet August Strindberg said, "Nobel money—some say dynamite money."

Idealism or remorse as motivator? Einstein and others ignored the fact that Nobel was extremely proud of all of his inventions and believed they were of great use to humanity, according to Michael Nobel, the great-grandson of Ludvig Nobel, Alfred's brother. He is convinced that remorse was not a motivating factor for his great-granduncle's creation of the peace prize.[2]

Rather, and as I will attempt to show in this book, Alfred Nobel was inspired by a higher purpose to contribute to a safer and more peaceful environment for all. Even in his earlier days, he believed his invention of dynamite—although it was not intended to be used as a weapon—could assist in preventing war. Concurrent with his then-strong belief in the deterrent effect of arms, Nobel once said in a discussion with a weapons manufacturer in Paris, "War must be made as deadly to the civilian populations back home as it is for the troops on the front lines. Let the sword of Damocles hang over every head, gentlemen, and you will witness a miracle—all wars will be stopped instantly if the weapon is called bacteriology."[3] As we shall see toward the end of this chapter, Nobel changed his mind about the deterrent effect of arms. However, his statement, and somewhat extreme opinion, negates suggestions that his involvement in the peace movement was merely a way to justify his investments in the arms industry.

Although his intentions were pure, Nobel also recognized that people might not comprehend his work or reasons behind his inventions.

"There is nothing in the world which cannot be misunderstood or abused," Alfred Nobel wrote to Bertha von Suttner, the love of his life and a major influence in his decision to establish the prize.

Dynamite was never created to be used in conflict. According to Michael Nobel, "Dynamite was not practical to use as a weapon. It was only meant to be used as an explosive building roads and tunnels. Nitroglycerine was completely unstable until Alfred made it safe."[4]

Understanding Nobel's intentions is crucial in order to evaluate the work of the Norwegian Nobel Committee whose job it is to select the Nobel Peace Prize winners. Intentions point to values, and without understanding and clearly defining those of Alfred Nobel, the committee can hardly execute his last will. To understand Nobel's values, we need to go back and look at his life.

Born in Stockholm on October 21, 1883, Alfred Bernard Nobel was the fourth son of Immanuel Nobel and Andriette Ahlsell. His family was one of engineers, descending from Olof Rudbeck, the best-known technical genius of Sweden's 17th century era as a great power in Northern Europe.[5]

Immanuel Nobel, also an inventor and engineer, left Sweden when Alfred was a child to build a successful business of manufacturing machine tools and explosives in Saint Petersburg. Yet young Alfred was raised in poverty. His mother managed, with the help of her family, to open a small grocery store in order to provide for her children after her husband left for Russia. Once Immanuel had established his business in Saint Petersburg, he sent for his family.

Finally, their living conditions improved, and the Nobel children were taught by private tutors, a sign of social status. By the time Alfred was seventeen, he spoke Swedish, Russian, English, French, and German fluently. Alfred had a wide range of interest and talents. Not only did he excel in chemistry and physics, he was also interested in literature and poetry. Alfred's father disliked his interest in literature and sent his son abroad to Sweden, Germany, France, and the United States to further his training in chemical engineering. Of all the places he visited as a young man, Alfred preferred Paris. There, he learned from the famous chemistry professor Théophile-Jules

Pelouze and, a turning point in his career, worked with Ascanio Sobrero, the young Italian chemist who invented nitroglycerine.

Nitroglycerine, a highly explosive liquid produced by mixing glycerine with sulphuric and nitric acid, was considered too dangerous for any practical use. It would explode in an unpredictable manner if subjected to heat or pressure. Nobel became fascinated with nitroglycerine and was determined to find a way to make it safe enough to be used in construction work. He returned to Russia in 1852 to work for the family enterprise, which was booming because of weapons orders from the Russian army, and he put all his efforts into developing nitroglycerine as a commercially useful explosive.

"SAFETY POWDER"

Attempting to stabilize nitroglycerine came at a cost. Manufacturing and transporting the substance caused several accidents at the Nobel family factory, and many workers died. Alfred Nobel took these accidents hard, but when his younger brother Emil was killed, he was dewvastated. However, he couldn't let his brother die in vain. Instead of giving up, the disasters only made him more determined to make nitroglycerine safe.

Finally, after years of hard work and tenacity, Nobel managed to create a more stable fluid form of nitroglycerine in 1863 that he named "blasting oil." Accidents during the manufacturing and transportation of his invention continued, nevertheless. After major improvements to stabilize the blasting oil, Nobel finally patented "Dynamite or Nobel's Safety Powder" in 1867.

Nobel borrowed the name dynamite from the Greek *dynamis*, meaning power, and added the oxymoron "Safety Powder," which is indicative of the duality that defined his life and career. His patent reads: "My new explosive, called dynamite, is simply nitroglycerine in combination with a very porous silicate, and I have given it a new name, not to hide its nature, but to emphasize its explosive traits in the new form; these are so different that a new name is truly called for."

Soon he was known in Germany as the Dynamite King (*Der Dynamiten-könig*). He had managed to both master the detonation process and find a safe way to transport his blasting oil without diminishing its power. By the end of the 1860s, he had opened dynamite factories in Sweden, Germany, Norway, Finland, and Austria; soon he had also opened in England and France.

His progress met with numerous hindrances. On the one hand, people wanted to copy his formula, and Nobel was constantly being pulled into legal disputes about patent infringements. On the other hand, he was criticized for bringing a hazardous product into the world. He was routinely blamed for accidents by the press, who called him "devil in the guise of a man," "merchant of death," and "mass murderer." Nobel cared what people thought of him and felt responsible for the deaths of his brother and all the other workers. Perhaps because he felt there was some truth in it, the negative publicity wounded him deeply and drained his strength. It also angered him. He once declared that, "lice are a sheer blessing in comparison with journalists, these two-legged plague microbes."[6]

The truth is, dynamite did facilitate violence. Indeed, assassins made use of this new and manageable explosive. In Russia in 1881, Tsar Alexander II was killed during a drive through the center of Saint Petersburg by the explosion of a dynamite-filled bomb. A year earlier, the tsar had barely escaped an attempt on his life when dynamite exploded underneath his dining room in the Winter Palace.

Some, including those in favor of the Russian tsar, thought dynamite made it too easy for revolutionaries to commit such terrorist acts. Others, such as Strindberg, in a poem from 1883, described Nobel as the man who had given the masses a chance to pay back the creator of gunpowder, Berthold Schwartz, who had made it possible for the aristocracy to maintain power:

> You Schwartz, a small deluxe edition, finely bound
> just for the nobles and the princely houses meant!
> Nobel! A budget-priced paperback, easily found
> since hundreds of thousands into the world were sent!

Strindberg called Nobel "the deliverer of ammunition to assassins."[7]

Some, such as General Henry du Pont, the head of Du Pont de Nemours, feared that dynamite would become a much more powerful alternative to gunpowder, which was Du Pont's business. Perhaps in an attempt to scare his customers from beginning to purchase from Nobel, he said, "It's just a question of time how soon a man who uses nitroglycerine will pay with his life."[8]

Nobel intended his invention to be used in large infrastructure projects such as railroads, roads, bridges, and tunnels where explosives would be essential. The early days critics would soon realize the utility of Nobel's invention. When Du Pont came to terms with the fact that dynamite was here to stay, his factory started manufacturing and selling Nobel's invention throughout the world. In fact, Du Pont was the main manufacturer of dynamite in the United States until the 1970s.

The construction of the Saint Gotthard Tunnel through the Swiss Alps was done using Nobel's dynamite. So was the Corinth Canal in Greece, as well as the Central Pacific Railroad in the United States.

A MAN ALONE

Even as his peers were criticizing him, and more sinister and rogue uses of his invention were made clear, Nobel pushed forward with an astounding work capacity. Instead of backing down, he continued with his business, he developed his empire, and he opened more factories.

An inventor, industrialist, and administrator, he worked to safeguard his patent rights, develop products, and establish new companies throughout the world, most of the time without any assistance. And this was before the internet or even the telephone. As an entrepreneur, according to professor Tore Frängsmyr, Nobel was "unbeatable."

He also dealt with all the people suing and criticizing him, but never apologized for his inventions.

"His life was hectic and stressful," according to Frängsmyr.[9] He pointed out that in letters Nobel wrote from Paris, he complained of being constantly hounded by people or, as Nobel put it, "pure torture."

People were crazy, he declared. Everyone wanted to see, interact with, and listen to him. Nobel wasn't interested in fame or fortune. He had dedicated his life to his inventions and to improving society, and he just wanted to be left alone to do his work.

Yet he still remained sensitive to what other people thought, and he attempted to change his public image by lecturing, visiting mining villages, giving demonstrations of the use of dynamite, and writing letters to newspapers. But he was also honest about the risks involved with explosives, and wrote, "Nobody should expect that an efficient blasting substance will become available to the general public without loss of lives."[10] Yes, Nobel was a man alone. He had sacrificed a lot for his mission, including his younger brother. He knew very few people with whom he could really talk. He had been in love once as a young man, and that woman had died. He did have a few friends, among them author Victor Hugo, who described him as "Europe's richest vagabond," because he moved around relentlessly.[11] After years of hectic traveling and working to set up his business and selling dynamite, Nobel decided to settle down in Paris in 1873. Having developed a love for Paris as a seventeen-year-old student, he wanted this glamorous city to be the center of his operation. At forty years old, he was a successful inventor, salesman, and businessman. He wanted to continue running his business, cultivate his admiration of French literature, and maybe even find love.

ENTER BERTHA

Nobel started searching for a comfortable house, and he found one at number 53 Avenue Malakoff. In this luxurious home, he had everything but a woman with whom to share it. It even had a greenhouse, "a winter garden," full of orchids, one of Nobel's passions. He imported a pair of the finest horses, another one of his passions, from Saint Petersburg for his carriage. As he had set up his business so that he no longer needed to constantly travel (he called his business trips "dynamite travel"), his life became predictable, and he felt lonely.

His house was frequently used for entertaining business relations, but Nobel didn't enjoy these superficial gatherings. He preferred to work alone in his laboratory, coming up with new inventions, rather than to socialize. At the end of his life, he held 355 patents. When feeling too isolated, he would walk to a nearby bistro and eat a simple dinner shared only by his most private thoughts.

However, he was aware that his self-imposed, emotional isolation bore risks.

"Unfortunately," he wrote, "it is true that in our life one who withdraws from educated society and neglects the interchange of ideas with thinking human beings finally becomes incapable of such interchange and loses respect for himself as well as the respect of others, which he had formerly earned and enjoyed."[12]

Not wanting to lose respect for others or himself, Nobel wanted someone to share his life with, but he realized that there were obstacles to overcome. First, Nobel's own notes make it clear that he thought himself too unattractive to arouse feelings of passion in a woman.

Always dressed in a dark suit with a white shirt and necktie, Nobel was short, pale, and unfit. By forty, he had already begun to walk with a slight stoop. Some said it was difficult to imagine he had ever been young. His dark brown hair turned gray at an early age, and he wore a neatly trimmed beard, as did most men of his time.

Second, he had a rather low esteem of the French women and their role in society.

"Personally I feel that the conversation of the Parisiennes is among the most insipid there is, while communication with educated and semi-emancipated Russian women is exquisitely pleasant," he wrote in a letter to his brother Robert. "Unfortunately, they have an antipathy to soap, but one cannot ask for everything."

Third, he also seemed to avoid placing himself in a position of emotional dependency. In a letter to his sister-in-law, Edla, he described himself as "a nomadic condemned by fate to be a broken shipwreck in life," and that he voluntarily excluded himself from "love, happiness, joy, pulsating life, caring and being cared for, caressing and being caressed . . . "

Maybe he was afraid that marriage would cost him his ability to run the Nobel enterprises. Although he didn't travel like before, his business and new inventions took up most of his time. He wrote that he was prepared to pay the high cost of solitude. Yet his unmarried state was not completely by choice. In a letter to his friend and colleague Alarik Liedbeck, he wrote, "Like others and perhaps more than others, I feel the heavy weight of loneliness, and for years I have been seeking someone whose heart could find its way to mine."

During a visit to Vienna in 1876, he decided to look for a woman to help him organize his life. He wanted someone to do more than fulfilling simple tasks such as copying letters and filing. He wanted a life partner, a wife. His advertisement in a Viennese newspaper read: "Wealthy, highly educated, elderly gentleman seeks lady of mature age, versed in languages, as secretary and supervisor of household."

This is how he met Countess Bertha Kinsky, who later became Bertha von Suttner and the first woman to win the Nobel Peace Prize. The beautiful thirty-three-year-old was a member of one of the oldest aristocratic Austrian families, but they were not rich, and she was required to work. With her education, skills, and aristocratic manner, she found a position as a governess to the children of the wealthy von Suttner family. The family's young son, Arthur, fell in love with Bertha, but the Baroness von Suttner opposed a marriage between her son and Bertha, seven years his senior, not only because of the age difference, but because of the inadequate dowry Bertha would bring. It was she who found Nobel's advertisement in the newspaper and convinced Bertha to apply for the position to get her away from her son.

Nobel was impressed by Bertha's handwriting and elegant choice of words, but he was probably also attracted to her beauty and the fact that she was unmarried. Although she was poor, Bertha's bearing and manner of expression were undeniably upper class, and Nobel was quickly convinced that she was more than qualified for the job. After a few letters back and forth, they soon came to terms, and Bertha left for Paris. Nobel waited for her train at the Gare de l'Est, and as soon as she arrived, they went by horse carriage to the Grand Hotel on Boulevard des Capucines, where he had reserved a suite for her while his house at Avenue Malakoff was being remodeled.

Bertha was pleasantly surprised by her new employer. "Alfred made a highly agreeable impression," she later wrote. "The 'elderly' gentleman the ad had prepared me for was nothing like the man I met: born in 1833, he was then forty-three years old, somewhat under average height, with a dark full beard, his face animated only by a mild glance from his blue eyes, his voice showing more melancholy than cynicism. Alternately sad and humorous—that was his nature. Little wonder Byron had become his favorite poet."

Their first meeting was a success for both of them. According to Bertha's diary, they had breakfast in the dining room of the hotel, and then they went to his house at Avenue Malakoff. After visiting his home, they continued their lively conversation in the Bois de Boulogne, a beautiful, massive public park on the western edge of Paris.

"Because of all the letters we had exchanged," Bertha wrote to her mother, "we did not feel as though we were strangers to each other."

Alfred, who was usually introverted, had an easy time talking to Bertha, and he even described his inventions and experiments to her. He also explained that, "I would like to invent a substance or a machine so frightfully effective and devastating that it would forever make wars altogether impossible."[13]

Bertha was still a few years from her crusading work for peace and her book *Lay Down Your Arms* (*Die Waffen nieder*, originally published in German in 1889), but she probably paid close attention to the Dynamite King's tales. She wrote in her memoir that much of Nobel's conversation centered on means of destruction, but that he ultimately believed that their true function was in peaceful activities, not for military purposes.

From that first day, Alfred was convinced that in Bertha he had found an equal intellectual and the perfect company. Bertha was also delighted.

"To speak with him about the world and people, about life and art, about problems of the moment or eternal problems, was an exquisite pleasure."

Although she enjoyed his company, she didn't love Alfred like she loved Arthur. Bertha must have realized that Alfred needed someone to care for him, someone who could be much more to him than a skilled secretary. It could not have come as too much of a surprise when a couple of days later, during lunch in the Bois de Boulogne, he asked her if her heart was taken. She explained as tactfully as she could that, in fact, she was engaged to Arthur von Suttner and had only temporarily broken it off because of his mother. She had responded to Alfred's advertisement, she said, to be financially independent.

Only a week after she arrived in Paris, Nobel had to travel on urgent business, and when he returned, Bertha had packed her things and returned to Vienna. She had sold a piece of family jewelry to pay for her hotel room, despite the fact that Nobel had intended to take care of her expenses. Only a couple of weeks later, she and Arthur von Suttner were married without his parents' consent. Ten years would pass before Arthur and his family had reconciled, and the couple moved into the family estate at Hartmannsdorf.

AN ARROGANT AND GENEROUS CITIZEN ACTIVIST

Alfred Nobel was heartbroken. Through his own writing, it was clear that Bertha remained his great love for the rest of his life. He also felt embarrassed and was convinced that he could never get any woman to love him. Then Nobel met Sofie Hess, who was selling flowers at a market in Austria. Although he was captivated by Sofie's beauty, she was no match for Bertha. Alfred was condescending and quick to point out her flaws.

"Sometimes I feel that your dog Bella acts with better judgment than you," he wrote in a letter. "At times you can bubble over with high spirits and be mischievous or lovely, but sensible—never! What you are lacking, so much the pity, is an understanding of the feelings and efforts of another human being. Yet that is where the secret of how to win someone's heart lies. It is truly woman's greatest virtue. But it presupposes a refinement and culture, which you are totally lacking."

And in another letter, "Our views of life—on the need for constant mental improvement, on our duties as human beings with a higher education—are so hugely different that we should never attempt to understand each other in these matters. It is with great pain that I draw the conclusion that my own nobility of soul has withered away, and, my head bowed in shame, I am stepping out of the circle of educated persons."[14] Still, despite his lack of respect for Sofie, Nobel kept seeing her and supported her financially for years. Sofie made him feel less lonely and she enjoyed his generosity. However, he never wanted to make the relationship official by marrying her. Ultimately, perhaps because she was tired of waiting for a commitment, Sofie cheated on Nobel and had a baby with another man. Only then did Nobel break off their relationship. He felt betrayed, not only by the fact that Sofie had gotten pregnant by another man, but because she was pretending to be Nobel's wife and claiming the baby was his.

"Sometimes I have a feeling that your family believes that my generosity and tolerance stem from pure stupidity," he wrote. "Imagine if I were poor and your family rich. Do you believe they would lend me a single kreuzer without interest or interest on interest? If you believe they would, you do not know them as well as I do . . . " Still, Nobel kept sending Sofie a generous allowance for the rest of his life and provided for her in his will.

Nobel's arrogance lived alongside his brilliance. But despite his flaws, he did not lack generosity, toward Sofie or anyone else. Success brought endless requests for donations from every corner of the world. Nobel gave, but he felt the demands tiresome.

"Each day the mail brings at least two dozen applications and requests for money amounting to at least 20,000 crowns (then approximately US $4,000)," he wrote. "That makes seven million crowns annually, which is why I must state that it would be better to have a reputation for being miserly than for being generous."

There were exceptions. A woman who worked for his household was getting married, and Nobel asked her what she would like for her wedding present. She amazed him by saying without hesitation, "As much as Monsieur Nobel himself earns in one day." Impressed and amused, Nobel agreed. The young woman received a monetary gift of 40,000 francs, the equivalent of US $110,000.[15]

Nobel wanted his money to come to mean something, and he wanted to help people, which is why he gave his fortune to different good causes in his last will. True to his wish to improve society to give people a chance, Nobel often helped people with potential and passion. In a letter to Bertha von Suttner, he once wrote, "there exists no eraser as for blackboards. I don't ask where their fathers were born, or what Lilliputian god they worship; helpfulness—the right kind—recognizes no national borders and seeks no confessions."

A DECLARATION OF LOVE

Was the peace prize inspired by Bertha von Suttner? She certainly maintained an influence over Nobel. He and Bertha kept in touch over the years, and they exchanged numerous letters. She was one of the few people in Nobel's life to whom he could speak honestly and freely. She became an avid crusader for peace, and they regularly conversed about issues relating to war and peace in their letters.

Nobel did have a passion for these issues before he met Bertha, but her work for peace and her peace association—not to mention his continuing love and admiration for her—stimulated his interest further. After he read her book *Lay Down Your Arms*, which had met worldwide success, he wrote her a heartfelt letter in April 1890:

> *Dear Baroness, Dear Friend,*
> *I have just finished reading your masterpiece. It is said that there are two thousand languages—which is 1999 too many—but surely your remarkable work must be translated into all of them. It ought to be*

read and reflected upon by each and everyone. How long did it take you
to compose this marvel? You will have to answer that question when
next I have the honor and the pleasure to press your hand in mine—
the hand of an amazon who so valiantly wages war against war . . .

Although the Dynamite King had become a member and donor of her
peace association—he even attended her Peace Congress in Bern in 1892—
he did not at first agree with her strategies of disarmament to obtain peace.

Once on a boat trip with Bertha and her husband during the Bern
congress, Nobel admired some of the large villas on the shore of the Swiss
lake. He said the money behind them was "spun by many little silkworms."

She responded sharply that, "dynamite factories are surely more profitable
than silk mills but definitely less innocent."

To which he quickly replied, "Perhaps my factories will end war quicker
than your congresses."[16]

Again, Nobel confirmed that he was not apologizing for inventing dynamite, nor was his will written out of guilt. Perhaps his competitive nature
and his ambition to prove himself played a part in his motivation for creating
the peace prize. As if he wished to move from Dynamite King to Peace King.
They may not have agreed on the strategy at first, but Nobel and Bertha did
agree that peace was a worthy cause.

LAST WILL

At fifty-four years old, this is how Nobel described himself:

"Alfred Nobel—pitiful creature, ought to have been suffocated by a
humane physician when he made his howling entrance into this life. Greatest virtues: keeping his nails clean and never being a burden to anyone.
Greatest weaknesses: having neither wife and kids nor sunny disposition
nor hearty appetite. . . . Important events in his life: none."[17]

With no wife or children with whom to share his success, Nobel was
lonely and miserable.

"He was a great entrepreneur and businessman," Michael Nobel confirmed, "and one of the richest men of his time, but he was unhappy."[18]

Nobel admitted in letters to relatives that he was afraid of dying alone and that his sacrifices and inventions wouldn't matter after he was gone. He drafted several wills before he finally signed the last one in 1895 at the Swedish-Norwegian Club in Paris. As it turned out, he had dedicated a big part of his fortune to the person who had "done the most or the best work for the brotherhood of nations and the abolishment or reduction of standing armies, as well as for the establishment and spread of peace congresses."

The words Nobel used might as well have been Bertha's. He may have changed his mind about the deterrent effect of arms, but he hadn't changed what was in his heart for Bertha.

He immediately informed her of its content, which was congruent with everything Bertha stood for. She was greatly touched.

"Whether or not I am still alive by then does not matter," she responded. "What you and I have given will live on."

In 1896, Nobel died at the age of sixty-three with only a servant present during a visit to his grand Italian home in San Remo overlooking the Mediterranean Sea. He wasn't surrounded by a wife or family. But he had managed to pass on his love of humanity and hope for a more united and peaceful world through his life work and last will. Although his last words didn't specifically express Nobel's values, his life and philanthropic endeavors, especially once he met Bertha, displayed his desire for peace, and for his peace champions to uphold a love of humanity, have the courage to stand up to greed and selfish leadership, and do work that unifies people through peaceful means.

In 1905, almost a decade after his death, the Norwegian Peace Prize Committee honored his values and awarded the prize to Bertha. She was the fifth recipient and first woman to receive Nobel's prize. His last will, and indeed the prize itself, is an undying love letter to Bertha and to humanity. The Norwegian Nobel Peace Prize Committee, however, would not always follow in his track in the years to come.

2

COMMITTEE OF SECRECY

It is not sufficient to be worthy of respect in order
to be respected.
—ALFRED NOBEL

NOBEL THOUGHT LONG and hard on what should become of his fortune after his death. He had no immediate family, and he wanted his money to continue to espouse a positive legacy. He wrote three wills and signed the final one on November 27, 1895, at the Swedish-Norwegian Club in Paris. Written in Swedish, the will contained fewer than one thousand words, or four handwritten pages.

Much in the same way he ran his business, doing most of the work himself without delegating, he wrote his will as a general outline of his intent rather than a detailed and meticulous document, which would cause issues when it came to actually enacting his wishes. The first issue with his will was he did not ask the different institutions beforehand if they would be willing to take on the tasks he willed to them. Unlike an agreement, a will is binding only for the party who signed it and cannot be forced upon the bequeathed. A single refusal could possibly have invalidated the will.

There were also complications with liquidating Nobel's properties and bringing the money back to his native Sweden. Nobel was domiciled in France and his assets were spread all over Europe. Liquidation meant paying taxes to the country where the property was situated, which would have reduced the amount to his charitable causes. Nobel's main executor, a young Swedish engineer named Ragnar Sohlman, wrote, "Had [Nobel] in any way conceived that the house in Paris could be viewed as his legal domicile, he would have shipped the stocks and bonds out of the country, just as we did. While he was alive, he constantly transferred the stocks and bonds from one place to another."[1]

Finally, and as expected, the will was contested by disappointed relatives, business partners, officials, employees, and other interested parties. Even King Oscar II, who disliked the fact that large amounts of money would end up leaving Sweden (this was after Sohlman had managed to bring Nobel's assets home to Sweden), encouraged Nobel's family members to "quash" it. According to Fredrik S. Heffermehl, former Norwegian supreme court judge and author of *The Nobel Peace Prize: What Nobel Really Wanted*, the king believed Nobel had been the victim of "misguided visionaries and misconceived internationalism."

Thanks to Sohlman's efficiency, intelligence, and initiative, the assets were transferred to Sweden and not taken by tax authorities in different countries. Nor were they consumed by lawsuits and attorneys' fees. To honor Nobel's will, Sohlman negotiated with estate managers, Nobel's heirs, the institutions that would confer the prizes, and with Swedish authorities. All of this took time. In 1900, four years after Nobel's death in 1896, the Nobel Foundation was set up in Stockholm to administer the prizes, as a result of these negotiations. Five years passed from Nobel's death until the first prizes were awarded in 1901 in the fields of physics, chemistry, medicine, literature, and peace.

WHY NORWAY?

Other than a small part of his fortune bequeathed to a few close to him, including nephews, nieces, friends, servants, and his former girlfriend Sofie Hess, Nobel wrote that, "The capital, invested in safe securities by my executors, shall constitute a fund, the interest on which shall be annually distributed in the form of prizes to those who, during the preceding year, shall have conferred the greatest benefit on mankind."[2]

This interest was to be divided into five equal parts. The first was for the most important discovery or invention in the field of physics. Another for the most important chemical discovery or improvement. Also awarded were outstanding achievements in physiology or medicine, literature, and finally, "to the person who shall have done the most or the best work for fraternity between nations, for the abolition or reduction of standing armies, and for the holding and promotion of peace congresses."

This last part has become what we today call the Nobel Peace Prize. Knowing what we know about Nobel's pride in his inventions and his belief in the deterrent effect of weapons, the last phrase of the will is a nod to Bertha von Suttner, who was an avid spokesperson for disarmament and strongly believed in peace congresses.

Every year on December 10, the date of Nobel's death, the prizes are given out. The Peace Prize, in accordance with Nobel's will, is the responsibility of the Norwegian Storting, or parliament. All the other prizes were kept in Sweden to be given out by Swedish nonpolitical institutions. The science prizes in physics and chemistry are administered by the Swedish Academy of Science, while the prize in medicine is awarded by the Karolinska Institute, a Swedish medical university. The Swedish Academy, which is in charge of the literature prize, was engulfed in a sexual assault scandal in 2017, which forced it to postpone the 2018 award.

A testament where one bequeathed most of one's fortune to charity was unusual at the time. In addition to the excluded relatives, Nobel's will was subject to much agitation and public discussion. His choice of Norway was especially unsettling, and many questioned why that country had been selected for something as prestigious as the peace prize. And by a Swede no less. Although Nobel didn't share his reasons, Scandinavian history might shed some light.

First, Norway was far behind Sweden in the areas of science, medicine, and literature, so it wasn't logical to put it in charge of those prizes. That left the peace prize.

The second reason was political. From 1814 through 1905, Norway was governed by Sweden. This so-called union with Sweden as the dominant partner was formed when Denmark—after having ruled over Norway for more than four hundred years—ceded Norway to Sweden in 1814. Having had no say in the matter, Norway was desperate to break free from this union. The bigger brother was not willing to let go. Many Swedes, including King Oscar II, felt that Nobel had insulted Sweden with his last will. Even though four of the five prizes were still in Sweden, they worried that Norway—the weaker party in this conflict—would gain power in the struggle between the two countries through the peace prize.

Nobel may not have intended a power struggle.

"I believe Alfred wanted to reinforce the union between the two countries," Michael Nobel said. "By giving the peace prize to Norway he was symbolically saying: we belong together in a peaceful alliance."[3] A third possible reason for Nobel's choice was a true wish for a more peaceful world. He wanted his money to have the greatest possible benefit to mankind. The Norwegian parliament had shown a strong interest in the European peace movement, and Norway was the first country to favor arbitration in international disputes.[4] Nobel also admired Bjørnstjerne Bjørnson, an influential Norwegian author, poet, and peace activist, who is famous for writing the lyrics to Norway's national song. Øyvind Tønnesson, historian and expert on the peace prize, suggested that Nobel might have feared the political aspect of the prize would diminish its significance.

"A prize committee selected by a rather progressive parliament from a small nation on the periphery of Europe," Tønnesson wrote, "without its own foreign policy and with only a very distant past as an autonomous military power, may perhaps have been expected to be more innocent in matters of power politics than would a committee from the most powerful of the Scandinavian countries, Sweden."[5]

Certainly, Nobel didn't want peace to be diluted by greed, selfish political leadership, or power games. Of all the European countries at that time, Norway must have seemed the most apolitical and impartial to Nobel, and one specifically focused on peace policies and agendas.[6]

No matter Nobel's reasons, the Norwegians were flattered and Parliament rapidly accepted the honor of awarding the prize. Perhaps Nobel's will contributed to Norway's confidence, because not long after, in 1905, it finally attained independence.

THE MIGHTY FIVE

Since 1901, the Nobel Peace Prize has been awarded by a committee consisting of five Norwegians elected by Parliament to sit on the Nobel Peace Prize Committee. Parliament, a unicameral legislature, consists of 169 members, elected by the Norwegian people every four years.

Each committee member is elected for a six-year term and can be reelected indefinitely. In the history of the committee, two members have served for thirty years. The members elect their own chairman and deputy chairman. Although the five committee members are responsible for the selection of a prize winner, they do not work alone. They are supported by the Nobel Institute, which was established in 1904 by the committee in accordance with the Nobel Foundation in Stockholm. The institute is situated in an elegant classical building at Henrik Ibsen Street 51, just behind the Royal

Palace. Its role is to aid the committee in selecting worthy prize winners and organizing annual events. Also assisting the committee are four permanent advisers, usually university professors in either history or political science. These are employees of the institute and answer to the director of the institute who also serves as secretary to the committee. The secretary's job is to give the five members guidance on Nobel's will and make sure the winner is selected according to the testator's intentions.

However, the role of director/secretary seems to have changed with the appointment of Geir Lundestad in 1990. Proactive and dynamic, Lundestad developed the annual prize-giving ceremony into a grandiose show, resembling the Grammy Awards. His goal was to put Norway on the map, and he has succeeded. The Nobel Institute has been transformed into an enterprise with considerable staff and operating costs, but also with a need for funding beyond the generous amounts granted by the Nobel Foundation.[7]

In 2005, Lundestad opened the permanent Nobel Peace Center in Oslo, a learning center boasting cutting-edge electronic technology and art. Delegations from all over the world, including the Museum of Modern Art in New York and Tate Gallery in London, have attended lectures and seminars held at the center. While these developments of themselves are positive, they also require substantial funding from the Norwegian government and businesses, which create doubts about the committee's independence.

Perhaps the success of his job went to Lundestad's head. He went from humble secretary to chair of a lavish business operation, and based on the way he presented himself and spoke on behalf of the committee, using the royal we, one might have mistaken him for a member—adding to the confusion about the Nobel committee's independence.[8]

"Lundestad has revolutionized the job and changed the position. Before, the secretary was more withdrawn," said Helge Pharo, professor in history and consultant to the Nobel Institute. The secretary's job is to stay in the background and offer guidance and support, not influence the committee's choices. Pharo added that the secretary's influence on the committee's decisions depends on the knowledge of the secretary. According to him,

Lundestad's knowledge and experience may have given him quite a lot of influence on the committee members.[9] However, Lundestad's knowledge combined with a big ego might have made him do more than that, tainting the idea of an independent committee. In Michael Nobel's opinion, Lundestad showed contempt for Nobel's vision of peace when he wrote in an October 17, 2007 *Aftenposten* article that, "the environment and climate, just like human rights, will soon be a natural part of the study."[10] Lundestad retired in January 2015, at seventy years old and after twenty-five years of service to the committee. The new secretary, Olav Njølstad, professor in history and philosophy and former research director at the Nobel Institute, seems to have taken the position back to its original form. In 2018, the concert in connection with the prize ceremony was canceled due to lack of corporate sponsors. Njølstad announced that there wouldn't be a concert in 2019 either. "We want to find a new concept we believe in and justify in terms of content, form, and finances," he said.

Even with a new secretary who seems to keep to his tasks, there are still reasons to question the committee's independence.

Although Nobel did not express in his will that the members must have political experience, the committee was filled exclusively with politicians until the 2013 election. One might argue that an interest in the peace movement should be a requirement for anyone wishing to become a member of the committee. This was expressed in several debates in Parliament and reflected the composition of the committee during its first decade in existence, up until World War II.[11] Bjørnson, a peace champion himself, is a perfect example. In 1903, there was a debate over a law professor's qualifications to become a member of the committee. What had the professor achieved in the service of peace to entitle him a seat on the committee other than being an expert in international law? asked one parliamentarian.

Back in those days, Parliament reflected on this question every time it was to fill the seats of the peace prize committee. After all, the committee's only job is to serve mankind by promoting peace. It is also supposed to be a body independent from Parliament and the government's politics.

The committee, however, hasn't always proven loyal to Nobel's will. Seeking allies right after its separation from Sweden, the Norwegian Nobel Committee selected Theodore Roosevelt in 1906. Roosevelt was more of a militarist, believing in the deterrent effect of arms, which was not in line with Nobel's intentions, and we will discuss Roosevelt in more depth in Chapter Four. When World War II ended in 1945, protecting Norway became even more important than world peace. The population expressed a strong sentiment of "never again an April 9," referring to the day in 1940 when the Nazis invaded Norway. From 1945, promilitary committee members were elected to the committee, and perhaps they were even encouraged to use their influence to serve Norway's political interests more than Nobel's intentions. The awards in 1945 and 1973, to Cordell Hull and Henry Kissinger, respectively, are frequently mentioned by Nobel historians as examples of the committee being motivated by a wish to strengthen ties with the United States during the Cold War.

By 1991, the Soviet Union had crumbled, the Berlin wall had fallen, and the Cold War was declared over. The threat of a possible attack by a foreign nation seemed distant. In 1999, instead of defending its border, Norwegian military forces under NATO were sent to fight abroad. By then, the committee's role as protector of Norwegian interests had become a habit. Additionally, in 1948, Parliament changed its role in electing members to the Nobel Peace Prize Committee. Ever since, a mathematical formula based on the previous election is used to award the winning political parties one or more seats on the committee. In principle, if a party got two-thirds of the parliament seats, it should also get two-thirds of the committee appointments. With a guarantee of a seat at the committee table, the winning parties of a parliamentary election are further discouraged to find and elect committee members who actually care about Nobel's wishes.

According to Heffermehl, since 1945, there has been a sharp deterioration in the quality of the committee members and their willingness to serve Nobel's last will.[12]

"The role of Parliament as such," Heffermehl wrote, "became an automatic, empty routine." According to Michael Nobel, the formula removes the prize further from Nobel's intentions.

"Parliament's task is to appoint those persons best able to sit on the committee—with regards to the objective of the prize," he said.[13] Instead of assuring the Nobel Committee's independence, the major political parties have used the prestigious seats on the committee to reward their own veterans.

Prior to 1935, the committee wasn't just reserved for civil servant veterans, it was filled with active politicians, which caused a conflict of interest on at least two occasions.

The prize of 1935—given in 1936—was awarded to Carl von Ossietzky, a German journalist, pacifist, and prisoner of the Nazis. The committee took a great risk with this award, as it went against Nazi Germany. Norway had been neutral during World War I, and the Norwegian government wished to remain impartial in future conflicts. Ossietzky, who was active in the German peace movement, warned in his writing that Germany was secretly rearming, which was in violation of the Versailles Treaty and Germany's own laws. For this, Ossietzky was sent to prison and then to a concentration camp, and although he had several opportunities to flee from Germany, he felt that his dissent would be more effective within the country than outside it. Ossietzky had a vast following campaigning for him to win the Nobel Peace Prize, but the Nazi government warned Norway that the prize would harm the relations between the two countries, and the Norwegian government did not wish to provoke Germany.

When the Nobel Committee still gave the prize to Ossietzky, two committee members, Foreign Minister Halvdan Koht, and former prime minister Johan Ludwig Mowinckel, resigned. They did it to create a distance between the committee and the Norwegian government, and in an attempt to appease the Germans. For the first and only time in Nobel Peace Prize history, the Norwegian king did not attend the prize ceremony.

While the Germans were not happy with Norway, and refused to let Ossietzky travel to Oslo to receive his prize, they did improve his conditions by transferring him to a private sanatorium, where he died in 1938 from tuberculosis and the effects of torture and hard concentration camp labor.

From then on, Parliament decided, no *active* member of the government could simultaneously be a member of the Nobel Committee. The potential conflict of interest was too great. In the 1970s, Parliament made another change, although it is not a formal rule. None of its members could serve on the committee either. Nevertheless, these changes haven't altered the fact that all the committee members have been political veterans.

That is, until the 2013 parliamentary election, when the Labor Party lost power for the first time in decades. Since before World War II, Norway's government had been dominated by the socialist Labor Party. As a result, the Labor Party secured more seats on the committee. The difference, however, between the political parties is minimal and all the major parties shared a promilitary line during the Cold War. Even the Conservative Party shares much of the political values of the more leftist Labor Party. (Fun fact: The Progressive Party, which is actually farther to the right of the Conservative Party, is still more moderate than the Republican Party in the United States.) Then, in 2013, a new coalition government between the Conservative Party and the Progressive Party was formed and maintained power in the latest elections in 2017.

This has led to changes in Parliament and ultimately in the Nobel Peace Prize Committee. In 2013, the Conservative Party, instead of picking one of their own, elected the first nonpolitician to the committee.

"Our last elected member, Henrik Syse, is not a politician," Nicolai Astrup, member of parliament for the Conservative Party said. Although Syse is the son of former prime minister Jan P. Syse, he has a long history in the peace movement and is a senior researcher at the Oslo Peace Research Institute. Astrup hoped that his party's appointment after the 2013 election would change the trend where the parties lost track of Alfred Nobel's intentions and seemed more focused on promoting the government's foreign policy.

However, as long as the committee is mostly filled with politicians, the Nobel Peace Prize Comittee's independence is questionable.

"It is very difficult for me to believe that a group of former politicians can be independent from the government," Michael Nobel said. "Many people say that it's not Nobel's prize, it's Stortinget's [Parliament's] own prize for whatever they deem a good cause." But he also expressed hope with the appointment of Henrik Syse.[14]

More recently, Parliament made another positive change toward the committee's independence. As of 2018, it cannot elect a new member to the committee who also has a leadership position in an international political body. This decision was made after much debate and criticism of former prime minister Thorbjørn Jagland, who chaired the Nobel Committee *and* led the European Council simultaneously. Because of this conflict of interest, Jagland was demoted from his position as Nobel chair in 2014, but is still a member of the Nobel Committee, a position he will hold until the end of 2020. Nevertheless, he will be the last Nobel Committee member to have also held office at an international political organization.

Conflicted interests create doubt as to the committee's independence. Still, the Norwegian government asserts time and again that the committee is impartial and that its choices have nothing to do with Norwegian or foreign politics. The committee itself concurs.

"[The committee] must never act under pressure from public opinion or from any form of political pressure," John Sanness, chair in 1981 said. "It is independent of all authorities, and its duty is to arrive at its decision in accordance with its best judgment and conviction."

These are big words from a group of political veterans who were chosen for their long and loyal service to their political party. Most of the peace prize winners have also been applauded by the government. That being said, the committee has made some decisions the Norwegian government was not happy with.

* * *

A COMMITTEE OF COURAGE?

The 1935 Ossietzky award is a clear example where the committee showed courage to make a decision solely based on Alfred Nobel's intentions, which is quite unusual. As we will see in future chapters, selections are almost wholly in harmony with the government's interests. But in the aftermath of the 1935 award, even the Nobel Committee itself tried to diminish the fact that the award went against the German government.

"It is quite obvious that the Nobel Committee, in awarding the prize to these different personalities, has neither shared all the opinions which they held nor declared its solidarity with all their work," Chairman Fredrik Stang said following the ceremony. "In awarding this year's Nobel Peace Prize to Carl von Ossietzky, we are therefore recognizing his valuable contribution to the cause of peace—nothing more, and certainly nothing less."

The real hero in that story is Ossietzky. The bravery of this one man against the giant Nazi government in an attempt to keep world peace is extraordinary.

Another nonpolitical choice came in 2010 when Chinese dissident Liu Xiaobo won. The committee, according to Lundestad, understood that its choice might have grave consequences for the political bond between Norway and China. Sure enough, since the 2010 award, the Norwegian government has been struggling to repair the broken relationship between the two countries, both politically and commercially.

In May of 2014, when the Dalai Lama, another enemy of the Chinese state, came to visit Oslo to commemorate the twenty-fifth anniversary of his Nobel prize, there was a heated debate in Parliament about whether or not to receive him. Norway has strong commercial interests in China, and, according to an article by Harald Stanghelle in *Aftenposten* on April 22, 2014, did not wish to upset this emerging superpower further. Parliament first thought to make the Dalai Lama enter through the back door, and they agreed that he should not be received in Lagtingssalen, the prestigious room all other prominent—although sometimes questionable—world leaders are received. In addition, most members of parliament, including the president, stated that they would not be present to welcome the Nobel laureate. In the weeks before his arrival, after even more pressure from China, the government decided that none of its members would be present at the meeting.

Foreign Minister Børge Brende said to *NTB* that it was with a heavy heart that the government declined to meet with the Dalai Lama. "But my job is to do what best serves Norway over time."

Current prime minister Erna Solberg, in an interview with NRK, said that she was against meeting the Dalai Lama, but that she would have congratulated the committee on its selection of Liu Xiaobo in 2010.

"You can't as a rule keep the same opinion if you have a different goal," she said in attempt to explain the discordance.[15] As a comparison, China's position didn't prevent President Barack Obama from receiving the Dalai Lama in February 2014.

Ossietzky, the Dalai Lama, and Liu Xiaobo demonstrate a peace prize committee independent from parliament and the government. However, many, including former secretary Lundestad, agree that this hasn't always been the case. According to him, nobody is interested in the principle of an independent committee. "They all have another agenda."[16]

Most of the time, the committee's choices are coherent with the government's view. Its members remain loyal to their party politics long after their retirement from the government and the line between the government and the committee is often unclear.

"With the whole of Norway's political power applauding the Nobel laureate, it is understandable that most countries don't believe in the committee's independence," said Erik Solheim, former member of parliament.[17]

"The government as a principle is always present at the prize ceremony and always has something positive to say about the selection," Lundestad confirmed. In addition, most members of parliament are present, demonstrating their support. The government is informed of the committee's choice one or two hours before the announcement, which gives it time to prepare a response.

"Within minutes following each and every award, the prime minister makes a public statement expressing what a wise and fair decision the committee has made. Every time, without exception," Erik Solheim said to NRK *Brennpunkt*.

When Yasser Arafat, Shimon Peres, and Yitzhak Rabin won in 1979, Prime Minister Gro Harlem Brundtland asserted "this is a joyful day, for everyone who has been wishing for conciliation in the Middle East."[18] The selections of the Dalai Lama in 1989 and of Liu Xiaobo in 2010 were similarly praised in the Norwegian press.

"It's a privatization of Norwegian foreign policy," Solheim said about the Nobel Committee.

Nevertheless, applauding the committee's choice one minute and refusing to officially receive the Nobel laureate the next, no matter the reason, may be viewed as hypocritical. Some believe it makes a mockery out of the Norwegian government and perhaps of Nobel's prize.

"Shall we let an Asian super-power dictate how strongly we speak up for injustice?" journalist Stanghelle asked.

In the end, Parliament's leader of the Committee on Tibet, Ketil Kjenseth, was allowed to receive the Dalai Lama at the parliament building, but not in the grand Lagtingssalen.

The answer to the question above from the Norwegian government appears to be "Yes."

THE ELECTION OF A WINNER

The committee votes on nominated candidates, and those eligible to nominate are numerous. According to the statutes of the Nobel Foundation, a nomination is considered valid if it is submitted by a person who falls within one of the following categories:

- Members of national assemblies and national governments (cabinet members/ministers) of sovereign states as well as current heads of states.

- Members of the International Court of Justice in The Hague and the Permanent Court of Arbitration in The Hague.

- Members of l'Institut de Droit International.

- Members of the international board of the Women's International League for Peace and Freedom.

- University professors, professors emeriti, and associate professors of history, social sciences, law, philosophy, theology, and religion; university rectors and university directors (or their equivalents); directors of peace research institutes and foreign policy institutes.

- Nobel Peace Prize laureates.

- Members of the main board of directors or its equivalent of organizations that have been awarded the Nobel Peace Prize.

- Current and former members of the Norwegian Nobel Committee.

- Former advisers to the Norwegian Nobel Committee.

Yet, despite sending out invitations to nominate each year, the committee receives relatively few responses. Perhaps if more people than the ones who receive an invitation knew of their eligibility, the Norwegian Nobel

Committee would receive more nominations. In 2009, the year Barack Obama won, there were 205 nominees. In 2016, the number of valid nominees was a record 376. The committee urges all who make nominations not to share the names of the candidates with the media. In fact, under the bylaws, the nominees and the committee's voting are confidential, as are the minutes that contain only the final decision. None of the discussions are reported. All information is held secret, and the records are sealed for fifty years after the fact.

This secrecy contributes to diminishing trust in the committee's independence. It is an obstacle to evaluating the Nobel Committee's work, and—except for leaks—little is known about the process, research, and basis for the decisions of the committee. It all remains a mystery.

If a committee member disagrees with the committee's choice, he or she is supposed to keep quiet about it. Or if the disagreement is too strong, that member can resign from the committee, as happened when Carl von Ossietzky won in 1935. In 1973, when Henry Kissinger and Le Duc Tho won the prize, two of the committee's five members resigned.

Another example is the 1994 award to the Arafat, Peres, and Rabin trifecta. On announcement day, Kåre Kristiansen held a second press conference to protest Arafat taking part in the award. A politician of the Christian Democratic Party, and a devout friend to Israel, Kristiansen said he had asked the committee to wait at least a year to see how the Oslo Accords were working in practice. The other members of the committee would not, and Kristiansen resigned as a result, honoring his strong belief that the 1994 prize was premature. Since the committee doesn't reveal its internal disagreements, the only way a committeee member can make their disagreement public is to resign.

Here is what we do know about the election process of a Nobel Peace Prize winner:

The deadline for the submission of nominations is February 1 of that election year, and that rule is interpreted strictly. When Anwar Sadat and Menachem Begin were awarded the prize in 1978 for the Camp David

Accords, the committee wished to include Jimmy Carter for his enormous efforts. However, he had not been nominated before February 1, so Carter was excluded in that year's award. He did win in 2002.

It's also public knowledge that the committee meets in late February or early March to conduct a first examination of the nominees. They come up with a shortlist of approximately twenty to thirty names, and they meet again in April to reduce the list further. The nominees (or cases) are studied up until the second Friday of October, when the committee makes its announcement of the winner. A simple majority vote is sufficient.

According to the statutes, the prize has to be awarded at least every five years, but it need not be given every year. If the committee believes no particular person or organization is worthy, it can skip the award that year. During World War I and World War II, when the Germans occupied Norway, the prize was postponed. There have been ten other occasions when no candidate was selected. Since 1973, however, it has been awarded every year.

Nobel also wrote in his will that the award should go to a "person," not to several persons. Two people shared the award the first two years it was given. The statutes were later adjusted to instruct that a prize can go to as many as three people at once, but not more. Since then, it has been divided many times, but only twice has it been given to three people—in 1994, when it went to Yasser Arafat, Shimon Peres, and Yitzhak Rabin of the Oslo Peace Accords, and in 2011, when it went to three African women, Ellen Johnson Sirleaf, Leymah Gbowee, and Tawakkul Karman, "for their non-violent struggle for the safety of women and for women's rights to full participation in peace-building work."[19]

Additionally, the Nobel Peace Prize is to be awarded to living persons. Only once has the prize been given to a person after their death: In 1961, it was awarded to Dag Hammarskjöld, the United Nations secretary-general from Sweden who was killed in a plane crash in September of that year. In 1974, the Nobel Foundation in Stockholm changed its statutes. There were to be no more posthumous winners. Only if a person is announced as the winner, and they die before collecting the award, will their estate be able to collect it.

SECRECY AND ARROGANCE

Since the beginning, Nobel's will and the foundation's statutes (established in Stockholm in 1900) have frequently been ignored by the committee.[20] In the early days, the committee and Parliament debated over how to follow Nobel's requirement that the prize should reward work done "during the preceding year." The Nobel Foundation statutes maintain that older works may be rewarded if their significance has not become apparent until recently.

"The prizes were meant to boost and encourage people in their careers," according to Jay Nordlinger's book *Peace, They Say,* not to "crown masters in twilight."

The committee has in practice done both. It cites the statute when it suits the members and dismisses it when it doesn't. When the Finnish diplomat Martti Ahtisaari was awarded the prize in 2008 in acknowledgment of his long career, Chairman Ole Danbolt Mjøs said, "It is not easy to take every sentence in Nobel's will absolutely literally."

In 2009, it gave the prize to President Barack Obama, who had barely taken office, in a hope for what he *might* accomplish. Thorbjørn Jagland, the chair that year, defended the committee's choice of Obama by asking who else had done more for peace during the preceding year than he? The secrecy behind the election process and the fact that corporations make donations to the Nobel Institute and peace prize concert add to the controversy. The committee acts as if it answers to no one and isn't accountable for any of its decisions. Its only loyalty seems to be to the members' political party.

"What they should have developed was Nobel's idea of peace, not their own," Heffermehl wrote. "The prize Nobel established was not for *peace* in general, it was a prize for *people who do determined work in certain ways and certain fields to end war.*" According to Heffermehl, the members abuse their responsibilities, and they are no longer respecting, if they ever did, Alfred Nobel's intentions.[21]

Michael Nobel has always had successful interactions with Norwegian companies and individuals. "Norway is a fantastic country. People's opinions are respected, as well as law and order," he wrote. "It is unfortunate that the Nobel Committee's decisions are conflicting with that." According to him, rewarding efforts for human rights and the environment—no matter how worthy the causes may be—are outside the scope of Nobel's last words.

"That the committee disregards the will and develops its own 'extended definition of peace,' is highly problematic and probably also illegal," Michael Nobel wrote.

But while the implementation of the prize and its intent might be up for interpretation and debate, Nobel's awarding Norway the honor of bestowing the prize boosted Norway's confidence on the world stage in a marked way. However, it was not in the way he envisioned.

NORWEGIAN
EXCEPTIONALISM

All Frenchmen are under the blissful impression that the brain is a French organ.

—ALFRED NOBEL

N OBEL DIDN'T GIVE instructions whether the selection process should be secret or transparent, but his values of peace and love of humanity suggest an intention of transparency. Yet the peace prize selection process takes place in secrecy. This secrecy reflects the attitude of the committee and, beyond that, the concept of Norway as better and morally superior to other countries. A poem by Henrik Wergeland in the early 19th century reflects the pseudo-patriotic spirit of Norway today. "We are one nation, an inch small, a fatherland we rejoice over and we are many. Our heart knows, our eye sees how good and beautiful Norway is."

While many nations have national pride, in Norway's case this feeling of superiority may come, in part, from having been suppressed and made to feel inferior for centuries, first by Denmark, and then by Sweden. When Nobel picked Norway, he saw it as a humble country, far removed from politics. The Norwegian Parliament was showing an unusual interest in the peace movement worldwide and had given a great deal of financial support to it. By Nobel's very selection of Norway, however, he may have enabled the Norwegian Nobel Committee to develop an arrogance with regards to the execution of Nobel's last will, meaning that the committee does as it pleases because it knows best.

As the Norwegian government was fighting for independence toward the end of the 1800s, the Nobel Peace Prize boosted its confidence as well as that of the population. Norway went from a marginalized state with zero power, to all of a sudden: *We matter. Somebody saw us and believed in us.* Not just anybody, Norway suddenly mattered to the greatest inventor and businessman at the time. The peace prize was the beginning of a new era for Norway, one of confidence and pride to be Norwegian. As confidence grew, so did innovation and wealth, largely helped by the later discoveries of hydroelectricity and oil. Both contributed to Norway's becoming one of the wealthiest countries in the world, which elevated the country's self-esteem further.

The Nobel Peace Prize put Norway on the map because of the many famous peace prize laureates, and suddenly, numerous nations were praising this peaceful and civilized country. Winston Churchill described it as "the prominent place the Scandinavian peoples hold in the struggle of civilized humanity for the betterment of the world."[1]

Ernesto Teodoro Moneta, the 1907 co-laureate, romanticized the war-mongering Vikings in his Nobel lecture: "your civic life today is as worthy of admiration in our time as was that of the bold Vikings in the days of war and armed conquest."[2]

Norman Angell, the 1933 laureate, parroted the image that Norway tries to project. "It is the little states, like this one of Norway, which have today evolved the highest civilization and the greatest social stability, have developed, more than others, the art of free and peaceful life together. They, more than others, may show the way by which the world may be led to security and peace."

The praise continues, even today. Year after year, the United Nations ranks Norway the most desirable place in the world to live. In a 2014 article, the *Huffington Post* listed twenty-five reasons why Norway is "the greatest place on Earth."[3] Norway as a society is put up on the same pedestal as the Nobel Peace Prize winner. It is viewed as a world peace champion.

Churchill did not know then that Norway would later produce missiles and arms in as much secrecy as it selects its peace prize winners. Omitted from Norway's self-marketing materials, most people still today are unaware of this profitable weapons enterprise, even within Norway. This small nation with just five million citizens ranks in the top twenty of the world's top arms exporters, according to the UN's Comtrade database and Nordic Page. According to Norwegian researcher Tove Lie, a lot of these weapons end up in war zones despite Norway's legislation against dealings with countries at war, and despite the fact that the Norwegian government is very much involved in resolving conflicts around the world.[4] The reason for this double standard when it comes to peace-related work and the state arms industry is purely financial. It is also human. We, as a society, want to do good. We want to protect our environment and our people, yet we are also caught up in profit and greed.

The state statistics bureau, SSB (Statistics Norway), released figures in 2018 showing that sale proceeds from Norway's weapon exports reached $436 million in 2017, marking an increase of nearly 80 percent from the previous year. Both sale and manufacturing of arms is important to the Norwegian economy, in terms of the job market, export revenue, and state taxes. Because the weapons industry is partly state-owned, revenue from exports has a positive impact on the national economy and the Norwegian people. *Aftenposten* reported that around half the value of the weapons exported went to fellow NATO member countries. Sales to non-NATO nations, however, were nearly triple those in 2016, mostly because Oman bought "weapons and weapon parts" for more than 1 billion Norwegian kroner (or approximately $111 million). That makes Oman, ruled by a totalitarian sultanate that Rasmus Hansson, spokeman for the Green Party, calls a "dictatorship," Norway's single-biggest weapons customer after it ordered and took delivery of a Norwegian Advanced Surface-to-Air Missile System (NASAMS) from the state-owned Kongsberg Gruppen.

Nevertheless, that Norwegian weapons end up in countries at war, "is a violation of the fundamental intentions in the foreign ministry's guidelines for export of defense material," Hansson told *Aftenposten* in January 2018. Hansson, who served the past four years as a Member of Parliament, has criticized Norway's weapons sales earlier and remains alarmed over the Norwegian defense industry's growth and activity.

Norway's weapons industry is in violation of Alfred Nobel's values. Yes, Nobel was also a businessman. But his dynamite was never created with the purpose of taking lives. Missiles, grenades, torpedoes, and ammunition are made with *only* the purpose of taking lives. Norway's status as a peace champion is incompatible with this state-owned industry. What's more, because of the blurred line between the Norwegian government and the Nobel Peace Prize Committee, the business of the state erodes trust in Nobel's prize further.

Parliament was mandated to select an independent committee free from ties to politics and commercial influences. Nobel made sure there would be enough financial support for the committee to operate independently, yet along the way, something changed. Because of the grand enterprise the peace prize has become, the institution also receives funding from the state and private corporations. In addition, the committee is filled with politicians who are loyal to the ruling parties in government. One is not unreasonable to question the Nobel Committee's neutrality. If the Nobel Committee is loyal to the Norwegian government, and perhaps to other sponsors—and otherwise feels it can do whatever it wants—how can it also work toward disarmament, which was Alfred Nobel's intention?

FROM UNDERDOG TO BULLY?

More than others. The best place on earth. Nobel's prize gave the peace movement in Norway a boost. Furthermore, it also gave the Norwegian people
confidence, but perhaps too much confidence. This was Nobel's way of
recognizing an insignificant and powerless country as special. Perhaps so
special that it could create its own definition of peace and disregard Nobel's
intentions and values. The country's financial situation, which benefits
hugely from weapons manufacturing, adds to this superior status. The
Government Pension Fund Global, which is Norway's sovereign fund, was,
in May 2020, the largest in the world, thanks to the discovery of oil in the
North Sea in the late 1960s.[5] Based on gross domestic product per capita
(GDP), Norway is ranked the second richest nation in the world, just after
Luxembourg, according to Focus Economics.

Before the discovery of oil, Norway was a modest country essentially
living off of farming and fishing. Post-World War II Norway, a country in
ruins, was slowly rebuilt with the aid of the Marshall Plan, or the European
Recovery Program, named after United States Secretary of State George
Marshall. The Marshall Plan consisted of monetary aid given by the United
States to rebuild Europe after the war and to prevent the spread of communism. Beginning in 1948, the Marshall Plan was in effect for four years and
had much to do with Norway's becoming a mixed economy. Norway's way
of saying "thank you," and of strengthening ties with the United States,
was to give the 1953 peace prize to General George Marshall. Though his
Marshall Plan did have concrete and lasting benefits for post-war political
stability in war-ravaged Europe, he was a military man until the end of his
career. The country he represented was also responsible for dropping nuclear
bombs on Japan.

During this reconstruction, the Labor Party was the major political faction
and imposed rationing of dairy products until 1949, and the rationing and
price control of housing and automobiles until 1960. Under the leadership
of Prime Minister Einar Gerhardsen, Parliament enacted many reforms,

including flattening income distribution, lessening poverty, and ensuring retirement programs, medical care, and disability payments for all citizens. The public sector grew and the divide between liberals and conservatives decreased.

This was a peaceful time in Norwegian history. The socialist speeches about solidarity, equality, and distribution of whatever wealth could be found were welcomed by those who had lived under scarcity and terror during the Nazi occupation. Besides a few years in the 1980s, the Labor Party stayed in power until the 2013 parliamentary election, when a Conservative Party-led coalition formed. Because the differences in the main political parties were minimal, the change in government hasn't had much impact. Erik Dalen, director of Ipsos Market and Media Institute (the Norwegian public opinion research institute) asserted that the majority of Norwegians still want to redistribute the wealth, maintain a high degree of general affluence, and minimize social differences. According to Ottar Hellevik, professor at the University of Oslo Faculty of Social Sciences, surveys also show that Norwegians gladly pay their taxes.

As the economy and country's self-esteem have grown, so has Norwegians' contentment with themselves. A 2013 survey by MMI shows that 90 percent of Norway's citizens are proud to be Norwegian. "We're not so proud that we've become wealthy," said Dalen. "But the wealth gives reason to believe that the way we have organized our society is correct and good. The wealth therefore contributes indirectly to the Norwegian pride."

A COUNTRY WITH SUPER POWERS

Norwegians, because of their newfound wealth and the Nobel Peace Prize, have a strong sense of supremacy as a society. Consider the role the country has taken as a mediator in the conflict in the Middle East. Norway functioned as a facilitator and mediator in the negotiations between Israel and Palestine that led to the peace accord in Oslo in 1993. In 1994, Nobel's medal was given to the parties involved in the Oslo Accords. In 2013, news media revealed that Norway had secretly been brokering talks from 2007 to 2010 between Afghanistan and the Taliban. Even recently, the Norwegian government helped negotiate a peace agreement between Colombian president Juan Manuel Santos and the FARC (Revolutionary Armed Forces of Colombia), which lead to Santos being awarded the 2016 Nobel Peace Prize.

"Norway is a secret super power within peace and reconciliation," said Henrik Thune, director of the country's foreign policy institute, NUPI. "We do much more than what's publicly known."

Thune and fellow researcher Leiv Lunde, of the Fridtjof Nansen Institute, affirmed that Norway has been involved in more than twenty peace negotiations around the world in the past ten years. Although a few of these talks have been reported on, most of them are not disclosed to the public. Perhaps the secrecy is understandable. Some of the facts might cause controversy. Norway partook in the NATO-led bombing of Libya, while it tried to arrange meetings between Libyan rebels and the Gaddafi regime. In September 2011, the leader of the Libyan transitional government even thanked Norway for the work it did to broker talks. Gaddafi's former deputy foreign minister, Khaled Al Gaaeem, also confirmed that talks with the rebels had been held in Oslo. Norwegian officials, according to an article by Nina Berglund, never commented on them. "In keeping with customary practice, the Norwegian diplomats' lips were sealed."[6]

According to Thune, foreign ministers are often skeptical as to what Norwegian peace-brokering efforts can accomplish. But they quickly realize, he said, how much influence Norway has, including access to US political leadership. The United States often asks Norway to act as a mediator with groups that leaders in Washington have difficulty dealing with. Brokering such deals gives Norway influence in return. Sometimes, as in 1994 and in 2016, Norway's involvement in the negotiations will even lead to a Nobel medal for the parties involved.

"The Norwegians," Jay Nordlinger wrote, "are thought to be a kind of conscience for the world, an example of civilization, and a prod to it."

Indeed, Norway does project an image of a perfect country, a culture of goodness, fairness, and solidarity for all. *Norwegian exceptionalism,* as it has been called, suggests that there is something better, nobler, and wiser about Norwegian people than those from other parts of the world.

Norwegians lecture, guide, and reprimand, using their $1 trillion and growing Government Pension Fund, commonly referred to as the Oil Fund, to discourage what they call unethical businesses practices and public policies in other countries. They will not invest in, or disinvest in countries they view as "unethical" in government, philosophy, or business, according to their ethics guidelines.[7] They seem to enjoy this role as judge of the world—usually self-appointed, and in one case, Nobel-appointed. One might say that Norway as a state has a high sense of its own worth and the money to back it up.[8]

Using the Nobel Peace Prize and Oil Fund to point fingers and to lecture, Norway finds it more difficult, however, to address its own weapons manufacturing and how these weapons end up in countries at war. The Norwegians themselves probably don't realize how two-faced this behavior is. It's become part of the culture.

In my book *The Mystery of the Lone Wolf Killer*, I wrote about Norway's strong group culture. The only acceptable way of standing out is not as an individual, but as a country, as a superior ethnic group. The individual by itself has little value. As much as the Norwegian people celebrate their country as the ultimate humane society, its system of strong state institutions discourages individual responsibility. Most people—outside of their close circle of friends—do not reach out to each other or to those less fortunate because they know it is not their job; the state will take care of everything and everyone. In this otherwise exceptionally evolved society, there is little personal involvement and philanthropy.

Most people, regardless of their country of origin, don't ask questions about their society. They take it at face value and accept it as is. As children, Norwegians are told that they must go out and be like the other children on the playground. They learn and adapt to the social rules in order to belong and be accepted. In Norway, this means not standing out or asking questions that are too critical of the status quo.

A strong group culture was necessary to survive and to rebuild Norway after the war. As a result, the Norwegian government became the ultimate group, and by Nobel's will, so did the Norwegian Nobel Committee. Nobel's last words may have been ignored for decades, yet very few dare to challenge the committee, which has allowed Parliament to elect politicians who are more loyal to the government than to Nobel. This culture has also reinforced the committee's belief that it can do what it wants and does not answer to anyone.

Yet mindsets alter with prosperity. The financial growth has led to a change in values in Norway's population, especially among the young. According to Hellevik, the young today rebel against the set ways of Norwegian culture. They're disobeying the law by not paying bus fares and by not respecting the speed limits on the roads.

"There is a new kind of morality in Norway," Hellevik said. "People want to think for themselves—it's part of a broad value change in this country at the beginning of the new millennium." This is the youngsters' way of rebelling against a culture where becoming invisible in a crowd seemed a better choice than standing out. That brings hope of change, also for the Nobel Peace Prize and the work of the committee.

MANY ROADS TO PEACE

However, as it now stands, any person who performed a great deed can win the Nobel Peace Prize, as long as the committee continues to ignore what Alfred Nobel actually intended. Let's take a look at the instructions he gave. His will contains six criteria to help the executors understand what kind of recipient Nobel had in mind for his award. The first two criteria refer to work done in the year preceding the award, while work that has "conferred the greatest benefit on mankind," applies to all of the five prizes. The next four apply only to the peace prize.[9] The winner shall be a champion of peace, having done "the best work for fraternity between nations, the abolition or reduction of standing armies," and finally for the "holding and promotion of peace congresses."

Knowing Nobel's criteria, it becomes clearer how the Nobel Committee has breached its job as the executor. The Nobel Peace Prize was not intended to award ending hostilities and caring for the victims, although they are valuable and vital humanitarian endeavors. It was meant, according to Heffermehl, to specifically reward *profound change* in society and to prevent war. Nobel's perspective was global, and he did not intend to reward conflict solving on a local level, within a country. His was a huge and highly specific criteria, which is why he stipulated that the prize need not be awarded every year. Yet, despite Nobel's intentions, numerous prizes have gone to such work outside the scope of his will in the peace prize's history.

As I will show in Chapter Four, after World War II, a promilitary sentiment presided in the Norwegian government, and Nobel's objectives of disarmament and peace congresses were ignored.[10] The peace congresses Nobel was referring to in his will were gatherings that started in the 1890s with the goals of achieving a better world by replacing military force and power struggles among nations with trust, cooperation, and binding international treaties. These congresses imagined law and agreements of disarmament as methods to avoid wars. Influenced by Bertha von Suttner, Nobel wrote his will with the idea that as long as military forces and weapons exist, there will always be a high risk of intentional or accidental violence. Although he had previously expressed that he believed in the deterrent effect of weapons, his last will showed that he had made a deliberate choice to position himself on the same side as von Suttner in the struggle against war. These gatherings for disarmament were therefore important to him.

Norwegian exceptionalism has made the committee turn a blind eye to peace congresses and even express that they are outdated.[11] Perhaps they are. Or perhaps the committee members' bond to the government and its political agenda is too strong. Peace congresses in various forms still very much exist.

Every three years, the International Peace Bureau holds a special meeting to bring together its members and supporters to discuss the challenges facing peace movements in an unstable and over-militarized world. The 2013 gathering in Stockholm explored the interrelationships between military intervention and the economy of war. On the agenda were what could be learned from military intervention in recent conflicts and what alternatives there were to military action. Also on the agenda was how to challenge the trend toward robot-warfare, as well as how to best support whistleblowers for peace. At the 2016 gathering in Berlin, the focus was on the economy that underpins the war system, on terrorism and intolerance, on disregard for the rule of law, and on inequalities and human rights.

Although the International Peace Bureau won the Nobel Peace Prize in 1910, it has been given little consideration by the committee since. Perhaps this can be explained by the minimal media coverage peace conferences receive. Other associations that fulfill Nobel's criteria are the International Association of Lawyers against Nuclear Arms and the International Physicians for the Prevention of Nuclear War. Neither of these has managed to get the Nobel Committee's attention.

Perhaps, because peace congresses don't receive much media attention, they don't bring the same glory to Norway and the Nobel Committee as other candidates, such as Barak Obama and Malala Yousafzai. But perhaps if these groups were recognized by the prize, they might gain more visibility for the work they are doing.

In recent years, the environment and humanitarian work have gotten attention by the Nobel Committee. In 2004, the peace prize was given a new dimension when Wangari Maathai was awarded for her efforts to empower women by starting a movement to plant trees in Africa. In 2007, when the committee selected Al Gore and the Intergovernmental Panel on Climate Change, it confirmed this new direction. While their work is both honorable and necessary, it's outside the scope of Nobel's will.

A testament is a legal document that must be respected unless it is invalidated by a court of law. The testator is free to change his or her mind at any time and alter the document, but death makes the will final. A bequest for cancer research must be used for that purpose. Only if cancer is cured can the funds be used for another cause, such as to eradicate HIV, for example. However, changing the purpose of a testament must be done though proper legal channels.

War has not ceased to exist, nor has the military been abolished. Nobel's testament has not attained its target. If Nobel knew that the Nobel Committee would not follow the letter of his will, he may have regretted entrusting the Norwegian Parliament with the execution of his will. The committee, however, does not agree and—in accordance with Norwegian exceptionalism—still believes it has complete discretion when it comes to the interpretation of Nobel's last words. Former secretary Lundestad defended the committee's stance by stating, "The committee thinks there are many roads to peace."[12] That may very well be true, but the Norwegian Nobel Committee's task is to follow Alfred Nobel's directions, not its own. One may not agree that disarmament is the best solution to prevent war, but that is beside the point.

Lundestad's comment is rare. Most of the time, the committee gives the silent treatment to any critics. The signal it sends out is strong. *This is how we do it, this is how we intend to continue, and there is nothing anybody can do about it.*

But maybe there is. Gunnar Jahn, committee chair for twenty-five years, kept a diary about his work and struggles in the committee that has been deposited at the National Library of Norway. It shows how Jahn fought to convince the committee to respect Nobel's will, but that he often lost. Although the committee is supposed to be an independent body, it still has a legal obligation to stay within the intentions in Nobel's will.

"If the Norwegian Nobel Committee refuses or is unable to keep within the mandate of Alfred Nobel," Michael Nobel wrote, "the Swedish Nobel Foundation has the possibility to intervene. The board of the Nobel Foundation has, since the amendment of the Swedish Foundations Act in 1996, a responsibility and a duty to make sure Alfred Nobel's intentions are followed." According to Michael Nobel, the credibility of his great-granduncle's legacy is today at risk.

Chairman Jahn never attempted to use the law to enforce Nobel's intentions. He voiced his opinions within the committee but never in public. Perhaps he didn't dare to. The individual is nothing against the group in Norwegian culture. Going up against the committee would have meant going up against the Norwegian political establishment and their unshakeable sense of Norwegian exceptionalism. No doubt there was and still is such an atmosphere within the Nobel Committee that places it and its decisions above the law. Their behavior and arrogance indicate that they feel they are "masters of the universe," according to Fredrik Heffermehl. The secrecy has given them power to say and do as they please, to respond to criticism, or to stay silent.

"The Nobel Committee has always practiced a broad concept of peace," Lundestad said in defense of the committee's decisions. Perhaps his statement was an accidental admission about the lack of regard the Norwegian Nobel Committee has always shown its founder's will and how they have used the prize as a way to further their own interests for decades.

4

PEACE PRIZE IN
A WORLD OF WAR

Let us grant that anything is better than war.
—ALFRED NOBEL

———

NOBEL MADE IT clear precisely what he wanted his peace prize to
recognize. In his own words, the winner shall be a champion of peace,
having done the "the best work for fraternity between nations, the "abolition or reduction of standing armies," and for the "holding and promotion
of peace congresses." Yet, the committee frequently ignores this part of the
testament and seems to focus only on work having "conferred the greatest
benefit on mankind." While this is part of it, it's not the only condition
stated in Nobel's will. On its own, what benefits mankind is too vague and
can be used to justify all sorts of means to achieve the goal, even military
action and war. As I will show throughout this book, Nobel's intentions have
continuously been interpreted loosely by the committee. In the early years

of the peace prize, the awards were often strategic and overt political decisions to strengthen Norway's foreign policies as well as sentimental postwar prizes—far from Alfred Nobel's actual intentions and values.

1906:
REWARDING THE ROUGH RIDER

In 1906, President Theodore Roosevelt won the prize for his back channel negotiations to end the 1904–1905 Russo-Japanese War. Roosevelt, the first American laureate, had the adversaries meet in Portsmouth, New Hampshire, and he successfully negotiated the Portsmouth Treaty on September 5, 1905.

The 1906 award was also the first controversial award. Roosevelt was more a champion of war than of peace, according to Asle Sveen, expert on Nobel Peace Prize history. "Nobel would have turned in his grave," Swedish newspapers at the time reported.[1]

A newspaper in Philadelphia wrote that it was perplexed that, "the militant champion of a large army and navy . . . should be crowned as America's great pacificator." According to the *New York Times*, "a broad smile illuminated the face of the globe when the prize was awarded . . . to the most warlike citizen of these United States."

Many considered Roosevelt a colonizer and a bully. Prior to his presidency, Roosevelt played a significant part in the Spanish-American War of 1898 that led to victory for the United States. The conflict started when the United States intervened in the Cuban War of Independence from Spanish reign. On May 6 of that year, Roosevelt resigned from his post as assistant secretary of the Navy and volunteered to lead a cavalry unit that would fight in Cuba against Spain. The war ended the same year with the Treaty of Paris, which favored the United States and allowed it temporary control of Cuba. The treaty also ceded Spanish colonial authority of Puerto Rico, Guam, and the Philippine Islands to the United States. As a result, the United States gained several island possessions around the globe.

Even Roosevelt himself would probably agree that he was not a champion of peace in Nobel's view. After all, this was the man who called pacifists "cowards," and said, "Speak softly and carry a big stick, and you will go far." He also said, "No man is worth calling a man, who will not fight rather than submit to infamy or see those that are dear to him suffer wrong." In his autobiography, he wrote, "the most important service that I rendered to peace was the voyage of the battle fleet around the world."

Roosevelt did share Nobel's view of courage. However, Roosevelt was a strong believer in the deterrent effect of using arms, and the way he often showed courage was by use of military force. This was a belief Nobel himself had originally shared, but came to reconsider by the end of his life. One example of Roosevelt's courage was shown during the famous Battle of San Juan Hill, near Santiago de Cuba, on July 1, 1898, which ended the Spanish-American War. Together with his cavalry unit, known as the Rough Riders (named after the rodeo act Buffalo Bill's Wild West and Congress of Rough Riders of the World), Roosevelt led a daring charge up San Juan Hill, encouraging his troops to continue the assault through enemy fire over open countryside. Roosevelt fought heroically in the front and with total disregard for his personal safety. The United States lost five officers and ninety-five enlisted men that day, but won the war.

No one can make a case against his bravery, but Nobel's prize is not given for military bravery. Roosevelt did, however, fulfill some of the criteria in Nobel's will. Because of the Portsmouth treaty, Roosevelt became one of the few Nobel laureates to meet the "preceding year" criteria in Nobel's will. He was also a passionate supporter of the International Court of Arbitration in The Hague, and submitted the dispute over the Pious Fund of the Californias between the United States and Mexico, the arbitration court's first case. The Pious Fund, established in 1697 to sponsor the Roman Catholic Spanish Jesuit missions in Baja California and the Franciscan Spanish missions in Alta California, became the object of litigation between the US and Mexico following the peace treaty that ended the war between the two countries in 1848, when the northern part of California was ceded to the United States.

The archbishop and bishops of the US state of California claimed that as citizens of the United States, they were entitled to receive money from Mexico according to a decree from 1842. Mexico refused on the grounds that the Pious Fund was no longer situated on Mexican territory. The United States won the arbitration case, ending the conflict between the two countries. Mexico continued to pay until 1966, when it negotiated to pay a lump sum that ended all future obligations to the Pious Fund.

Although these actions deserved commendation, the 1906 award was probably motivated by something other than Roosevelt's achievements for peace. Norway had broken free from Sweden a year earlier and was eager to strengthen its independence. It had tried to appoint one of the younger sons of King Edward VII of Great Britain as the new king of Norway in an attempt to strengthen the bonds with Great Britain. King Edward VII, however, didn't wish to get involved in the conflict between Norway and Sweden. Lacking options and pressed for time, the Norwegian government selected Prince Carl of Denmark, leaving itself still tied to its former ruler. Jørgen Løvland, the Nobel Committee's chairman at the time, was also Norway's foreign minister, and he was seeking allies. Befriending the president of the fast-emerging United States of America with the Nobel medal may have seemed like a sound strategy should Norway's independence again be threatened.

1912:
ELIHU ROOT—YET ANOTHER MAN OF WAR

In 1912, in an ironic move, the committee selected another man of war to receive the prize of peace. Born in Clinton, New York, in 1845, Elihu Root was one of the leading corporate attorneys in the United States and served as president of the American Bar Association, before he gave up his career in law to serve his country. In 1899, President William McKinley asked Root to take the post of secretary of war. Coming out of the Spanish-American

War, McKinley said he needed a lawyer for the job, not a military man. Root responded that he would be honored to represent "the greatest of all our clients, the government of our country."

As United States secretary of war from 1899 to 1904, Elihu Root reorganized and modernized the administrative system of the Department of War. He established new procedures for promotion, founded the National War College, enlarged West Point, and opened other schools for special branches of the service. Root also created a general staff, restored discipline within the department, and strengthened control over the National Guard. He transformed the army from an unrelated collection of small frontier outposts and coastal defense units into a modern, professionally organized military machine comparable to the best in Europe. According to Henry L. Stimson, who was later appointed to Root's position, "No such intelligent, constructive, and vital force" had occupied that post in American history.[2]

It was for his accomplishments as war secretary that Root was awarded the Nobel medal.

Root "had to settle a number of particularly difficult problems," Committee Secretary Ragnvald Moe said in his speech at the 1912 award. "It was he who was chiefly responsible for organizing affairs in Cuba and in the Philippines after the Spanish-American War."

Root did devise a plan for returning Cuba to the Cubans. He also wrote a charter for the governance of the Philippines designed to ensure a democratic and independent government, free to protect its local customs.

Then, when he was appointed secretary of state under President Theodore Roosevelt, Root maintained the "open door" policy in East Asia, a policy he had helped frame as secretary of war. He negotiated the so-called "Gentlemen's Agreement" with Japan, which facilitated the immigration of Japanese workers to the United States, and promoted amicable relations with South America.

Root also sponsored the Central American Peace Conference held in Washington, DC, in 1907, which resulted in the creation of the Central American Court of Justice, an international tribunal for the judicial settlement of disputes. He negotiated numerous international arbitration treaties, and—along with Lord James Bryce—instituted the Permanent American-Canadian Joint High Commission for the settlement of future problems between the two countries.[3]

No doubt, Root was excellent at his job as both secretary of war and of state. But did he share Nobel's intention and values of unity by peaceful means and a love of humanity?

Let's take a look at Root's own words.

"To deal with the true causes of war," he said in his Nobel speech, "one must begin by recognizing as of prime relevancy to the solution of the problem the familiar fact that civilization is a partial, incomplete, and, to a great extent, superficial modification of barbarism. The point of departure of the process to which we wish to contribute is the fact that war is the natural reaction of human nature in the savage state, while peace is the result of acquired characteristics."

In his speech, Root went on to justify humans' attraction to war, calling it mankind's original civil and social condition. Humans, according to Root's analysis, were savages prone to war, and peace by consequence could be acquired like good table manners. To achieve such good manners, war was not to be excluded. In the aftermath of receiving the Nobel medal, Root started advocating for military preparation in the, according to him, likely event the US would enter World War I. Later, he had reservations about President Wilson's vision of the League of Nations. Through his own words, and later action, Root was certainly no peace champion by Alfred Nobel's definition. As with the 2006-award, the Nobel Committee was likely still motivated by a wish to strengthen Norway's ties with the United States.

1920:
THE LAUREATE WHO LED HIS COUNTRY TO WAR

In most of the years during World War I, the Nobel Peace Prize was not awarded. Europe was in shatters, confusion reigned, and handing out a prize for peace during unprecedented bloodshed was the last thing on anyone's mind.

In 1920, after the war had ended, the prize went to President Woodrow Wilson, who led the United States across the ocean and into that war. Wilson served two terms as president, from 1913 to 1921.

In 1916, Wilson ran for reelection on the slogan "He kept us out of war." During the first years of battle in Europe, Wilson insisted on keeping the United States neutral. He even offered to mediate. Then he changed his mind. Germany began sinking US ships, and there was pressure on him to react. Germany also incited Mexico to go to war against the United States. On April 2, 1917, less than a month after Wilson was sworn in for a second term, the man who "kept us out of war" asked Congress for permission to attack Germany.

"It would look as if Europe had finally determined to commit suicide, as Carlyle thought it had at the time of the French revolution—and the only way we can help is by changing the current of its thought," Wilson said, justifying changing his mind about going to war.[4] Apparently, his way of changing the current was by sending in the troops. What had been a European conflict then became a world war.

In Europe, many were relieved when the United States joined the war. Massive American effort slowly tipped the balance in favor of the Allies. After the Germans signed the armistice in November 1918, Wilson went to Paris to try to build an enduring peace. A few months later, in January 1918, he laid out his aims and visions for a postwar Europe in his address to Congress. His Fourteen Points were a declaration of ideals, and the last point would establish "a general association of nations . . . for the purpose of affording mutual guarantees of political independence and territorial integrity to great and small states alike." Wilson presented his Fourteen Points at a peace conference in Paris, and the League of Nations was formed.

For these efforts, Wilson was awarded the Nobel medal. But there were at least two issues with this award.

First, Wilson never managed to get his own country to become part of the League of Nations. When he later presented the Versailles Treaty, containing the Covenant of the League of Nations, to the US Senate, he asked, "Dare we reject it and break the heart of the world?" They did. The United States never became a member of this League.

Second, the Versailles Treaty of 1919, which was the premise for the League of Nations, was deeply flawed. Wilson's efforts in the formation of the League were futile. This "gigantic world monument, which President Wilson erected in 1918," Norwegian Prime Minister Johan Ludwig Mowinckel said, "to the glory of his own country and for the happiness and salvation of the world," would not leave the world a happy place for long.

The Germans based their signature to the armistice on Wilson's Fourteen Points, hoping for equitable peace as the US president had promised. "Our task at Paris is to organize the friendship of the world," Wilson said, "to see to it that all the moral forces that make for right and justice and liberty are united and are given a vital organization to which the peoples of the world will readily and gladly respond."

Although Wilson encouraged "peace without victory," the reality of the Versailles Treaty was far from equitable. According to Article 231 of the treaty, "The Allied and Associated Governments affirm, and Germany accepts, the responsibility of Germany and her allies for causing all the loss and damage to which the Allied and Associated Governments and their nationals have been subjected as a consequence of the war imposed upon them by the aggression of Germany and her allies."

As many history books have pointed out, the Versailles Treaty was a travesty on many levels. Instead of an amicable agreement all parties could live with, it left Germany broken. The Versailles Treaty was no peace treaty, it was a punishment for Germany. Rather than a just and stable peace as Wilson had promised in his Fourteen Points, the Germans felt humiliated and betrayed. It deprived the country of a significant part of its territory, including some seven million people and all of its overseas possessions. Alsace-Lorraine became, once again, part of France, and Belgium was enlarged in the east with the addition of the former German border areas of Eupen and Malmedy.

The treaty's harsh conditions damaged Germany's integrity and the German people's morale. It was one thing to impose limitations on the German military, banning the use of heavy artillery, gas, tanks, aircrafts, and submarines. But the treaty also required Germany to pay the enormous reparation cost of the war to the Allies, ruining Germany financially for the unforeseeable future.

In Germany, the treaty was referred to as "The Dictate." Its list of demands and orders from the Allies created a deep resentment in the German population against the Western powers. Adolf Hitler used these feelings of betrayal to gather support during his years in politics, which finally led to his election as chancellor in 1933. He promised the German population that it would rise again and become a great and once more proud nation. Hitler not only delivered hope to the German people, he delivered employment and prosperity. They would have followed him anywhere, and most of them did. Hitler didn't miss the opportunity to accuse the democratically elected Weimar government of betraying Germany by signing the Versailles Treaty. The Germans' distrust in democracy fueled Hitler's plan to turn his country toward authoritarianism, and eventually the Nazi dictatorship.

While Hitler was preying on the losses the Treaty of Versailles caused Germany for his own political gain, Wilson returned to the United States claiming victory. Determined that Congress would ratify the accord, Wilson enthusiastically campaigned for it across the nation. Nevertheless, that treaty he considered a triumph was a complete betrayal of the values of peace, justice, and friendship he had praised in the weeks and months prior to the Versailles Conference. It was also a betrayal of the hopes that millions of Germans had placed in Wilson and his Fourteen Points. Not even his own Senate believed in the Fourteen Points. The German people were right. The Versailles Treaty resulted in Hitler starting World War II, which brought bloodshed and destruction on a level the world had never seen. However, the effects of the Versailles Treaty continued to be felt after the war.

Among other territorial rearrangements under that treaty, the former German province of East Prussia was split in 1924 and given to Lithuania and Poland (after World War II, the region was split between Poland and Russia), the Sudetenland—a predominantly German speaking area situated in the vicinity of the Sudeten mountain range—was given to former Czechoslovakia (as of 1993 the Czech Republic), and Yugoslavia was formed as a union of the Serbs, Croats, and Slovenes. Creating new and unnatural borders and nations did not create unity and peace long term. Instead, it led to massive upheaval and, eventually, to the Bosnian War between the Serbs and Croats, which lasted from 1992 to 1995.

The committee didn't know the disastrous outcome of the Versailles Treaty when it gave Nobel's prize to Wilson. To the committee, Wilson was a candidate who not only gave the world hope of a new and peaceful world order, but also played an important part in strengthening Norway's political ties with the United States.

1925:
CHARLES G. DAWES—HELL AND MARIA

In 1925, the Nobel Peace Prize Committee gave the medal to Vice President Charles Gates Dawes of the United States. The rationale behind this award was the Dawes Plan, a short-lived economic strategy that gave Germany a new schedule and new terms for reparations after World War I. Dawes shared that year's award with Sir Austen Chamberlain, the British foreign secretary, one of the three men responsible for the Locarno Treaties.

The Dawes Plan was initiated in 1923, when the League of Nations invited Dawes to chair a committee to deal with the issues around the German reparations of World War I. Dawes provided this committee with a report—the Dawes Report, submitted in April 1924—"providing facts on Germany's budget and resources, outlining measures needed to stabilize the currency, and suggested a schedule of payments on a sliding scale."[5] The Allied occupation of the Ruhr industrial area had contributed to the hyperinflation crisis in Germany, partially because of its disabling effect on the German economy. Dawes's plan provided for an end to the Allied occupation, which would reduce the inflation, and proposed a payment plan for the damages Germany could possibly live with.

The Dawes Plan has been viewed as the beginning of the seven agreements of Locarno of 1925, which were meant to tie up loose and inadequate ends from the Versailles Treaty.

"No more war!" French foreign minister Aristide Briand declared to the League of Nations. "From now on it will be for the judge to decide what is right. Just as individual citizens settle their disagreements before a judge, so shall we also resolve ours by peaceful means. Away with rifles, machine-guns, cannons. Make way for conciliation, arbitration, peace!"

Dawes did his task as a financial planner, but—unlike Briand—he didn't speak much about peace. Nevertheless, his plan became part of the efforts to reconcile Germany with the rest of Europe. According to Sir Austen Chamberlain, the other winner of the 1925 prize, "The outstanding work of the Dawes Committee greatly facilitated our task." Chamberlain had been part of negotiating the Locarno Treaties, which fixed Germany's western borders and stipulated that arbitration would be used to resolve international disputes. The agreements also demilitarized Germany and made it part of the League of Nations.

The Locarno Treaties were like putting a Band-Aid on Germany's broken pride and integrity. It did nothing to actually heal the wound. Dawes had made a payment plan for Germany, but this plan didn't resolve the underlying sense of injustice and resentment the Germans felt after the Versailles Treaty forced them to pay excessive punitive damages. Perhaps the Nobel Committee started to realize they made a mistake when they rewarded Woodrow Wilson for the Versailles Treaty. Perhaps the committee thought that by honoring the Locarno Treaties, it could somehow magically make everything better. Although the Locarno Treaties were greeted with celebration around the world, they ended up worthless, and may be viewed as foolish in hindsight. Just a few years later, World War II broke out. Nevertheless, the Nobel Committee cannot be expected to foresee what happens after the prize, and the men behind the Locarno Treaties did deserve to be honored.

The manner in which the Nobel Committee gave out the prize to Dawes and Chamberlain creates a doubt as to Dawes's credibility as a peace champion. That year's prize was only announced in 1926, together with the 1926 winners—Aristide Briand and Gustav Stresemann—who had, with Chamberlain, crafted the Locarno Treaties. It may look as if the committee didn't have any worthy candidates to choose from in 1925, but did not want to skip a year despite the fact that they are allowed to. Skipping a year (when there is no excuse of a war) takes courage, because that makes a statement that none of the candidates were peace champions. Perhaps that is why the committee grouped Chamberlain with Dawes—because they didn't find Dawes worthy on his own.

Whether or not the Nobel Committee found Dawes to be a worthy peace champion on his own is uncertain, but it did admire his financial planning, according to the Nobel Peace Prize website. When he was appointed US director of the Bureau of the Budget in 1920, according to the Nobel site, Dawes used his knowledge and experience in finance to reform the budgetary procedures, saving the US government about two billion dollars in the first year.[6]

Perhaps the committee also enjoyed Dawes's forthright and fearless nature. During World War I, he went to Europe as a purchasing agent for the American forces and was made brigadier general. When Congress investigated charges of waste during the war, Dawes responded to one particular question about overpaying for the use of French mules by retorting:

"Helen Maria, I'd have paid horse prices for sheep if the sheep could have pulled artillery to the front!" After that, Dawes was nicknamed "Hell and Maria."[7]

Dawes was elected the thirtieth vice president of the United States in 1924, on President Calvin Coolidge's ticket. He didn't accomplish much during his term as vice president, perhaps because he didn't get along with the president. Soon after the election, Dawes sent a letter to Coolidge saying he wouldn't be attending the cabinet meetings. It is believed that this was the beginning of the feud between the two.[8]

Perhaps it also amused the Nobel Committee that Dawes, in a Senate address on the day of President Coolidge's inauguration, criticized the Senate rules and seniority system and, as a result, overshadowed Coolidge and angered the Senate.

"I should hate to think," Dawes said, "that the Senate was as tired of me at the beginning of my service as I am of the Senate at the end."

Dawes's relationship with President Coolidge and the Senate is relevant because, as later chapters will show, the Norwegian Nobel Committee has a love-hate relationship with the US government. While Norway has sought to strengthen ties with the US, it also frowns upon some of the US leaders, and the committee seems to enjoy a Nobel prize winner who dares to oppose these leaders.

No matter the motives of the committee, Dawes, who was born in Ohio in 1865, is known more for his music than for his work in public service or the fact that he won the Nobel Peace Prize. His "Melody in A Major" was the only No. 1 pop single cowritten by a United States vice president, not to mention Nobel winner. "It's All in the Game," which incorporated Carl Sigmund's lyrics to Dawes's tune, was a 1958 hit for Tommy Edwards. (Edwards's version reached number thirty-eight on Billboard's All Time Top 100.) In 1951, the year Dawes died, violinist Fritz Kreisler recorded it and made it his signature encore. Louis Armstrong, Dinah Shore, Nat King Cole, Barry Manilow, and Elton John have also covered it.

1929:
OUTLAWING WAR

The years following World War I were filled with the belief that the world could not survive another war, and the Nobel Committee's choice in 1929 reflects that sentiment. That year's award went to Frank B. Kellogg, secretary of state under President Coolidge from 1925 to 1929. Kellogg, an ambassador to Great Britain as well as a judge in the Permanent Court of International Justice at The Hague, was the coauthor, with Aristide Briand of France, of the Kellogg-Briand Pact, which made war altogether illegal.

On the tenth anniversary of America's entry into World War I, April 6, 1927, Foreign Minister Briand proposed a treaty between France and the United States guaranteeing "perpetual friendship" and prohibiting war. France had been hit hard by World War I and, still feeling threatened by its German neighbor, it was seeking alliances. The State Department represented by Kellogg gave the proposed bilateral agreement a lukewarm reception. They worried that such an arrangement could be interpreted to require the United States's intervention in case the sovereignty of France was ever threatened.

A few months later, Kellogg finally countered the proposal with a larger treaty for all nations to sign. Kellogg saw this treaty as "the greatest accomplishment of my administration" and, perhaps, a way to win the Nobel Peace Prize. Upon learning that he had been nominated, he sent the press release to his wife with a note saying that if he could realize this pact, "I think it quite likely I would get that prize."

The signatories to this treaty would renounce war and use arbitration as an instrument of national policy. Also known as the Pact of Paris, the treaty was signed in the French capital on August 27, 1928, initially by representatives from fifteen countries. Altogether, sixty-four countries, including Germany, Italy, and Japan, joined. Ironically, Benito Mussolini called the pact "transcendental," and the Japanese praised this "sublime and magnanimous treaty."

Did Kellogg actually believe that an agreement where the parties renounce war would actually prevent war? Did he truly believe that much in humankind? Or was his work motivated by a wish to become a star and shine in the light of the prestigious Nobel medal? His own admissions seem to indicate the latter. A true peace champion cares more about humankind than his own personal gain.

Although abdicating war was an inspiring thought, it turned out to be unrealistic. The Kellogg-Briand Pact also left too many loopholes, which the Nobel Committee missed. No country would renounce the right to self-defense, nor the definition of what construed self-defense. The United States would not forsake the Monroe Doctrine, which stated that any European attempts to colonize or interfere with states in North or South America would be viewed as acts of aggression, requiring US intervention. There were no sanctions either if a signatory country were to use illegal force. The signatory states signed this treaty because there were no obligations to be held to and no sacrifices to be made.

The Nobel Committee may have been fooled by wishful thinking. Joseph Stalin was not. "They talk about pacifism," Stalin said, "they speak about peace among European states. . . . All this is nonsense."

The member states soon realized that there was no way to enforce the pact or to sanction those who broke it. Three years later, in 1931, Japan invaded Manchuria. In 1939, Germany invaded Poland, and World War II began. Although the Kellogg-Briand Pact looked good on paper, the committee was likely motivated by something more than a naive idea of peace. The 1929 award to US Secretary of State Kellogg served, yet again, as a tool to reinforce the political bond between Norway and the United States.

5

INCONSISTENT CHOICES

For my part, I wish all guns with their belongings and
everything could be sent to hell,
which is the proper place for their exhibition and use.
— ALFRED NOBEL

A RE THE INCONSISTENCIES surrounding the peace prize and its
recipients indicative of political fluctuations? Most of the early prize winners had *some* of the characteristics of peace champions, even if the political
benefits of awarding them the prize were also evident. After World War II, the
committee's choices seem to have strayed further away from Nobel's instructions
and have included labor organizations and bankers. The committee has also since
extended peace to include the environment, human rights, and humanitarian
work. Sometimes the committee follows the few requirements stipulated in
Nobel's last will, but often it does not. Sometimes the cause is good, but the
motivations unclear. Other times the motivation is nakedly political.

1944:
POST-WORLD WAR II SENTIMENTALISM

The only Nobel Peace Prize medal that was awarded during Nazi Germany's occupation of Norway (from 1939 to 1945) was in 1944, when the prize went to the International Committee of the Red Cross (ICRC). The committee waited, however, to announce and hand out this prize until 1945 after the Germans had capitulated.

The ICRC, a humanitarian organization founded by Henri Dunant in Geneva in 1863, might seem like a worthy prize winner at first glance. The organization is based on volunteer work around the world, and was founded to protect human life and health, to ensure respect for all human beings, and to prevent and alleviate human suffering. However, Alfred Nobel didn't include such work in his will. One might argue that humanitarian work can actually create a more peaceful world, but that's a different discussion—one I will come back to at the end of this book.

Even if humanitarian work was part of Nobel's last will, the Red Cross may not have qualified as a peace champion. The Red Cross showed indifference to Jewish suffering and death during the Holocaust when it stopped applying pressure on Nazi Germany to improve prisoners' conditions in the concentration camps. The organization made erroneous reports about the dangers for the Jewish population and was even accused of accepting Nazi propaganda. Perhaps the ICRC tried to keep its reputation as a neutral party. No matter the reason, the organization hardly showed the courage and love of mankind that Nobel asked of his peace champions, let alone lived up to its own values as an organization. As early as May 1944, the ICRC's failed response to this genocide was known to the outside world and should also have been known to the Nobel Committee.

The choice of the Red Cross seems mostly motivated by sentiment and safety—after all, the Red Cross had won the prize before in 1917. Had it not been for its insufficient response to the Holocaust, the organization would also have been a safe choice because of its admirable values. Perhaps the

1944 award was the committee's way of saying "we know we've been quiet for a while, but we're still here," and here is a safe, palatable choice, even if it is not necessarily a worthy peace champion.

1945:
THE "FATHER OF THE UNITED NATIONS"

The 1945 award went to Cordell Hull for his role in helping to establish the United Nations. The League of Nations had failed and ceased to exist in April 1945, and the United Nations took its place. Hull served as secretary of state under President Franklin D. Roosevelt for eleven years, the longest anyone has ever served in that position. In 1943, while the war was still raging, Hull drafted the UN Charter, another international resolution designed to prevent war. This time the United States became a signatory state, which added to the credibility of the UN and confidence that the members—this time—would keep the peace. What the committee apparently overlooked was Hull's anti-Semitic tendencies as well as the discriminatory policies of the entire US State Department under Hull. Only six years earlier, Hull had demanded that President Roosevelt turn away the ship SS *St. Louis,* which was carrying 937 Jewish refugees seeking asylum from Nazi persecution. Hull was a Democrat from Tennessee, and the Southern Democrats were a political party for white Americans who had defended slavery during the Civil War and had racist values. The Southern Democrats did not want Jewish refugees on American soil, and Hull threatened to withdraw support from Roosevelt in the upcoming elections if he allowed the refugees in.

The ship had first attempted to reach Cuba but was stopped before it arrived on shore. Cuba had just changed its policy on receiving refugees and refused to take the passengers of the *St. Louis.* The captain then decided to turn to the United States. In a telephone conversation between Hull and Henry Morgenthau, Jr., Secretary of the Treasury, on June 5, 1939, Hull made it clear that the passengers could not legally be issued US tourist visas as they had no return addresses. He also pointed out that the issue at hand was between the Cuban government and the asylum seekers. The United States had nothing to do with it.

Roosevelt gave in to Hull's pressure and turned the ship away on June 6, 1939. It returned to Europe, and although the United States did work with Britain to find safe asylum for the refugees, the United States by and large failed in doing that, as more than a quarter of those who had been aboard that ship later died in the Holocaust.

The following year, in September 1940, another ship from Portugal, the *Quanza*, with Jewish refugees onboard, tried to acquire visas to enter the United States. Hull declined again. However, this time First Lady Eleanor Roosevelt managed to bypass Hull's refusal through another State Department official, and the Jewish refugees onboard this ship were finally allowed to disembark in Virginia.

On a different occasion during the war, American Jews sought to raise money in order to save Romanian Jews from mass murder. Again, Hull refused to come to their rescue. To send money out of the United States during wartime, two government agencies, the Treasury Department and the State Department, had to sign a simple release. Henry Morgenthau, Jr., signed immediately. Hull's State Department delayed, during which time many Jews died in the Transnistria concentration camps.

Hull was hardly a peace champion. But there were reasons he appealed to the Nobel Committee.

Not only was Hull rewarded for his role in the creation of the United Nations, the committee also pointed out his role in the good-neighbor policy of the Roosevelt administration. This policy focused on bringing international harmony to the Americas. Nobel Committee chair Gunnar Jahn also spoke about Hull's devotion to lower tariffs and free trade, hailing him as "representative of all that is best in liberalism, a liberalism with a strong social implication." Free trade and social liberalism are commendable accomplishments, although not what Nobel had in mind for his prize recipients, and certainly not recipients who turned a blind eye to genocide.

Hull's reticence to engage with the worsening situation that faced European Jews under Nazi Germany, and the unfavorable attitude he maintained toward the Jewish community to bolster his future political ambitions, add up to a glaring oversight by the Nobel Committee.

1953:
GEORGE C. MARSHALL—MILITARY CAREER MAN

"Nobel's peace prize is not given to Marshall for what he accomplished during the war," Nobel Committee member C. J. Hambro said in his 1953 presentation speech, but rather for what he had done afterwards.

Secretary of State George Catlett Marshall, Jr. received that year's prize for the European Recovery Plan, better known as the Marshall Plan, a financial proposition set up to rebuild European economies after the end of World War II and to prevent the spread of communism.

Still, Hambro spoke about Marshall's past military accomplishments in his presentation speech.

"The United States had no military strength that could prevent war or even an attack on America," Hambro said. "And Marshall, who saw the total war approaching, and his own country powerless, clearly realized the truth of Alfred Nobel's words: 'Good intentions alone can never secure peace.'" Nobel's words were from a time when he still believed in the deterrent effect of arms. By the time he wrote his last will, however, Nobel had changed his mind about the use of weapons. Hambro used an outdated statement from Nobel in an attempt to justify awarding the 1953 prize to a general of the United States Army.

The committee was not alone in being impressed with Marshall's leadership of the Allied Forces during World War II. Winston Churchill hailed him as the "organizer of victory."

Marshall, who was born in 1880 into a middle-class family in Uniontown, Pennsylvania, was a military man his whole career. After graduating from the Virginia Military Institute in 1901, he was immediately commissioned to second lieutenant in the US Army. Prior to World War I, he was posted to various positions in the United States and the Philippines. He served as an infantry platoon leader and company commander during the Philippine-American War and in several other guerrilla uprisings.

After the United States declared war on Germany in April 1917, Marshall was assigned to help oversee the mobilization of the First Division for service in France. In mid-1918, he was posted to American Expeditionary Forces headquarters in Chaumont, France, where, under the mentorship of General John J. Pershing, he was a key planner of American operations. Marshall was instrumental in the planning and coordination of the Meuse-Argonne Offensive, which contributed to the defeat of the German army on the Western Front.

Between World Wars I and II, Marshall worked in a number of positions in the US Army, focusing on training and teaching modern, mechanized warfare. In July 1938, he was assigned to the War Plans Division in Washington, DC, and subsequently reassigned as deputy chief of staff. In that capacity, Brigadier General Marshall attended a conference at the White House at which President Franklin D. Roosevelt proposed a plan to provide aircraft to England in support of the war effort. Although he knew the plan lacked logistical support or training, Marshall failed to voice his disagreement. He was willing to risk American soldiers' lives, sending them unprepared into a conflict that the United States wasn't even part of. As a military man, perhaps Marshall was eager for his country to get involved. Perhaps his willingness to sacrifice American lives should have ended his career. Instead, President Roosevelt promoted him to general and chief of staff of the United States Army. Marshall was sworn in as chief of staff on September 1, 1939, the same day German forces invaded Poland. He held this post until the end of the war in 1945.

Under his leadership, the US Army expanded forty times its size by 1942, into a military force of more than eight million soldiers. To do this, Marshall approved an abbreviated training schedule for men entering the army, focusing particularly on basic infantry skills, weapons proficiency, and combat tactics. The new men were often not even trained to use their own rifles or weapons systems and, once in combat, many were killed or wounded, usually within the first three or four days.[1] Marshall may have been a skilled organizer, but his willingness to send untrained American soldiers to battle in Europe—although perhaps not unusual practice at that time—was not the behavior of a responsible leader concerned with the well-being of his men.

After President Harry S. Truman appointed Marshall US secretary of state in 1947, Marshall became the spokesperson for the State Department's ambitious plans to rebuild Europe.

In the devastation and ruins of Europe's cities, the Soviet Union and its many associated Communist parties were gaining followers desperate for any promise of assistance. Lack of food and material goods aided the communist cause. Further, the Russian forces were the first on the scene after Hitler's fall and were looked upon as saviors in Germany and Eastern Europe. The United States countered with the four-year Marshall Plan. Beginning in April 1948, the US proposed to rebuild war-devastated regions, remove trade barriers, modernize industry, and make Europe prosperous once again.

Marshall's ultimate goal—the defeat of Communism—became the beginning of another war, which would last more than four decades: The Cold War. According to Michael Cox and Caroline Kennedy-Pipe's 2005 report *The Tragedy of American Diplomacy? Rethinking the Marshall Plan,* the European Recovery Program was also offered to the Soviet Union. However, the United States demanded that all participating countries detach themselves from Communist influence, a demand that was evidently unacceptable to the Soviet Union.[2]

As Chairman Jahn was handing Marshall the Nobel medal and diploma, three journalists started protesting by shouting "Hiroshima" and "Nagasaki." To these protestors, Marshall was no peacemaker, but instead represented the country that had dropped nuclear bombs on Japan. As they dropped leaflets from the balcony at the audience below, Jahn leaned over to Marshall and said with contempt "Communists."[3]

Marshall—remaining calm—smiled back at Jahn as if he agreed, according to Nordlinger.

Even as he accepted the Nobel medal, Marshall spoke about the grave conse-quences of demilitarization, which he believed had resulted in the invasion of South Korea. "There has been considerable comment over the awarding of the Nobel Peace Prize to a soldier," he said. "I am afraid this does not seem as remarkable to me as it quite evidently appears to others. I know a great deal of the horrors and tragedies of war."

Marshall's militarization continued long after World War II. As Secretary of Defense from 1950 to 1951, Marshall made military preparations for entering the Korean War. On September 30th, he sent a classified message to General Douglas MacArthur ordering troops to cross the border into North Korea. "We want you to feel unhampered tactically and strategically to proceed north of the 38th parallel," the message stated. By the looks of it, Marshall wanted war.

Massive militarization and disregard for human life—including his own soldiers. That doesn't sound anything like a peace champion according to Nobel. Even his efforts to rebuild Europe weren't done with the well-being of the European population in mind. It was about power.

Some people believe in the deterrent effect of arms and a strong military, like Nobel once did, although his last will made his final opinion on that matter clear.

1986:
ELIE WIESEL—A SENTIMENTAL FAVORITE, BUT WHY?

The 1986 Nobel Peace Prize was awarded to the author and Holocaust sur-vivor Eliezer "Elie" Wiesel. According to the committee, Wiesel emerged as "one of the most important spiritual leaders and guides in an age when violence, repression and racism continue to characterize the world." [4]

Wiesel, who was born in 1928, spent his life writing about the Holocaust, and was a spokesperson for human rights and for justice. Professor and political activist, Wiesel is the author of fifty-seven books, including *Night* (translated from the French version *La Nuit*), based on his experiences in the concentration camps of Auschwitz and Buchenwald.

Many supporters campaigned for him to the Nobel Committee for several years prior to 1986, and he, like President Jimmy Carter, was nominated countless times.

"I was not proud of my Nobel," Kissinger wrote to Wiesel, "but I am proud of yours." Even the Norwegian king expressed to Wiesel that if he could have voted, he would have voted for him. The committee called Wiesel a "messenger to mankind." It stated that through his struggle to come to terms with "his own personal experience of total humiliation and of the utter contempt for humanity shown in Hitler's death camps," as well as his "practical work in the cause of peace," Wiesel had delivered a powerful message "of peace, atonement and human dignity." *Night* later became part of Oprah Winfrey's book club and a New York Times best seller.

Wiesel is probably as close to a peace champion as one can get, if we include human rights work. However, the motivations of the Nobel Committee are not as clear. The committee members may have been motivated by trying to balance the political consequences of the previous year's award. In 1985, the Nobel Peace Prize was awarded to the International Physicians for the Prevention of Nuclear War, a group that was founded in 1980 by a Boston-based group of American and Soviet doctors. One of its cofounders, Dr. Yevgeny I. Chazov, had been the personal physician of the top Soviet leadership and a member of the Communist Party Central Committee since 1982. He had also been Russian deputy minister of health since 1968. The group, and by extension the Nobel Committee, urged President Ronald Reagan to stop all nuclear testing.

"Various well-placed Norwegians," the *New York Times* reported in 1986, "said one of the committee's most basic impulses was to seek 'balance' in its awards from year to year—and that the choice of Mr. Wiesel would offset that of the International Physicians group in 1985." This was, after all, in the middle of the Cold War, and with the 1985 award, the committee had taken a stand against the United States. The award to the International Physicians group was probably more to the liking of the Kremlin than the White House, the *New York Times* noted. But in 1986, it would be the other way around. Wiesel was far from a darling of the international socialistic political elite, unlike some of the previous Nobel winners, including Swedish UN Secretary-General Dag Hammarskjöld (winner in 1961), Polish dissident and leader of the workers' union, Solidarity, Lech Walesa (1983), or South African anti-Apartheid and human rights activist Desmond Tutu (1984). Vehemently anti-Communist, Wiesel was a strong supporter of the Jewish state and was not afraid to speak up and stick his head out.

"We must always take sides," Wiesel said in his acceptance speech. "Neutrality helps the oppressor, never the victim. Silence encourages the tormentor, never the tormented."

Some of Wiesel's opinions, however, may have gone too far, even for his supporters.

"For me, the Jew that I am, Jerusalem is above politics," he wrote in the *New York Times* on April 18, 2010. "It belongs to the Jewish people and is much more than a city; it is what binds one Jew to another in a way that remains hard to explain. When a Jew visits Jerusalem for the first time, it is not the first time; it is a homecoming."

Wiesel's position on Jerusalem was criticized by Americans For Peace Now, a nonprofit Jewish organization with the aim to achieve a comprehensive political settlement to the Israeli-Palestinian conflict.

"Jerusalem is not just a Jewish symbol," Americans For Peace Now stated. "It is also a holy city to billions of Christians and Muslims worldwide. It is Israel's capital, but it is also a focal point of Palestinian national aspirations."

Wiesel has also been criticized in Israel. The Israeli newspaper *Haaretz* published an article by Yossi Sarid accusing him of being out of touch with the realities of life in Jerusalem.

In *The Holocaust Industry*, professor Norman Finkelstein reproached Wiesel for promoting the "uniqueness doctrine" which holds, according to Finkelstein, the Holocaust as the paramount of evil and therefore historically incomparable to other genocides. Finkelstein also blamed Wiesel for playing down the importance of other massacres, especially the Armenian Genocide, and spoiling efforts of raising awareness of the genocide of the Romani people executed by the Nazis.

Wiesel's stance on the political situation in the Middle East was surely not in line with the Norwegian left-wing dominated committee, who sympathized with the Palestinian cause. So, if they didn't agree with him, what made the committee select Wiesel? Especially, since Simon Wiesenthal, another Holocaust survivor and human rights activist, was also a candidate that year. Wiesenthal, who was known as the "Nazi-hunter," dedicated his life to bringing those who had carried out the genocide to justice, and according to Tom Segev's book *Simon Wiesenthal: The Life and Legends*, "Missing out on the prize was the biggest disappointment of Wiesenthal's life. He brought it up again and again, as if he had been the victim of a great injustice, until his dying day."

Again, politics enter the equation. This time, possibly to the amusement of the committee, Wiesel was fearless in publicly opposing Ronald Reagan, a hated figure among the Western European political elites. In 1985, President Ronald Reagan was planning a trip to visit a German military cemetery with Chancellor Helmut Kohl. Among the two thousand graves there, it appeared that fifty belonged to former SS soldiers. This caused upheaval in the United States. In April that year, Wiesel visited the White House to receive the Congressional Gold Medal. During his speech, he begged Reagan to stay away from the cemetery.

"That place, Mr. President, is not your place. Your place is with the victims of the SS."

In the end, Reagan did go through with his visit, although he also made a trip to the concentration camp at Bergen-Belsen in an attempt to calm public opinion. Nevertheless, Wiesel's stance against Reagan must have pleased the Norwegian Nobel committee. Perhaps it pleased them enough to award him the medal. Two candidates. Similar qualifications. One prize. And while both Wiesel and Wiesenthal were human rights activists, and not, strictly speaking, peace champions according to Nobel's will, they both deserved to be honored. But Wiesel was the one who confronted Reagan, and he won.

* * *

SOMETIMES THE COMMITTEE'S selections are far from peace champions but benefit Norway politically, like in the case of Cordell Hull, which
helped strengthen Norway's ties with the United States, and George C. Marshall, who, in addition to strengthening political ties, benefitted Norway with
financial aid after World War II. Sometimes, the winners are praiseworthy,
but their work is outside the scope of Nobel's will. With Nobel's knowledge
of human nature, he might not have been surprised if he were alive.

"I intend to leave, after my death, a huge fund for the peace idea," he
once wrote, "but I am skeptical as to its results."

6

PISTOLS AMONG
THE OLIVE BRANCHES

Hope is nature's veil for hiding truth's nakedness.
—ALFRED NOBEL

ALTHOUGH SOME OF the Nobel Peace Prize recipients are only marginally qualified to win the award according to Nobel's parameters, a few stand out as outrageous, even tragic, choices, that defy even the broadest definition of a peace advocate. In these cases, Norway put politics before reason. So eager was this once-modest country to flex its political muscle, that it rewarded some of the world's worst examples of humanity.[1]

One such an example is the 1994 medal to Yasser Arafat for his participation in the Oslo Accords, a peace agreement made between the Palestine Liberation Organization and Israel. Arafat shared that year's prize with the Israeli prime minister Yitzhak Rabin and Israeli Foreign Minister Shimon Peres. While Rabin showed real efforts to keep the peace—Rabin even paid with his life—few would equate the concept of peace with the actions of Yasser Arafat.

The Nobel Committee, however, had demonstrated over and over again to varying degrees that they did not mind that a laureate did not fit Nobel's idea of a peace champion. Instead, by constantly making up new definitions to suit different needs and different times, it has eroded our trust in the Nobel Peace Prize over the years. The committee's role, according to chairman Francis Sejersted, is not to "hand out certificates of good conduct," but to "reward practical work for peace." With this, Sejersted tried to justify what is perhaps the most controversial peace prize in history.

YASSER ARAFAT—THE ARMED LAUREATE

Although honorable, the committee's rationale for the 1994 award—to "serve as an encouragement to all the Israelis and Palestinians who are endeavoring to establish lasting peace in the region"—turned out to be a joke. Even a minority of the Nobel Committee thought so, and Kåre Kristiansen resigned in protest. Kristiansen said that Arafat's past was "too filled with violence, terrorism, and bloodshed, and his future too uncertain to make him a Nobel Prize winner." Kristiansen was also worried this award would "give the wrong signal to other violent organizations in the Middle East and other parts of the world."

His concerns about Arafat were not unfounded. Five days before the committee announced its selection, Hamas (an offshoot of the Egyptian Muslim Brotherhood) kidnapped an Israeli soldier named Nachshon Wachsman. Although Hamas was not part of PLO, Arafat did have ties to the Muslim Brotherhood, and he did not publicly condemn Hamas' attacks on Israel. On October 14, the day of the Nobel Peace Prize announcement, Israel ordered a raid to try to save Wachsman. The raid failed and Wachsman was killed along with one other soldier. In the evening, Rabin announced that he would "happily give back the Nobel Peace Prize to bring back the lives of the soldiers who fell."

As a result of Israel's raid, Arafat refused to make peace and to allow the Palestinians their state, as was stipulated in the Oslo agreement. However, according to a report by Israel's Ministry of Foreign Affairs, Arafat had violated the Oslo Accords numerous times even before the Norwegian Nobel Committee decided to award him the Nobel Peace Prize.

Under the 1993 Oslo Accords, Arafat was to refrain from inciting violence against Israel and to take measures to prevent others from engaging in it. However, Israel's Ministry of Foreign Affairs reported numerous violations of the Oslo Accords by Arafat, including a speech Arafat made on January 7, 1994, in Gaza, where he said that "The heroic intifada, which has entered its seventh year, is an extension of the 29-year-old Palestinian revolution and will go on relentlessly. . . . It is continuing, continuing, continuing."[2] At a mosque in Johannesburg, South Africa, on May 10, 1994, Arafat said, "The jihad will continue. . . . You have to understand our main battle is Jerusalem. . . . You have to come and to fight a jihad to liberate Jerusalem, your precious shrine. . . . No, it is not their capital. It is our capital." At a rally in Gaza in November 1994—between the announcement of the prize and the prize giving ceremony—Arafat said, "Our people will continue with its jihad."[3]

Not only was his past "too filled with violence, terrorism, and bloodshed," but his future was, too. Arafat proved Kristiansen right. The PLO leader immediately "reverted to terror," according to Nordlinger, "like an uncured drunk to the bottle." According to Kristiansen, the other members of the committee were hoping the prize would "motivate him to stay on track. That, of course, didn't happen, but the committee will never acknowledge that."

To understand why the Norwegian Nobel Committee would give Arafat Nobel's prize, we have to go back in time and look at the evolution of conflict in the region and Arafat's role in it. The conflict between the Jewish state of Israel and the Palestinians began with the creation of Israel in 1948. After World War II and the Holocaust, the global Jewish community demanded a recognized Jewish state in the Holy Land region of the Middle East between the Jordan River and the Mediterranean Sea.

The struggle began over land—Palestine, the area both groups claimed—not over differences in religious beliefs. Following the war of 1948–1949, the Holy Land was divided into three parts: The State of Israel, the West Bank (of the Jordan River), and the Gaza Strip. The Jewish claim that this small area referred to as the Holy Land—approximately 10,000 square miles, or about the size of Belgium—is rightfully theirs based on the biblical promise to Abraham and his descendants. The Jews also needed a haven from European anti-Semitism. Palestinian claims to the land are based on their continuous residence in the country for hundreds of years and the fact that they represented the demographic majority until 1948. They reject the notion that a biblical-era kingdom constitutes the basis for a valid modern prerogative. If Arabs engage the biblical argument at all, they maintain that since Abraham's son Ishmael was the forefather of the Arabs, then the land God promised belongs to the Arabs too.

When the United Nations segregated an area of the former British possessions of the Trans-Jordan regions for Israel, some 700,000 Islamic Palestinians found themselves without a homeland. The Palestinians and their Arab supporters in Egypt, Syria, and Jordan immediately went to war with the new state of Israel in 1948. Israel won the war, validating its right to exist. In major wars in 1967 and 1973, Israel overtook more Palestinian areas, including the Gaza Strip near the Israeli border with Egypt, the West Bank of the Jordan River, the Golan Heights near Israel's border with Syria, and the Sinai Peninsula, which Israel later returned to Egypt.

Born in Cairo in 1929, Arafat grew up in Cairo and Jerusalem during this turbulent time. His Palestinian mother died when he was five years old, and he was sent to live with his maternal uncle in Jerusalem. His earliest memories reek of extreme violence. Arafat used to tell stories of British soldiers breaking into his home in Jerusalem when he was a child and beating his family members. After four years in Jerusalem, his father brought him back to Cairo where an older sister took care of him and his siblings.

Arafat, a man who lived his life underground and always on the move, made no secret of his willingness to settle differences with violence. After all, violence was the only response he had learned growing up. As a teen-ager, Arafat was already smuggling arms into Palestine to be used against the British and the Israelis. When he was nineteen, during the war of 1948 between Israel and the Arab states, Arafat left his studies at the King Fuad I University (later Cairo University) to fight against the Jews in the Gaza area.

After the Arabs were defeated and the state of Israel was established, he applied for a visa to study in the United States and went to the University of Texas. At first glance, Arafat looked like any other international student in the United States. Having recovered his spirits from losing the war against Israel, he returned to Fuad University to major in engineering, but he spent most of his time leading a group of Palestinian students who were planning attacks against Israel.

Earning his degree in 1956, Arafat worked briefly in Egypt, and then settled in Kuwait, where he was employed in the department of public works before successfully running his own contracting firm. His profits went to his political activities and to Fatah, an underground network of terrorist cells he founded with some friends in 1958. He also kept close connections to the Muslim Brotherhood that originated in Egypt, a transnational Muslim terrorist organization. The following year, Fatah began publishing a magazine advocating armed struggle against Israel, and by the end of 1964, Arafat left Kuwait for Jordan to organize raids against his enemy, who was attempting to push Palestinian people from their homeland and make it part of Israel.

A number of groups were formed in this period to counter the Israeli forces and expansion on Palestinian land, but they weren't necessarily coop-erating. PLO was established under the sponsorship of the Arab League, which brought together a number of guerilla groups, including Fatah, to all work to free Palestinian land occupied by Israel. The Arab states preferred a more conciliatory policy than Arafat's and Fatah's, but after the Arab states were defeated by Israel in the 1967 Six-Day War, Fatah emerged as the most powerful and best organized group within PLO. Subsequently, Arafat became the PLO executive committee chair. Now under Arafat's reign, PLO ceased being a puppet of the Arab states, who wished to keep the Palestinians quiet, and instead became a full-fledged terrorist organization based in Jordan.

Disturbed by the group's guerilla attacks and other violence against Israel, King Hussein of Jordan soon expelled the PLO from his country. The organization then moved to Lebanon, and because of that country's weak central government, Arafat was able to run PLO practically as an independent state.

"Our basic aim is to liberate the land from the Mediterranean Sea to the Jordan River," he said in 1970. The objective was to uproot the Zionist entity from Palestinian land.

Two major incidents in 1972 reveal how far Arafat was willing to go to obtain his goal. A Fatah subgroup called Black September hijacked a Sabena flight on its way from Brussels to Lod, Israel, via Vienna and forced it to land at the Ben Gurion International Airport in Lod. A shootout at the airport followed, and twenty-four civilians, including Popular Front for the Liberation of Palestine's spokesman Ghassan Kanafani, were killed. In retaliation, PLO bombed a bus station two days later, killing eleven civilians.

Then, at the Munich Olympic Games, Black September kidnapped and killed eleven Israeli athletes. According to Mohammed Oudeh, also known as Abu Daoud, one of the masterminds behind the Munich massacre, "Arafat was briefed on plans for the Munich hostage-taking."

PLO received massive international criticism after these attacks and were eventually ousted from Lebanon by Israeli troops. Although Arafat had to close down Black September and stop PLO's attacks outside of Israel, the West Bank, and Gaza Strip, he managed to keep PLO active by moving its headquarters to Tunis. With little sympathy from the international community, this was a problematic time for Arafat and PLO. He was also forced to be on the move and keep the details of his life secret due to the many assassination attempts by Israeli intelligence agents.

In 1974, Arafat addressed the UN General Assembly, saying he was holding an olive branch for peace in one hand and a freedom fighter's pistol in the other.

"Do not let the olive branch fall from my hand," he said as a warning.

The Norwegian government was touched by Arafat's speech. Norway, a supporter of Israel since its inception, started to develop sympathy with the Palestinian cause. Israel was backed by the big and powerful United States of America, but no one seemed to care about the suffering of the Palestinians. Labor Party politicians (the ruling party) began meeting with Arafat and showing support for Palestinian demands.

At the end of 1987, the Palestinian population in the West Bank and Gaza began a mass uprising against the Israeli occupation. This *intifada* (or "shaking off" in Arabic) implicated hundreds of thousands—many of them children and teenagers without any resistance experience—who demonstrated massively, went on strikes, refused to pay taxes to the Israeli government, boycotted Israeli products, and established underground "freedom" schools. Regular schools had been closed as a reprisal for the uprising. Although it mostly comprised nonviolent resistance, the Intifada also included throwing stones and Molotov cocktails, and erecting barricades to impede the movement of Israeli military forces.

In 1988, Arafat made another attempt to attract sympathy from the West. In a speech at a special United Nations session held in Geneva, Switzerland, Arafat declared that PLO renounced violence and supported "the right of all parties concerned in the Middle East conflict to live in peace and security, including the state of Palestine, Israel, and other neighbors."

The Norwegian government and Nobel Peace Prize Committee were swayed. They now thought a peace agreement with Israel was possible. After overcoming the setback when PLO supported Iraq in the Persian Gulf War of 1991, the peace process began, leading to the 1993 Oslo Accords.

It would appear that Arafat was awarded the Peace Prize by the Nobel Committee for having opted for the olive branch by signing the Oslo Accords in Washington in 1993. But, while he did extend an olive branch and even signed the peace agreement, Arafat had proven again and again that he was not to be trusted. Even before his speeches at the UN and peace negotiations in Oslo, Arafat was known for gaining sympathy from the West in public, while secretly ordering violence at home.

"Arafat would condemn operations by day," Mohammed Dahlan, an old Arafat lieutenant, proudly said, "while at night he would do honorable things." Those honorable things, according to Nordlinger, meant more violent attacks, including the suicide attack of the Tel-Aviv-Jerusalem bus on July 6, 1989, killing sixteen people, and the Mehola Junction suicide bombing between two buses on April 16, 1993, in which two people were killed and twenty-one wounded. Arafat arrived at the peace prize ceremony in Oslo in December 1994 wearing his .357 Magnum revolver handgun manufactured by Smith & Wesson. In a concession to Norwegian and Nobel sensibilities, he reluctantly removed his gun before the ceremony began. He had clearly chosen the freedom fighter's pistol instead of the olive branch, and no doubt this had always been his choice.

Arafat died in 2004 in France at the age of seventy-five, a warmonger until the end.

YITZHAK RABIN—THE BONE BREAKER

Using terms like "force, power, and beatings," Israeli prime minister Yitzhak Rabin warred his way into history. But that was not how he intended to live his life.

"At the tender age of sixteen," he said, "I was handed a rifle so that I could defend myself—and also, unfortunately, so that I could kill in an hour of danger."[4] He dreamed of becoming a water engineer, which he thought was an important profession in the dry Middle East. Nevertheless, the struggles between Israel and Palestine put an end to his dreams, and instead Rabin devoted his life to the ongoing war. Under the leadership of Rabin, Israel attempted to smash the 1987 Intifada uprising using military power. Soldiers were instructed to break the bones of demonstrators. From 1987 to 1991, Israeli forces killed more than one thousand Palestinians, many of them under the age of sixteen. Israel engaged in massive arrests and had, at one point, the highest per capita prison population in the world. The country also instituted secret police that executed targets at close range and snipers who killed from a distance. No doubt to avoid war crimes allegations, Israel denied such targeted killings for years.

However, at the beginning of the 1990s, the situation in the region seemed to improve. Because of Egypt's peace treaty with Israel in 1979 and the Arab cooperation with the United States in defeating Iraq in the Persian Gulf War of 1991, new doors opened to possible Israeli-Palestinian peace. Although known as a bone breaker, because of his tough stance on Palestine, Rabin welcomed the idea of finding a peaceful solution to the conflict. However, he knew that talking directly to the PLO leader would be difficult.

Norway offered to provide a place where the two parties could hold secret meetings, and for several months in 1992, the diplomats gathered in a secluded, wooded area near Oslo. Fourteen secret meetings took place as well as many other unofficial talks during walks in the Norwegian forest.

The result of these meetings was a declaration of principles, or the Oslo Accords. The agreement included Israel's recognition of PLO as Palestine's official representative, PLO's renunciation of violence, PLO recognizing Israel's right to exist, and agreements as to the division of the land.

Rabin played a leading role in the peace negotiations and was perhaps one of the few who actually believed in the process. When he and Arafat signed the accords on the White House lawn in September 1993, President Bill Clinton announced that the "Children of Abraham" had taken new steps on a "bold journey" toward peace. After the children of Abraham had signed and shaken hands, Rabin said to the PLO leader, "We who have fought against you, the Palestinians, we say to you today, in a loud and a clear voice, enough of blood and tears . . . enough!"

In accordance with the pact, PLO moved to validate its renunciation of violence with a change of organization and name from PLO to Palestine Authority or PA. Israel showed willingness to change by giving up territory in Gaza and the West Bank. Despite the setback of the Wachsman ordeal, Rabin was adamant about keeping his end of the agreement, even though many Jews protested the accords and felt that Rabin had betrayed Israel by believing in Arafat. Unlike Arafat, the Israeli prime minister would not give up or back down. He insisted that as long as he had a majority in the Knesset, the unicameral national legislature, he would not take their objections into account. The protesters, he said, "can spin around and around like propellers," but he would continue on the path of the Oslo Accords.

Even though peace had not been achieved, the Palestinians held an election in 1996, in accordance with the Oslo Accords, where Arafat was elected president of the Palestine Authority. True to his character, however, he kept his dictatorial governing style over the newly established Palestine and continued with terrorism until his death in 2004.

Rabin was no warmonger like Arafat. He actually wanted peace. But he was perhaps no champion of peace in Nobel's view either. For one, when Israeli soldier Wachsman was kidnaped, Rabin refused to negotiate with the Palestinian kidnappers. Instead, he ordered a raid in retaliation, which officially ended the peace. During his leadership, with whatever means he had available, he protected his country against an enemy that wished to eradicate his people, even if that meant killing more than one thousand Palestinians, many of them as innocent as the Israelis he wanted to protect. Acknowledging that he was perhaps not a worthy recipient during his Nobel lecture, he said, "Military cemeteries in every corner of the world are silent testimony to the failure of national leaders to sanctify human life."

A year later, he was assassinated at a peace rally by an Israeli extremist for his convictions and wishes for peace.

SHIMON PERES—FATHER OF ISRAEL'S ATOMIC BOMB

Minister of foreign affairs under Yitzhak Rabin, Shimon Peres was in charge of the negotiations with PLO on the Israeli side, and he shared the 1994 peace prize with Rabin and Arafat. The inclusion of Peres, a surprise to some Nobel watchers, was a tribute both to his enduring vision of a Middle East at peace and the brilliance of his diplomacy in achieving the breakthrough agreement with the PLO, according to the *Los Angeles Times*.

"We made the choice this way because we found it too difficult to distinguish between the efforts of Rabin and Peres," committee chair Francis Sejersted explained.

When Rabin was killed, Peres took over as prime minister, and in 1996, he founded the Peres Center for Peace with the aim of "promot[ing] lasting peace and advancement in the Middle East by fostering tolerance, economic and technological development, cooperation and well-being."

Although it would appear that he was a man of peace, that is not exactly true. In fact, Peres continued his predecessor's "force, power, and beatings" policy, which would also be continued by the prime ministers who succeeded him. During the years that followed, and especially during the second Intifada that started in 2000, the Israeli forces started using heavy artillery to keep the Palestinians at bay.

Peres was later elected president of the Knesset, where he remained until he retired in 2014, at the age of ninety-one. He died two year later, in 2016. Perhaps his most important accomplishment was organizing his country's nuclear program. Known as the father of Israel's atomic bomb, Peres can hardly be viewed as a Nobel peace champion.

THE AFTERMATH OF THE OSLO ACCORDS

In retrospect, it's easy to be wise. With the 1994 Nobel Prize, however, awarded to the parties of the Oslo Accords, peace didn't even last until the announcement of the prize, let alone the prize ceremony. Kåre Kristiansen, the committee member who resigned in protest, worried that the 1994 award would damage the Nobel Peace Prize's reputation. Could there be any doubt, he asked, "that this award is going to downgrade the prize and weaken respect for it?"

His concerns were well founded. The world was outraged.

"Has the Nobel Prize become an insult to peace?" was the headline in a 1994 *Daily Mail* article written by British historian Max Beloff.

Deputy editor of *The Observer* Adrian Hamilton called it a "peace of opportunism rather than one of principle."

Yelena Bonner, the widow of the 1975 laureate Andrei Sakharov said, "to this day, I cannot understand and accept the fact that Andrei Sakharov and Yasser Arafat . . . share membership in the club of Nobel laureates."[5]

Part of the problem may have been in the premise for the agreement. The 1993 Oslo Accords were intended to set up a framework that would lead to the resolution of the ongoing Israeli-Palestinian conflict. PLO was in a weakened state during the secret negotiations in Oslo and his lack of options was probably why Arafat agreed to the talks in the first place.[6] The organization had no support from the neighboring Arab states and had been worn down by the Israeli military.

The Israeli people were unhappy with Rabin and the agreement. The Palestinians also felt humiliated and betrayed by the Oslo Accords and by Arafat. Their discontent, combined with corruption in the Palestinian Authority, led to a second Intifada in 2000, which turned out much bloodier than the first.

During the first three weeks of this uprising, Israeli forces shot one million bullets at unarmed Palestinian demonstrators. On some occasions, armed PA policemen, often positioned at the back of unarmed demonstrators, returned the fire. Seeing the protests as acts of aggression, Israel consciously escalated the use of force to avoid a protracted civil unrest. Soon, they started using tanks, helicopters, and F-16 fighter planes in a full-scale war on the Palestinians, who used the intensification of force to attract international sympathy.

The war between the Israelis and the Palestinians has still not ended. In November 2000, Hamas and Islamic Jihad, later joined by the Popular Front for the Liberation of Palestine and the Fatah-affiliated al-Aqsa Martyrs' Brigade, began conducting suicide bombings and other armed operations against Israel. There were more than 150 attacks from 2000 through 2005, compared to twenty-two incidents from 1993 to 1999 by Islamist opponents of the Oslo process.

Hezbollah, operating out of southern Lebanon, began a series of attacks against Israel, culminating in the 2006 Israeli-Hezbollah War. The Israelis then elected the conservative Benjamin Netanyahu as prime minister. Distrustful of a recognized Palestinian state, Netanyahu put no effort into following up on the terms of the Oslo Accords. Several attempts, notably by the United States, have been made to reach a peace agreement between Israel and its Arab neighbors. The one initiated by Barack Obama in 2009 came to a halt a year later when US negotiators failed to persuade Netanyahu's coalition government to renew the moratorium. The United States also failed to convince PA's Mahmoud Abbas to resume negotiations and to end all settlement activities on occupied territory.

Tension has been rising again in Jerusalem since the summer of 2014. An attempt by the US Secretary of State John Kerry to revive a peace process failed, and the two sides are farther apart than ever. Although the conflict used to be about the possession of land, it has become more defined by religion since Israel captured the West Bank in 1967. Perhaps that was why the Palestinians chose a synagogue for the attack on November 18, 2014 that killed four Jewish worshippers. The two Palestinian attackers were also shot.

Since President Donald Trump recognized Jerusalem as Israel's capital on December 6, 2017, there has been another spike in violence and the number of deaths is increasing.

Many Palestinians believe Israel is preparing to allow Jews to pray in the compound of the al-Aqsa Mosque in Jerusalem, the third holiest site for Muslims after Mecca and Medina. The Israeli government has denied this. The Palestinian president Mahmoud Abbas has called for Palestinians to defend al-Aqsa, and the Israeli government has condemned such defense as an incitement to terrorism.

In May 2017, the Israeli cabinet held its weekly meeting in tunnels below al-Aqsa Mosque, on the fiftieth anniversary of the Israeli occupation of East

Jerusalem, "to mark the liberation and unification of Jerusalem"—a move that infuriated Palestinians.

During Friday prayers in July 2017, thousands of Palestinians came out to pray in the streets outside of Lion's Gate, one of the entrances to the Old City. Peaceful demonstrations were violently suppressed by Israeli forces, resulting in hundreds of injuries.

President Abbas, who continues to assert that he is against the use of violence, has been overshadowed in recent years by Hamas, the more extreme Islamist rival of Fatah in the Palestinian national movement. Hamas has declared war numerous times.

As of 2019, the Israeli government continued to enforce severe and discriminatory restrictions on Palestinians' human rights. It has restricted the movement of people and goods into and out of the Gaza Strip and facilitated the unlawful transfer of Israeli citizens to settlements in the occupied West Bank, according to a 2019 Human Rights Watch report. That same report confirms that Israeli forces continue to respond to demonstrations for Palestinian rights on the Gaza side with excessive lethal force. Between March 30 and November 19, 2019, security forces shot and killed 189 Palestinian demonstrators, including 31 children, and wounded more than 5,800. Demonstrators threw rocks and Molotov cocktails, used slingshots to hurl projectiles, and launched kites bearing incendiary materials, which caused significant property damage to nearby Israeli communities.

The Israeli army also launched intermittent air and artillery strikes in the Gaza Strip during this same period, killing thirty-seven Palestinians. Palestinian armed groups fired more than one thousand rockets and mortars toward Israel from Gaza as of November 13, 2019. All of which amounts to a major increase in violence from previous years, according to the Meir Amit Intelligence and Terrorism Information Center. The vicious circle of conflict seems to have no end.

The 1994 prize may be viewed as an attempt to resolve conflict in the Middle East, and also the committee's, perhaps flimsy, hope to promote Norway as a peacemaker through the 1993 Oslo Accords, in which Norwegian diplomats were instrumental in brokering the deal between Israel and Palestine. Do not forget that few believed that the Oslo Accords would establish a lasting peaceful coexistence between the parties. Norway was now a major player in global politics, if only momentarily, and the prize drew international attention to that fact. Norway didn't have to say, "Look how great we are." The prize said it all.

Surely the Norwegian government wanted to copy the success of the 1978 Camp David Accords, in which President Jimmy Carter brokered a peace agreement between Israel and Egypt. For that, the committee awarded the 1978 peace prize to the Israeli prime minister Menachem Begin and Egypt's president Anwar Sadat.

1978–PEACE PRIZE CEREMONY IN A FORTRESS

Before the Oslo Accords, there had been other attempts at finding a resolution to the conflict in the Middle East. On September 17, 1978, President Sadat, Prime Minister Begin, and President Carter signed the Camp David Accords, laying the groundwork for a formal peace treaty between Egypt and Israel.

Egypt had previously waged four wars on Israel, starting with the country's founding in 1948, but now Sadat was seeking peace. After twelve days of secret negotiations lead by Carter at the presidential country retreat at Camp David, Maryland, the parties finally signed two framework agreements. As a result, a peace treaty was indeed signed on March 26, 1979, after which Israel returned the whole of the Sinai Peninsula (seized in the 1967 war) to Egypt. In return, Egypt granted Israel full diplomatic recognition and promised to end the violence.

For their efforts, the 1978 Nobel Peace Prize was awarded to Sadat and Begin. As mentioned in Chapter Two, the committee wanted to include Carter, but was forced to leave him out because he hadn't been nominated within the February 1 deadline.

Unlike the Oslo Accords, the Camp David Accords were a success and peace has been upheld between Israel and Egypt ever since. However, one question remains: does a successful peace agreement automatically erase a laureate's sins and make them peace champions? The people in the Middle East, for whom this peace agreement mattered the most, seemed to think not. The Arab world felt betrayed by Sadat's willingness to make peace. Even Arafat had an opinion.

"As far as the Palestinian people are concerned," he declared, "the Nobel Prize has been shared by two fascists with a black history."[7] By "fascist," he may have thought that Sadat had acted disloyal to his people and the Arab world by making a deal with the enemy. As described earlier in this chapter, Arafat was not willing to make peace with that enemy, even after he signed the Oslo Peace Accords.

As a consequence of Sadat's peace efforts, Egypt's membership in the Arab League was suspended (and not reinstated until 1989). There was also trouble within Egypt. Various Islamic groups called for the Egyptian president to be overthrown and replaced by a government based on Islamic theocracy. Sure enough, the last months of Sadat's presidency were marked by internal uprising.

The one with the darkest history of the two 1978 winners, however, was the Israeli prime minister Menachem Begin. Of Polish descent and heavily marked by the Holocaust, Begin was a Zionist who fiercely believed Jews had a right to return to the Holy Land. These beliefs led him to head Irgun Zvai Leumi, an underground terrorist faction, which in 1946 blew up a wing of the King David Hotel in Jerusalem, the head-quarters of the British administrators of Palestine. Ninety people were killed in the attack, including Jewish and Arab hotel employees, as well as British officials. Begin was also responsible for Irgun's infamous attack on the Arab village Deir Yassin in 1948, where more than two hundred men, women, and children were killed. The British authorities placed a price of £10,000 on the "grim-faced, bespectacled" Menachem Begin's head for his terrorist acts.

"My friends and I labored to educate a generation," Begin once said, "to be prepared not only to toil for the rebuilding of a Jewish state but also to fight for it, suffer for it and, if needs be, die for it."

Begin, like any other person, had more than one side. According to the *New York Times,* he was a brilliant politician, and could be "soft-spoken, mild-mannered, and personable." On the other hand, he called "every German a Nazi, every German a murderer." In general, however, Begin was considered a right-leaning hard-liner in the West, and many were dismayed that Sadat had to share the prize with him.[8]

This discontent showed at the 1978 Nobel prize-giving ceremony in Oslo, as well. That December, Begin traveled to Oslo to receive the prize, but Sadat did not show up. His official reason, and a valid one, was that no peace treaty had been concluded yet. The Camp David Accords were merely preparations for an agreement. The real reason Sadat didn't show, however, was that he was already paying a steep prize for his peace efforts back home in the Arab world. Standing next to Begin in Oslo, showing the world they were cohorts, would just make it worse.

Because of the many threats to Begin's life, the prize ceremony was moved from the University of Oslo to Akershus Festning, a fortress standing on a cliff above the Oslo fjord. Mass demonstrations ensued in this otherwise peaceful city, and Begin was transported by helicopter from the airport to the royal palace and from there to the fortress. At the ceremony, Begin repeated what Carl Christian Berner, former president of the Norwegian Parliament, had said during his speech at the very first peace prize ceremony in 1905.

"The Norwegian people have always demanded that their independence be respected," Begin said. "They have always been ready to defend it. But at the same time they have always had a keen desire and need for peace."

The same applied to Israel, he asserted. Begin may have had a point, but that didn't qualify him for Alfred Nobel's prize. The years following the 1978 award would show Begin's true nature. In 1982, he led Israel to war against Palestinian guerillas in Lebanon, which, according to the *New York Times,* "enmeshed Israel in the lethal sectarian politics of Lebanon." This invasion was a response to years of border harassment, but as the Israeli forces bombed the Lebanese capital for ten weeks, "criticism and anguish arose."

Many Norwegians felt that the prize to Begin should have been revoked, and there were discussions in Parliament. The Nobel Committee responded the way it usually did when criticized: with silence.

Sadat is a different story. He showed considerable bravery when he traveled to Jerusalem in November 1977 to meet Begin and address the Knesset in an attempt to find a solution in their conflict. He was subject to numerous assassination attempts in the short years following the award, and ultimately paid with his life. He was murdered on October 6, 1981, by religious fundamentalists associated with the Muslim Brotherhood. Part of the plot against him were two men who later became infamous. Omar Abdel-Rahman, also called the "Blind Sheikh," was convicted in the 1993 World Trade Center bombing. Ayman al-Zawahiri, who later became the second most important man in al-Qaeda, took Osama bin Laden's place in the organization when bin Laden was killed by US forces in 2011.

Both the 1978 and 1994 awards have been viewed as insults to peace and to Alfred Nobel.

"Perhaps this is the moment," British historian Beloff wrote in the *Daily Mail* about the 1994 award, "to abolish the Nobel Peace Prize altogether."[9]

7

DEVALUING WOMEN

*It is my express wish that in awarding the prizes no
consideration be given to the nationality of the candidates,
but that the most worthy shall receive the prize,
whether he be Scandinavian or not.*

—ALFRED NOBEL

Promoting women is important to the Norwegian government. The Law of Gender Equality,[1] which was passed in 1978, is supposed to ensure the recruitment of women in typically male-dominated professions. The law requires 40 percent female representation in public-appointed offices and councils, and the Municipal Act of 1993 requires 40 percent female representation in the Municipal Council.[2] Universities in Norway with typically more male students have installed a system of extra points for female applicants, incentivizing the acceptance of women into those studies, and in 2007, Parliament passed a law requiring boards of listed companies to have a gender balance of at least 40/60.

Norway prides itself on having come farther than most other countries with more women on boards, in government, and in leadership positions than any other country. Nevertheless, there is still work to do. Although systems and regulations have been put in place, only 22 percent of Norway's top leadership positions are filled with women, according to the 2018 CORE Topplederbarometer.

Why is that? Norway has an equal education system, laws, and equality awareness campaigns, yet women are not equally present in leadership. Here is where the Nobel Peace Prize comes in. The problem of gender inequality runs deeper than any regulation or quota. In today's society, we lack female role models. Yes, we have examples of female leaders, but these women have often adopted a masculine form of power and end up leading with an iron fist. Without being conscious of it, women maintain a dysfunctional system of competition and distrust. According to professor Phyllis Chesler, women often don't help other women, which means that the few female leaders we have don't necessarily act as role models.[3] Unlike laws and regulations, Nobel's prize has a chance of making a difference by choosing female peace champions that have not given away their own feminine power and who are willing to help and support other women to rise up and take an active part in our society to the benefit of mankind and our planet.

Alfred Nobel understood the importance of such women for our society. It was a woman, Bertha von Suttner, who inspired Alfred Nobel to create the Nobel Peace Prize in the first place. As of 2019, however, only fifty-three women have won the prize since its inception, while 866 men have been awarded (in addition to the twenty-four organizations that received the prize). While this imbalance has been in accordance with society's patriarchal model of power, it's time for it to change. The committee realizes that and has, in recent years, made efforts to nominate and select women. The problem is that the committee doesn't seem to have values in place to guide it in its selection process. As a result, the committee sometimes selects women who are true peace champions according to Nobel's vision. Other times, the women are as far from role models as some of the male recipients. This chapter will show examples of both.

MOTHER TERESA:
THE GREATEST HUMANITARIAN
OF THE TWENTIETH CENTURY

Agnes Gonxha Bojaxhiu, better known as Mother Teresa, won the Nobel Peace Prize in 1976 as a reward for dedicating her life to humanitarian work. She was no doubt one of the greatest humanitarians of the twentieth century, and if humanitarian work was part of the scope, she would have been a clear Nobel peace champion. Her entire life is still an inspiration to others.

Born in 1910 in Skopje, the current capital of the Republic of Macedonia, Mother Teresa was committed to helping others from an early age.

"My child, never eat a single mouthful unless you are sharing it with others," her mother told her. "Some of them are our relations," she responded when young Mother Teresa asked who the people at their table were, "but all of them are our people."

At eighteen, she went to Ireland to join the Loreto Sisters of Dublin, where she took the name Sister Mary Teresa after Saint Thérèse of Lisieux. A year later, she went to India, and after her First Profession of Vows, she was assigned to teach at Saint Mary's High School for Girls, a school dedicated to the city's poorest Bengali families.

Mother Teresa learned to speak Bengali and Hindi fluently, taught geography and history, and dedicated herself to alleviating girls' poverty through education for nineteen years, the last few as the school principal. As was customary, she took on the name of "Mother" when she made her final vows to a life of poverty, chastity, and obedience.

In 1946, while riding a train from Calcutta to the Himalayan foothills for a retreat, she heard Christ speak to her, telling her to abandon teaching to work in the slums of Calcutta aiding the city's poorest and sickest people. After having received permission to leave the Loreto convent in 1948, she walked into the city in the blue-and-white sari she would wear in public for the rest of her life, with the goal to help "the unwanted, the unloved, the uncared for."

Over the course of the 1950s and 1960s—through her newly founded sisterhood Missionaries of Charity—she established a leper colony, an orphanage, a nursing home, a family clinic, and a string of mobile health clinics. In February 1965, Pope Paul VI encouraged her to expand internationally. By the time of her death in 1997, the lay volunteers and members of Missionaries of Charity numbered more than four thousand. The 610 groups were located in 123 countries on all six continents.

Mother Teresa was hailed for being a meek and selfless nun, qualities our society has traditionally appreciated in a woman. It is not her selflessness, however, that makes her a role model for modern women and future generations. We, as a society, have been conditioned to believe that a woman can only be worthy of praise by ceasing to exist—by sacrificing her own needs to serve others. In my opinion, that belief is outdated. No one has to be selfless to be a decent human or a role model. On the contrary, this is a burden for any young woman to bear—to know that she must give up her own life to save others, whether in the role of being a mother or a leader. Being caring and compassionate are admirable qualities in both men and women. But we also shouldn't model to our children that a woman has to sacrifice herself in order to be worthy of praise. Our children don't need to watch more selfless women. They need to watch women who save themselves first and then take responsibility for the world. Mother Teresa was much more than a meek, selfless nun. She proved to be a powerful woman with influence to make a real difference.

Although praiseworthy, she wasn't perfect. Sometimes, she voiced her opinions quite aggressively, just as she did during her Nobel acceptance speech when she spoke against women's right to abortion. While I personally don't agree with her, I respect her opinion. Perhaps she could have showed more tolerance toward those who didn't share her views.

"We speak of peace," she said in her acceptance speech, "I think that today peace is threatened by abortion, too, which is a true war, the direct killing of a child by its own mother. . . . Today, abortion is the worst evil, and the greatest enemy of peace . . . Because if a mother can kill her own child, what will prevent us from killing ourselves, or one another? Nothing." She also believed birth control was a sin.[4]

According to the late Christopher Hitchens, author of *The Missionary Position: Mother Teresa in Theory and Practice*, Mother Teresa's anti-abortion message has been used to fuel several anti-abortion political machines throughout Europe—particularly in Ireland—and even in the United States. In giving her the peace prize and therein providing her yet another international stage, the committee may have paved the way for her to do the work of the Catholic Church and attack women's choices head on with arguments that still echo today.

Hitchens also claimed that Mother Teresa was a hypocrite. According to him, she consoled and supported the rich and powerful, allowing them all manner of indulgence, while preaching obedience and resignation to the poor. In the April 1996 issue of *Ladies' Home Journal,* she voiced her opinion on the separation of her new friend Princess Diana from Prince Charles. "It is good that it is over. Nobody was happy anyhow," she said. She was surely right. However, while she recognized the royal couple's right to divorce, she had only just finished advising the Irish electorate to vote against a national referendum that proposed the right to civil divorce and remarriage.

It has also been alleged that dying people in the hospices were refused pain relief while Mother Teresa herself accepted hospital treatment and medication. According to a 2016 *Huffington Post* article by associate editor Krithika Varagur, "Doctors observed unhygienic, 'even unfit,' conditions, inadequate food, and no painkillers—not for lack of funding, in which Mother Theresa's world-famous order was swimming, but what the study authors call her 'particular conception of suffering and death.'" Professor and author Geneviève Chénard wrote in the *New York Times* that "Mother Teresa believed that suffering made you closer to God."

Mother Teresa was friendly with powerful people who supported her mission. Some of these people were of questionable character. During a visit to Jean-Claude Duvalier, former president and dictator of Haiti, she praised

"Baby Doc" and his wife for their love of the poor Haitian population, while it was public knowledge that Duvalier had continued his father Papa Doc's totalitarian regime, in which thousands of Haitians were tortured and killed. Baby Doc was also known for a notorious lavish lifestyle while his people starved. Hundreds of thousands fled the country during his presidency.

She also accepted a large donation from Charles Keating, the American lawyer, real estate developer, and financier, who in 1999 pleaded guilty to four different counts of fraud, for which he spent time in prison. She also used his private jet when visiting the United States. During Keating's trial, Mother Teresa made a character statement in his favor, even though it was quite clear that Keating had stolen the money from small investors.

In Mother Teresa's defense, many powerful people have surrounded themselves and been supported by those of questionable characters. Perhaps the fact that she is a woman makes her a target of more scrutiny because we, as a society, expect women to be irreproachable.

According to Hitchens, Mother Teresa encouraged members of her order to secretly baptize dying patients, without regard to those patients' religion. Perhaps she did. Maybe she was more indulgent with the rich and famous than with the poor. Nevertheless, her flaws don't erase her accomplishments of improving people's lives around the world. They make her human. She had all of Nobel's values: an unconditional love of mankind, courage to do her calling—often in very difficult circumstances—and a wish for unity and peace. The case is not so clear for the next female Nobel Peace Prize winner.

RIGOBERTA MENCHÚ: THE "TARNISHED LAUREATE"

Guerilla fighter Rigoberta Menchú was awarded the 1992 prize "in recognition of her work for social justice and ethno-cultural reconciliation based on respect for the rights of indigenous peoples."

There are two issues with that year's prize. First, Nobel had not originally thought his prize should go to human rights related work, or to those working to prevent internal conflict within a country. But even if such work was within the scope of the Nobel Peace Prize, that year's candidate was perhaps no peace champion or role model. Let's take a look at the details of Menchú's life and how she managed to attract the Nobel Peace Prize Committee's attention.

Born on January 9, 1959, to a poor farm family, Menchú has dedicated her life to publicizing the predicament of Guatemala's indigenous peoples during and after the civil war (1960–1996), and to promoting native rights in her country. Raised in the K'iche' branch of the Mayan culture, she became involved in social reform activities through the Catholic Church and particularly in the women's rights movement. Her work aroused opposition in influential circles, especially after a guerilla organization established itself in the area. The Menchú family was accused of taking part in guerrilla activities, and her father, Vicente, was imprisoned and tortured for allegedly having participated in the execution of a local plantation owner. After his release, he joined the recently founded Committee of the Peasant Union (CUC), the local rebel organization. In 1979, Menchú, too, joined CUC. That year, her brother was arrested, tortured, and killed by the army. The following year, her father was killed when a small band of rebels—led by him—captured the Spanish Embassy in protest of the government's policies. Security forces stormed the building, and most of the rebels were killed. Shortly afterward, her mother also died after being arrested, tortured, and raped.

Menchú became increasingly active in CUC, and in 1980, she was a main figure in a CUC strike for better conditions for farm workers on the Pacific coast. She was also active in large demonstrations in the capital. She joined the radical 31st of January Popular Front, where her contribution consisted mainly in educating the native farmers in resistance to massive military oppression. In 1981, fearing for her safety, Menchú went into hiding in Guatemala before she fled to Mexico. Her new life consisted of organizing resistance efforts from abroad. In 1982, she took part in founding the joint opposition body, the United Representation of the Guatemalan Opposition.

From Mexico, Menchú went to France, where she met Elisabeth Burgos-Debray, a Venezuelan-French anthropologist and activist. Burgos-Debray convinced Menchú to tell her compelling story and made a series of taped interviews, which in 1983 became *I, Rigoberta Menchú*, a ghostwritten autobiography alternating idyllic scenes of K'iche' culture with disturbing accounts of war and death in modern Guatemala. A best seller that was translated into several languages, it touched people around the world—including the Nobel Peace Prize Committee.

In 1986, she became a member of the National Coordinating Committee of CUC, and the following year, she narrated *When the Mountains Tremble*, a film about the struggles of the Mayan people.

Menchú's efforts in shedding light on the extreme violence in her country and on the predicament of the indigenous peoples were noble. Her family and other countrymen were subjected to true horror by the Guatemalan government. The only problem was that Menchú had lied about her part in the events. For more than a decade after the publication of *I, Rigoberta Menchú*, anthropologist David Stoll investigated Menchú's story, researching government documents, reports, and land claims (many filed by Menchú's own family), and interviewing former neighbors, locals, friends, and enemies. In his 1999 book *Rigoberta Menchú and the Story of All Poor Guatemalans,* Stoll claimed that Menchú had altered her personal story, as well as her family's and the village's, to attract sympathy for the guerrilla movement. He concluded that Menchú's book "cannot be the eyewitness account it purports to be," because the Nobel laureate repeatedly described "experiences she never had herself."[5]

Using Stoll's book and other sources, the *New York Times* conducted its own research of Menchú's story and came to the same conclusion. According to the *New York Times*, the land dispute central to the book "was a long and bitter family feud that pitted her father against his in-laws, and not a battle against wealthy landowners of European descent who manipulated government agencies into trying to drive her father and other Indian peasants off unclaimed land."[6]

Menchú made up that she watched a younger brother starve to death while she was forced to do hard plantation work, and a particularly emotional episode where she and her parents were forced to watch as another one of her brothers "was being burned alive by army troops." This brother was actually killed in entirely different circumstances when the family was not present, according to the *New York Times*.

Contrary to Menchú's statement in the first page of her book that "I never went to school," and could not speak Spanish nor read or write until shortly before she dictated the text of her book, the *New York Times* article asserted that she "in fact received the equivalent of a middle-school education as a scholarship student at two prestigious private boarding schools operated by Roman Catholic nuns."

The article also pointed out that because she spent much of her youth in boarding schools, it is unlikely that she could have worked as an underground political organizer and spent up to eight months a year laboring on coffee and cotton plantations, as she describes in great detail in her book.

Menchú maintained for some time that she was proud of the book, and she denied using it as a tool to gain publicity. Those questioning its honesty had a racist political agenda, she said. Then she changed her mind and blamed any inaccuracies on her ghostwriter.

"I am the protagonist of the book, and it was my testimony," Menchú said when later interviewed by the *New York Times*, "but I am not the author." She then described her relationship with Burgos-Debray as "nonexistent" because of a disagreement over publishing royalties.

The peace price committee probably didn't know this about Menchú when they selected her. Still, the question remains if the peace prize to her should be revoked. The Nobel Committee's response to that question was clear. Geir Lundestad, former director of the Norwegian Nobel Institute, said in a telephone interview that he was aware of Stoll's manuscript and had no reason to doubt its veracity. Nevertheless, he said, "There is no question of revoking the prize." He added that the decision to award Menchú "was not based exclusively or primarily on the autobiography," and that her purpose in telling her story the way she did "enabled her to focus international condemnation on an institution that deserved it, the Guatemalan army."

That may be true. Nevertheless, there are other issues to consider. A true peace champion shares the values of Alfred Nobel: his love of humanity, his courage to stand up for what's right, and efforts to seek peace and unity between peoples through peaceful means. Menchú was a guerilla fighter who supported violence to defend her cause. Also, a peace champion is supposed to be an inspiration, a beacon of hope, and encouragement to all of us to become peace champions in our own lives. When a laureate lies about their life, and then, when busted, puts the blame on someone else, that behavior erodes trust and credibility in the peace prize as an institution, and it also harms the efforts of the cause and the people they are championing. Perhaps, in future cases, the committee should consider revoking a prize if it later turns out that a laureate tarnishes the award's mission.

The committee's refusal to consider revoking that year's prize may have been motivated by something else: the Norwegian government's negotiations between the Guatemalan government and the guerrilla organizations, which finally led to a peace agreement in 1996. With the committee's strong ties to the government, it is not unfair to ask whether revoking Menchú's award would also have downplayed the Norwegian efforts in those negotiations.

ELLEN JOHNSON SIRLEAF:
THE AFRICAN "IRON LADY"

The Nobel Committee gave the 2011 prize to three African women, among them Liberia's former president, Ellen Johnson Sirleaf, for her "non-violent struggle for the safety of women and for women's rights to full participation in peace-building work." The committee declared that Sirleaf—known as Africa's "Iron Lady"—was a leading "promoter of peace, justice and democratic rule."[7]

If that had been the case, Sirleaf would have been a true peace champion. But it's not. Born in the Liberian capital of Monrovia in 1938, Sirleaf left her country with her husband to study at Madison Business College in Wisconsin and then went to Harvard, where she gained a master's in public administration. She then returned to Liberia and worked for the government when Samuel Doe seized power in a coup d'état in 1980.

Several of the other ministers were executed, but she was open to cooperating with the new dictator and became finance minister in Doe's administration. After she publicly criticized Doe and the People's Redemption Council for mismanagement, she fled Liberia and moved to Washington, DC, where she had an impressive career in the World Bank, Citibank, and as director of the United Nations Development Program.

At the beginning of the First Liberian Civil War in 1989, Sirleaf supported Charles Taylor's rebellion against Doe and helped raise money for the war. Because of this, Sirleaf was later unsuccessfully banned from politics by the Truth and Reconciliation Commission, established in 2006 by Sirleaf herself.[8]

In 1996, the hostilities ended due to the presence of peacekeeping forces. This ceasefire allowed for the 1997 general election, in which Sirleaf opposed Taylor as the presidential candidate for the Unity Party. After much controversy, she placed second to Taylor who remained in his position as president. Sirleaf left the country soon after and went into exile in Abidjan.

In November 2005, after Taylor had retired, Sirleaf won the presidential election and became the first woman to lead an African nation. *Forbes* magazine named her one of the world's most powerful women in 2006. The following year, she was awarded the Presidential Medal of Freedom—the United States' highest civil award—allegedly for her personal courage and unwavering commitment to expanding freedom and improving the lives of people in Liberia and across Africa. In 2010, as the only female and African head of state, Sirleaf was named by both *Newsweek* and *Time* as one of the best leaders in the world. The same year, *The Economist* praised her as "arguably the best president the country has ever had."

The Nobel Committee swallowed the international praise, possibly without doing any research on its own. Liberia experts around the world wondered how Sirleaf could be deemed worthy of the world's most prestigious prize. A year after she received the Nobel medal, NRK's *Brennpunkt* made a documentary that addressed whether Sirleaf had told the truth about her relationship with warlord Taylor, and if she in fact had obtained safety for women in her country the way she and the Nobel Committee asserted.

"I didn't see what Johnson Sirleaf had done to deserve the peace prize," Stephen Ellis, Liberia expert living in Amsterdam, said, "because she didn't bring peace to Liberia." How thorough is the committee in its research of the nominated candidates? asked *Brennpunkt*. Since the committee's work stays secret for fifty years, the answers are not easy to find.

"Few other persons better satisfy the criteria in Alfred Nobel's will," Chairman Thorbjørn Jagland said at the 2011 ceremony. In the audience sat Labor Party representative Marit Nybakk and committee member Ågot Valle, who had nominated Sirleaf.

"It was about time that the Nobel Peace Prize went to women," Nybakk said. She was surprised that NRK would raise critical questions, as if being a woman was qualification enough.

Brennpunkt's journalists contacted ten of the world's most prominent Liberia experts, and not one of them said the Nobel Committee had contacted them. "I was amazed," Ellis said to the Norwegian journalists, "it just didn't occur to me that Sirleaf was one of the people the Nobel Committee would consider." In his opinion, had the committee made inquiries in Liberia, they would have eliminated her as an eligible candidate for the peace prize. According to Ellis, during Sirleaf's presidency, she restored the same style of governance—with a corrupt administration—that brought the country into war in the first place. Had the committee contacted him, he would have told them so, he said. The fact that they did not, indicates that the Nobel Committee didn't care to learn who Sirleaf really was, nor what she had done for peace. All that mattered to them, it seemed, was that she was Africa's first female president and that she was being praised in the international press.

Adekeye Adebajo, another Nigerian expert on Liberia, said that the perception of Liberia's former president is divided. On the one hand she can be described as a "very hardworking and dynamic person," but on the other hand, "her role in supporting Taylor's rebellion sends the wrong message in terms of awarding her the peace prize."

Liberia's fourteen-year-long civil war, which began in 1989, was inhumane and brutal. "Nobody should expect miracles from me," Charles Taylor declared back then, "I'm not Jesus Christ." Taylor managed to get rid of the dictator Doe, but his methods included ethnic cleansing and the use of child soldiers.

Taylor set up roadblocks, according to an official US report, and in one roadblock called "No Return," more than two thousand people—who were considered Doe supporters or part of Doe's ethnic group—were randomly killed in 1990 alone.[9]

Abdullai Kamara, an independent political analyst in Liberia, said that it is the common perception in the country that Sirleaf was one of Taylor's supporters from the United States. In 1990, Sirleaf made a written declaration to the US Congress where she pledged her loyalty to Taylor, asserting that she believed he could bring democracy back to Liberia.

Taylor was tried and found guilty of war crimes and crimes to humanity including terror, murder, and rape, by the International Criminal Court (ICC) in The Hague. In April 2012, he was sentenced to fifty years in prison.

Courtenay Griffith, Taylor's attorney, asserted to NRK's journalists that Sirleaf was one of three cofounders of Taylor's organization, the National Patriotic Front of Liberia (NPFL). He also confirmed that Sirleaf used her position in the World Bank to lobby Western governments to support Taylor's government. Sirleaf has admitted to supporting Taylor but denies having ever been involved in NPFL and says her monetary aid was limited to US $10,000. Griffith claims Sirleaf raised more than one million US dollars for the organization. In 1990, in spite of difficulties traveling in Liberia, he said, she made it to the northeastern part of the country to meet with Taylor and his soldiers.

In the end, Sirleaf turned on Taylor and helped the ICC prosecute him. Could Taylor's attorney's statements about Sirleaf be motivated by revenge? Perhaps, but Griffith is not the only one to say this about Sirleaf. Tom Woewiyu, the third cofounder of NPFL and defense minister in Taylor's administration, confirmed Griffith's story to *Brennpunkt*. Woewiyu, who now lives in Philadelphia, asserted that he wanted the truth to come out about Sirleaf's role in Liberia's civil wars. Taylor was responsible for the military aspects, he said, whereas Sirleaf was in charge of the political and financial side of the uprising. She was the political leader of Taylor's regime.

NRK attempted to obtain a statement from Sirleaf in regard to Woewiyu's strong accusations against her. She refused to respond. In her 2010 autobiography with the not-so-humble title, *This Child Will Be Great*, she wrote that she did sympathize with Taylor at first, but that she was never part of NPFL. She also contended that she withdrew her support for Taylor in the summer of 1990, when she discovered the atrocities he had committed.

"Sirleaf withdrew her support of Taylor because he and the NPFL refused to hand the presidency over to her as she had expected," Woewiyu said. According to him, her disconnection with NPFL had nothing to do with the atrocities.

"Apparently the Nobel Committee was misled," he said. "They didn't do enough research into the so-called peace achievements that Sirleaf had made in Liberia." Since she came into power in 2005, "she has re-armed the heart of Liberia," Woewiyu stated.

It appears that the committee naively swallowed the Liberian president's word as well as the praise in the international press without asking the difficult questions. It believed Sirleaf's and her government's statements that life for the people of Liberia had improved since she became president. "The monstrous numbers of rape have diminished," Jagland said in his presentation speech.

In Monrovia, no one understands how those conclusions were founded, or who gave this evidence to the committee, according to NRK *Brennpunkt*. When asked, Secretary Lundestad refused to give any information on the committee's sources. The Norwegian Refugee Council's database contains statistics on rape of women and children in Liberia from 2009 to 2012, but there are no reliable numbers before 2009, Musa Kanoe told NRK, and the situation is still chaotic. The truth is that no one knows if the number of rape cases has gone up or down under Sirleaf's government. A weak justice system in Liberia combined with an extremely corrupt police force does not help bring clarity to the situation. This is the reality in the country where Sirleaf was president from 2006 to 2018.

The committee praised Sirleaf for the fact that women have been given more chances of getting an education in Liberia under her leadership. This is also an unsubstantiated statement, according to Jessica Hanson, who has worked in education in Africa for several years. There is an increase in young girls enrolling in schools, she said when interviewed by NRK, but the girls do not stay. Out of ten of them, starting in the first grade, there may be only two or three left in the fourth grade, she said. Parents do not have the money to send all their children to school, so they prefer to send the boys. There is also a problem of teachers sexually abusing girls, according to NRK's research. The numbers Sirleaf's government shared internationally to show how education of women has improved are incorrect, according to Hanson.

Sirleaf's administration also officially acknowledged the cruel practice of genital mutilation of young women. It did so by giving out circumcision licenses to teachers in so-called bush schools all over the country.

"Ellen is a darling of the West," journalist Mae Azango said to NRK, "but here in Liberia, everybody knows that Ellen isn't a darling." Azango broke the taboo when she wrote about the practice of female mutilation in the newspaper *Front Page Africa* in the spring of 2012. She said that women were angry with Sirleaf and did not want to vote for her because she did not seek the interest of women. Nevertheless, her efforts for human rights, especially women's rights, were one of the main reasons the Nobel Committee awarded her the prize.

Sirleaf's lack of support for the Truth and Reconciliation Commission—which was founded by her—after the wars in Liberia, is another reason she shouldn't have received the peace prize. This commission attempted to ban her, as well as fifty other politicians, from holding any public positions for thirty years.

"When you look at the role Sirleaf had before she became president," Norwegian Liberia expert Morten Bøås said, "and the fact that she hasn't managed to bring much needed stability and unity to the Liberian people since she became president, my conclusion is that she did not deserve the Nobel Peace Prize."

Sirleaf is most certainly not the role model for other women the Nobel Committee wanted her to be. And she is no worthy peace champion.

* * *

WHILE THE COMMITTEE'S intentions might have been in the right place for both the 1992 prize to Menchú and the 2011 award to Sirleaf, these prizes "tokenize" women instead of honoring women's contributions to peace. The fact that a woman is a leader, perhaps even trendy in terms of media coverage, does not automatically make her a role model to other women.

The Nobel Peace Prize Committee has had other women in its pool of candidates to choose from. PeaceWomen Across the Globe (PWAG) is an organization based in Bern, Switzerland, that aims to increase the visibility of women promoting peace worldwide. The organization, previously known as 1000 PeaceWomen, began as an initiative to nominate women from more than 150 different countries for the 2005 Nobel Peace Prize. The nomination was notable for including relatively unknown women who have made significant contributions to world peace.

One of these women was Cora Weiss, President of the Hague Appeal for Peace. Weiss has been a peace activist since the early 1960s, when she led Women Strike for Peace, a US national movement initiated by mothers who discovered the hazardous effects nuclear testing had on cow's milk and the babies who consumed it. Their efforts played a crucial role in the adoption of the Limited Test Ban Treaty of 1963, and they were among the first Americans to oppose the Vietnam War.[10]

As a leader in the anti-Vietnam War movement, Weiss organized demonstrations, including the largest one on November 15, 1969, in Washington, DC. She organized the exchange of mail between families and POW's in Vietnam which revealed names of those alive.[11] Weiss traveled to Vietnam and arranged for the return of some of these prisoners.

At home, she was a volunteer teacher in the New York City public school system.

"I have marched, petitioned, written letters, gone to jail, spoken out, and joined organizations, and I have concluded that peace education may be the most sustainable work we can engage in," she said. "To reach peace, as our mentor, Betty Reardon, the founder of the International Institute of Peace Education, says, we need to teach peace." Reardon, who was 90 years old at the time of this writing, is another worthy candidate for the Nobel Peace Prize.

Peace education, according to Weiss, means teaching for and about human rights, gender equality, sustainable development, disarmament, nonviolence, social-and economic justice, and traditional peace practices, including how to solve conflict.

"How did your grandmother resolve problems with your grandfather? Did she kill him?" Weiss asked. "We need to bring peace education to formal and informal learning for girls and boys, women and men. We need to teach through participation, welcoming critical inquiry and reflection so we can prepare everyone for democracy and an active role in society."

Weiss was among the drafters of what became UN Security Council Resolution 1325 on Women, Peace and Security. She has spent her life as an activist for human rights, women's rights, and peace. The Norwegian Nobel Committee even referred to Resolution 1325 at the 2011 ceremony honoring Sirleaf.

While our world needs more female role models—and we must encourage the Nobel Committee to continue to seek out female candidates—the committee must also make sure these candidates are worthy peace champions, not just women in leadership positions who have adopted an outdated power model, which led to distrust, violence, and war in the first place. Being chosen because of one's sex and not because of one's qualifications is far from empowering. Perhaps it is even condescending. Despite noble intentions, such practices devalue women, and use them.

8

UNITED NATIONS: A LOVE AFFAIR

Good intentions alone will not assure peace, nor,
one might say,
will great banquets or long speeches.
—ALFRED NOBEL

—⁓—

THE UNITED NATIONS and its forerunners have received more Nobel Peace Prizes than any other organizations.[1] The first Nobel Peace Prize in 1901 went to Frédéric Passy, one of the founders of the Inter-Parliamentary Union. In a like manner, the committee honored the League of Nations through Woodrow Wilson in 1919, and in 1945, the United Nations through Cordell Hull. In 1954, the prize went to the UN High Commissioner for Refugees, in 1965 to the United Nations Children's Fund (UNICEF), and in 1982 again to the UN High Commissioner for Refugees.

The end of the Cold War and of the rivalry between the United States and the Soviet Union brought high hopes of a more assertive UN in the 1990s. President George H. W. Bush spoke of a "new world order," according to an article by Max Boot in *Foreign Affairs*. Presidential candidate Bill Clinton talked about giving the United Nations more power and even its own standing military force.[2]

Selecting an organization such as the UN for the Nobel Peace Prize may seem like the safe choice, especially because the UN was founded to prevent war between its member countries. Also, in a culture where the individual has little value outside the group, as I explained in Chapter Three, it's not surprising that the Norwegian Nobel Committee wishes to promote organizations. This organization is particularly close to Norway's heart, since Norway considers the United Nations a check on American power, and the UN is the closest to a world government we have yet achieved.[3]

Although an international organization governing for world peace is a noble idea, the UN hasn't always lived up to Nobel's idea of a peace champion. Yet, the Norwegians have continued to have an unwavering faith in the United Nations and its peacekeeping forces. So much, in fact, that the organization received the Nobel Peace Prize again in 1988 and 2001.

1988:
THE UN PEACEKEEPING FORCES

"Our determination has to be channeled into the United Nations," committee chairman Egil Aarvik said as he presented the 1988 prize to the UN Peacekeeping Forces. "This is the best hope for the future of the world—indeed its only hope!"[4]

There are several issues with the 1988 award. By definition, the UN Peacekeeping Forces go against what Alfred Nobel stipulated in his will. His peace prize, according to his last will, was meant to go to work for disarmament. Sending in military troops, no matter who sends them, is not what Nobel intended.

"How can a peace prize go to a group that is military in nature?" Colman McCarthy, a columnist for the *Washington Post* wrote about the 1988 Nobel Peace Prize. "How can peace be created by the same methods of organized violence—fighting with military weapons—that destroyed it?"[5]

While McCarthy raises a valid point, the UN Peacekeeping Forces are only supposed to use weapons as a last resort. The peacekeepers' role is to monitor and observe peace processes in post-conflict areas and assist excombatants in implementing the peace agreements they may have signed. The assistance comes in many forms, including confidence-building measures, power-sharing arrangements, electoral support, strengthening the rule of law, and economic and social development. The peacekeepers—often referred to as "blue berets" or "blue helmets" because of their light blue hats or helmets—include soldiers, police officers, and civilian personnel. Peacekeeping is guided by three basic principles: Consent of the parties, impartiality, and the use of force solely in self-defense or in protecting the mandate.[6]

Peacekeeping has unique strengths, according to the UN's own website, including legitimacy, burden sharing, and an ability to deploy and sustain troops and police from around the globe, integrating them with civilian peacekeepers to advance multidimensional mandates. UN Peacekeepers provide security, political, and peace-building support to help countries make the early, but difficult, transition from conflict to peace. As we shall see, the peacekeepers haven't always managed to keep their promise.

Who decides when and where to send the UN Peacekeepers? The United Nations Charter gives the UN Security Council the power and responsibility to take collective action to maintain international peace and security, and therefore most peacekeeping operations are established and implemented by the Security Council. All troops belong to the UN member countries who send them, and while they remain members of their respective countries' armed forces, they serve under UN operational control. Therefore, the peacekeepers do not constitute an independent UN army.[7]

Peacekeeping was initially developed during the Cold War to resolve conflict between states by using unarmed or lightly armed soldiers, and these operations have grown over the years. In 1993, the annual cost was

US $3.6 billion, reflecting the big operations in the former Yugoslavia and in Somalia. With the increase in operations around the world, the cost rose to $5 billion in 2006. Approved resources for the period from July 1, 2018 to June 30, 2019 was $6.7 billion, according to the UN Peacekeeping Fact Sheet. As of October 31, 2019, there had been a total of seventy-one operations since 1948, and thirteen are active as of December 2019.[8]

Many of the peacekeeping forces' operations have been successful. In El Salvador and Mozambique, the blue berets provided ways to achieve self-sustaining peace by making sure that the ceasefire agreements were respected.

According to journalist and author David Bosco, in a May 30, 2013 *Foreign Policy* article, the UN Peacekeeping Forces, even with profound limitations, manage to mitigate ongoing conflict and help prevent the recurrence of conflict once it has subsided.[9]

In recent years, however, the peacekeepers' neutrality and efficiency have been questioned and criticized. Sometimes, soldiers get involved in conflicts when they shouldn't. Other times, they don't protect the mandate they are supposed to protect. Bosco reported that when Congolese M23 rebels advanced on eastern Democratic Republic of the Congo's largest city, Goma, in November 2012, the UN Peacekeepers stood by, never firing a shot in order to prevent the attacks on Goma. One reason behind the peacekeepers' inaction is the complex situation in the country, with a government that has no interest in protecting its citizens. People who don't believe their leaders have their backs are much more likely to join terrorist groups or rebels, and trying to stop them without also changing the fundamental issues in the country's leadership is near impossible. Perhaps the UN's involvement leads to more violence in such cases. Nevertheless, "That dismal performance revived a longstanding debate about the value of the UN's signature activity," Bosco wrote. "The spectacle of Syrian rebels capturing dozens of peacekeepers in the Golan Heights has reinforced the perception of impotence."

Let's take a look at some of the peacekeeping efforts that have failed terribly.

SOMALIA

The UN Peacekeeping Forces have been deployed to Somalia since 1992. In 2012, the UN Security Council increased the African Union peacekeeping force in Somalia to nearly 18,000 troops in an attempt to defeat rebels—notably the threat from the Muslim extremist group al-Shabaab—and help stabilize the country after more than two decades of war and chaos. Somalia's root problem, however, is governance, or the lack thereof.[10] The UN has spent decades attempting to work with discredited governments in Mogadishu, not knowing which clan leaders to address. According to *The Guardian*, "Somali clan politics work by consensus and through representatives who establish a proven track record. Legitimacy is not built by elections. The donors are beholden to the countries that finance them, not the Somalis they supposedly serve. . . . At worst, the money that pours in as a result of the drought feeds the corrupt government that produces the next disaster."[11]

In addition to the issues of governance and corruption in Somalia, there has been no ceasefire agreement or consent between the parties involved, which would have facilitated the UN's role as keeper of peace. Taking into account the challenging issues in the country, perhaps the Somalia operation lacked manpower or the necessary political support to implement the mandate.

Today, Somalia is still a country ravaged by political instability, famine, and chaos. While the UN may not be to blame for Somalia's problems, the blue berets didn't always act in the best interest of the Somalian people. CNN reported pictures from a Belgian newspaper showing two UN soldiers holding a Somali boy over a fire.[12] As this chapter will show, this kind of behavior—which is the antithesis of championing peace—on the part of the UN Peacekeepers is perhaps more frequent than we would like to think.

* * *

BOSNIA

The Bosnian War raged from March 1992 to December 1995. The war involved several factions, mainly the Republic of Bosnia and Herzegovina and those of the self-proclaimed Bosnian Serb and Croat entities within Bosnia and Herzegovina. The UN Peacekeeping Forces were sent in, but failed to prevent the conflict from escalating.

The war started as a result of the disintegration of the Republic of Yugoslavia. Following the Slovenian and Croatian secessions from Yugoslavia in 1991, the multiethnic Bosnia and Herzegovina—inhabited by Muslim Bosnians or Bosniaks (44 percent), Orthodox Serbs (31 percent), and Catholic Croats (17 percent), passed a referendum for independence on February 29, 1992.

The Bosnian (Orthodox) Serbs, however, rejected the referendum and, immediately following the United States's and the European Union's recognition of Bosnia and Herzegovina on April 7, 1992, the Serbs began firing on the capital of Sarajevo. The Serbian forces continued to attack towns with large Bosniak populations, and the ethnic cleansing of the Muslim Bosniaks accompanied the outbreak of war. Although the Serbs were primary perpetrators and the Bosniaks the primary victims, the Croats were also among the victims and perpetrators. Within six weeks a coordinated offensive by the Yugoslav People's Army (JNA), paramilitary groups, and local Serb forces brought roughly two-thirds of Bosnian territory, including Sarajevo, under Serb control until the end of the war in 1995.

Under the command of the Bosnian Serb general Ratko Mladić, the Serbs killed more than eight thousand Bosnian Muslims (Bosniaks) in the atrocious Srebrenica massacre in July 1995. A Serbian paramilitary unit known as the Scorpions, officially part of the Serbian Interior Ministry until 1991, participated in the Srebrenica massacre, along with several hundred Russian and Greek (also Orthodox) volunteers.

Kofi Annan, the UN secretary-general, described the mass murder as the worst crime on European soil since World War II.[13] According to a June 27,

2005, resolution by the US House of Representatives, the aggression and genocide during the Bosnian War "ultimately led to the displacement of more than 2,000,000 people, an estimated 200,000 killed, tens of thousands raped or otherwise tortured and abused."

Only a NATO bombing campaign, led by the United States, ended the war in Bosnia four years after its beginning. The UN Peacekeeping Forces were unable or perhaps unwilling to do anything. A complex conflict with extreme violence, just like in Congo, may have been the reason for the UN's failure. According to the Human Rights Watch Report, UN forces were outnumbered by the Serbs, who were able to enter the so-called "safe-areas" the UN troops were supposed to protect. The Serbs took UN soldiers hostage and threatened to kill them if the UN didn't allow the Serbs to continue their slaughter within the safe areas. Other UN soldiers were forced to undress and hand over their uniforms, weapons, and vehicles to the Serbs, who would continue raping, torturing, and killing Muslims while posing as UN soldiers. Tadeusz Mazowiecki, former prime minister of Poland and the special rapporteur for the former Yugoslavia for the UN Commission on Human Rights, resigned from his job because of his frustration with the UN soldiers. According to him, the failure of the UN Peacekeeping Forces to protect the "safe areas" were due to a "lack of consistency and courage displayed by the international community and its leaders."[14]

RWANDA

Another failure was the horrific 1994 Rwandan genocide. During the approximate one-hundred-day-massacre from April to July 1994, the governing Hutus slaughtered the Tutsi population as well as moderate Hutus. More than 800,000 people were killed—about 20 percent of Rwanda's population and 70 percent of the Tutsi tribe.

During the slaughter, the UN Peacekeeping Forces watched and did nothing to protect the Tutsi minority. The United Nations and in particular some of its member countries including the United States, Great Britain, and Belgium, were criticized in international press for their inaction, including failure to strengthen the mandate of the UN Assistance Mission for Rwanda (UNAMIR) peacekeepers. "What's the point of the peacekeepers when they don't keep the peace?" was the headline in *The Guardian* from September 17, 2015. [15]

The conflict between the Hutus and Tutsis went on for decades. The country was first ruled by the elitist minority Tutsi tribe, which created a strong resentment in the Hutu population, whom they treated like slaves. That led to uprisings and the Hutus taking power. The conflict continued between the Hutu-led government and the Rwandan Patriotic Front, which was largely composed of Tutsi refugees whose families had fled to Uganda in the 1950s following the earlier waves of violence.

International pressure on the Hutu-led government of Juvénal Habyarimana resulted in a ceasefire in 1993 with intent to implement the Arusha Accords that would create a power-sharing government between the two tribes. Many conservative Hutus, including members of the Akazu—an informal organization of Hutu extremists close to the president—were dissatisfied with the agreement and viewed it as conceding to enemy demands. The Hutu population was afraid the RPF would reinstate the Tutsi monarchy and enslave them.

Genocidal killings began when, on April 6, 1994, an airplane carrying Hutu President Habyarimana and Burundian president Cyprien Ntaryamira was shot down on its descent into Kigali, and all passengers were killed. Blaming the Tutsis for the plane crash, Hutu soldiers, police, and militia started killing key Tutsi and moderate Hutu leaders. Checkpoints and barricades were erected, and the Hutus used the Rwandans' national identity cards to systematically verify people's ethnicity and kill the Tutsi. The Hutu forces recruited or pressured Hutu civilians to arm themselves with weapons including machetes, clubs, and other blunt objects. The civilians were encouraged to rape, maim, and kill their Tutsi neighbors, and destroy or steal their property. In the end, despite being outnumbered by the Hutus, the Tutsis managed to seize control of the northern part of the country and capture Kigali in mid-July 1994, bringing an end to the genocide.

Why didn't the UN Peacekeepers manage to protect its mandate and prevent the genocide? Part of the problem is the political interests of the UN member states. The UN Security Council's decisions to intervene "are increasingly dominated by the narrow politics of *quid pro quo* among the five permanent members who tend to form odd coalitions around any specific situation," according to Sudhir Chella Rajan, a senior fellow at Tellus Institute, where he leads the Program on Global Politics and Institutions. "This is true especially of so-called 'humanitarian interventions,'" he wrote, "where strategic interests of the five are typically more significant than any truly human needs." As an example, Rajan points to the eagerness to protect Kuwaitis under Iraqi occupation in 1991, while failing to keep the peace in Rwanda.[16]

In his 2004 book *Tower of Babble: How the United Nations has Fueled Global Chaos*, Dore Gold, former Israeli ambassador to the UN, criticized the organization's moral relativism in the face of genocide and terrorism. The modern United Nations has, according to Gold, become diluted to the point where only seventy-five of the 184 member states "were free democracies, according to Freedom House," a Massachusetts-based research institute and think tank. He believes this dilution has made the UN more amenable to dictatorships.[17]

The United Nations has admitted to failing to prevent the genocide in Rwanda. In 1994, Kofi Annan was appointed Head of the United Nations Department of Peacekeeping Operations (DPKO), and in a UN report on the Rwanda massacre, Annan was criticized for not delivering warnings about the upcoming genocide.[18] According to Michael Barnett, a UN senior official at that time, DPKO failed to pass on information that could have strengthened a case for intervention to the Security Council. Jean-Pierre Twatzinze, one of the leaders within the Hutu paramilitary organization Interahamwe, confirmed the location of the organization's hidden weapons reserve. He also told UN officials that he "had been ordered to compile lists of Tutsis in Kigali which he thought were to be used 'for their extermination.'"[19]

"The issue was not that the information wasn't there," German UN expert Andreas Zumach told *Deutsche Welle*. "But there was a total unwillingness by all fifteen member countries of the Security Council and other countries in the General Assembly to provide troops." It was very obvious, according to Zumach, that in none of the western capitals was there sufficient interest to avoid a genocide in Rwanda.

This disinterest was also reflected in the peacekeeping forces on the ground. *The Guardian* reported on April 12, 1994 that within the sight of the peacekeeping forces, a Rwandan woman was hauled along the road by a young man with a machete. "He pulled at her clothes as she looked at the foreign soldiers in the desperate, terrified hope that they could save her from her death." None of the troops moved. "It's not our mandate," said one soldier, leaning against his jeep as he watched the condemned woman, the heavy rain splashing at his blue United Nations badge.

"The 3,000 foreign troops now in Rwanda are no more than spectators to the savagery," Michael Barnett said. Some did more than just watch. In 2000, the United Nations was sued for complicity to genocide in Rwanda. The soldiers were accused of handing over families to the enemy instead of defending them.[20, 21]

Perhaps these soldiers acted on their own initiative. Others did not. The French government, in particular, was criticized for actively supporting the Hutu genocidal regime.[22, 23]

While the UN stood on the sidelines, French soldiers actively protected and aided the French-speaking Hutus against the more Anglophone Tutsis. In a 2008 article, the *New York Times* quoted a Rwandan government report stating that, "French soldiers themselves directly were involved in assassinations of Tutsis and Hutus accused of hiding Tutsis." The report was compiled by a team of investigators from the Rwandan Justice Ministry. French officials were accused of giving political, military, diplomatic, and logistical support during the genocide to Rwanda's extremist government and the Hutu forces that slaughtered minority Tutsis and politically moderate Hutus.[24]

If the UN Peacekeeping Forces are to be considered a peace champion, they should at the very least be expected to protect innocent people from getting brutalized and killed when they can, and otherwise stay as neutral in the conflict as possible. That didn't happen in Rwanda.

Perhaps the UN's inaction in Rwanda has to do with its failed operation in Somalia. The UN had been burnt by the high number of casualties among its soldiers in Somalia, and the member countries who sent soldiers didn't want to repeat the disaster. "For many at the UN," Barnett said, the moral compass pointed "towards New York," and not at Rwanda. By this, he meant that the UN hesitated to get too involved in a PR-risky operation that could damage the prospects for future peace-building operations.[25]

UN PEACEKEEPING FORCES AND SEXUAL VIOLENCE

Perhaps worse than anything else are the sexual crimes—especially against children—committed by some UN soldiers in several of the countries where they are deployed. According to Jay Nordlinger, everywhere the blue berets were stationed they raped, ran prostitution rings, demanded sex in return for food, and tortured.[26]

Although these crimes were perhaps not as systematic as Nordlinger claims and the perpetrators certainly didn't act according to orders, they still represented the UN. It is revolting that the UN, which is supposed to protect innocent civilians, is responsible for such crimes. In the 1996 UN study *The Impact of Armed Conflict on Children*, former first lady of Mozambique Graça Machel stated that, "In 6 out of 12 country studies on sexual exploitation of children in situations of armed conflict prepared for the present report, the arrival of peacekeeping troops has been associated with a rapid rise in child prostitution."

These discoveries have contributed to the doubts about the efficiency of the United Nations and its peacekeeping forces. According to journalist and human rights activist Gita Sahgal, prostitution and sexual abuse crop up wherever humanitarian intervention efforts are set up. "The issue with the UN is that peacekeeping operations unfortunately seem to be doing the same thing that other militaries do. Even the guardians have to be guarded."[27]

In 1999, Kathryn Bolkovac went to Bosnia as part of a UN mission. She discovered numerous individuals in the Bosnian and UN police—which was made up of some 1,800 officers from forty-five countries—who were not only abusing trafficked prostitutes, but were on the traffickers' payroll. In a 2012 interview with *The Telegraph*, she said that the UN soldiers were paid to give warnings on raids, return girls who escaped, or let the traffickers know where they could collect the girls they had "dumped somewhere on the border," so they could be recycled back into the system. "Free access to the girls was an added perk," she said.[28] Although these were despicable acts of certain rogue operators within the UN Peacekeeping Forces, these revelations have further eroded trust in the UN.

The UN leadership was appalled when the information of sexual crimes came out.

"Sexual violence . . . needs to be treated as the war crime that it is; it can no longer be treated as an unfortunate collateral damage of war," Zainab Hawa Bangura, UN representative of Sexual Violence in Conflict, said.

The fact remains, however, that in several cases, the UN peacekeeping missions have failed. Having been named peace champion in 1988 certainly didn't make the UN Peacekeeping Forces any more champions of peace than they had been prior to the award, and since the scandals have come to light, the Nobel Committee has had to re-evaluate its former laudatory relationship with the UN.

2001:
THE UNITED NATIONS AND KOFI ANNAN

On Presentation Day of 2001, Oslo's City Hall transformed into a Nobel laureate hall of fame, including Desmond Tutu, Rigoberta Menchú, and Jody

Williams, all of them honoring one hundred years of Nobel Peace Prizes. That year, Nobel's medal went to the United Nations and its secretary-general, Kofi Annan. The committee wished "in its centenary year to proclaim that the only negotiable route to global peace and cooperation goes by the way of the United Nations."[29] The question remains, however, whether the UN and Kofi Annan were worthy peace champions.

Born in Ghana in 1938, Kofi Annan—who has been called "president of the world" and the "secular pope"—worked for the United Nations his entire career. Beginning as a budget officer for the World Health Organization in 1962, he was the first secretary-general to emerge from the UN bureaucracy. In 1993, he was put in charge of the peacekeeping operations, and he was still responsible for these operations during the Srebrenica massacre and the Rwandan genocide in 1994. Certainly not peace champion-worthy achievements.

In 1995, Annan and the UN started the Oil-for-Food Program, which was supposed to relieve the suffering of civilians as the result of the UN's imposition of sanctions on Iraq following Iraq's invasion of Kuwait in 1990. The Oil-for-Food Program ended in 2003 with a corruption scandal, in which Annan and his son were allegedly implicated. An investigation from 2003 to 2005, led by former Federal Reserve chairman Paul Volcker, looked into accusations that some of the program's profits were unlawfully diverted to the government of Iraq and to UN officials.[30]

According to a report released on February 3, 2005, by Volcker's commission, much of the food aid supplied under the program "was unfit for human consumption." The report further stated that the US $64 billion Oil-for-Food Program was so poorly managed that Iraqi leader Saddam Hussein collected $1.7 billion in kickbacks from participating companies and $11 billion in oil-smuggling profits. Among the most volatile allegations probed by Volcker were suspicions that Annan had steered lucrative Iraqi oil contracts to a Swiss company, Cotecna, which had Annan's son, Kojo, on its payroll.[31]

At first Kofi Annan denied having had any meetings with Cotecna. Later in the inquiry, however, he recalled that he had met twice with Cotecna's chief executive Elie-Georges Massey. The Inquiry Committee found there was insufficient evidence to indict the secretary-general on any illegal actions. Nevertheless, it did find "ethically improper" behavior by Benon Sevan, a Cypriot national who had worked for the UN for about forty years and who was appointed by Annan to the Oil-for-Food Program. Sevan repeatedly denied the charges and argued that he was being made a "scapegoat."

Volcker's report listed both Western and Middle Eastern companies that benefited illegally from the program and was highly critical of the UN management structure and the Security Council's oversight.[32, 33] Although Volcker's investigation didn't find enough evidence against Annan for unethical behavior, it tainted his reputation as head of the UN.

The Norwegian Nobel Committee didn't know the details of this scandal when it selected the UN and Annan as Nobel peace champions in 2001. They would have known, however, about the UN's failure in both Bosnia and Rwanda, and the soul-searching and skepticism that should have come in the intervening years between the 1988 awarding of the prize to the UN, and then the fiascos in Bosnia and Rwanda in between, clearly did not take place.

Perhaps it didn't matter so much whether the UN and Annan were worthy of Nobel's prize. In 2001, the committee had another agenda. The committee chairman made it clear at the Nobel ceremony that the 2001 prize was more than a declaration of Norway's love to the UN. It was a warning to the United States and President George W. Bush not to act against terrorism without the UN's consent. Announcing the prize one month after al-Qaeda's terrorist attacks on September 11, 2001, the UN must have supremacy in any fight against Islamic terrorists, Chairman Gunnar Berge implied in his presentation speech.[34]

Annan, of course, agreed in full.

"In every great faith and tradition," Annan held, "one can find the values of tolerance and mutual understanding." These values must be defended against those who believe "that there is one people in possession of the truth, one answer to the world's ills, or one solution to humanity's needs." States can only "serve the interests of their citizens by recognizing common interests and pursuing them in unity."

The 2001 prize received criticism, including from the Israeli government. A year before the Nobel announcement, in October 2000, three Israeli soldiers were kidnapped and killed by Hezbollah terrorists. The terrorists had crossed the Israeli border disguised as UN soldiers, wearing the UN uniforms, and using a vehicle with UN insignia. Legitimate UN Peacekeepers had made a video that constituted evidence to this event, however, the organization denied for months that it was in possession of the video. A year later, in 2001, it finally handed over a copy so heavily edited that the terrorists could not be identified. Because of the UN's lack of cooperation, Israel was unable to locate the soldiers before they were killed.[35] Why the UN refused to assist the Israelis is unknown. Perhaps its lack of cooperation was a wish to stay out of Israel's conflicts in the Middle East. Kofi Annan did, however, admit that it could have been more helpful in order to try to save the Israeli soldiers.

"It is clear that serious errors of judgment were made, in particular by those who failed to convey information to the Israelis which would have been helpful in an assessment of the condition of the three abducted soldiers," Annan's spokesman said.

Annan "regrets this error," but he did not regret hiding the identity of the terrorists. As a neutral organization, he asserted, they couldn't do otherwise. Annan was right, of course. The UN is supposed to be a neutral party in conflicts. However, Hezbollah is considered a terrorist group by most countries in the West. According to UN Security Council resolution 1566, adopted by unanimous vote, the UN condemns terrorism as a serious threat to peace. Understandably, the Israelis thought this neutrality between a member country and a terrorist group was appalling.[36]

The Israelis were not the only ones who expressed criticism of that year's prize. "Conspicuous dissent came from survivors' groups in Rwanda and Bosnia," the *Washington Times* wrote, "two nations grievously failed by UN peacekeeping missions in the mid-1990s, when Mr. Annan was head of that department."[37]

The chairman of a Rwandan group said, "He has a heavy responsibility in the Rwandan genocide. It is a pity, it is unfortunate—he should not have been awarded that Nobel Prize."

In his 2003 book *Shake Hands with the Devil: The Failure of Humanity in Rwanda*, Canadian and former general Roméo Dallaire—who was force commander of the United Nations Assistance Mission for Rwanda—blamed the lack of response to the genocide on Annan. Dallaire asserts that Annan held back UN troops from intervening, and that he refrained from providing more logistical and material support. Annan failed, according to Dallaire, to provide responses to his repeated faxes demanding access to a weapons depository in order to defend the endangered Tutsis.[38] As I mentioned earlier in the chapter, the UN's reticence to repond to the crisis in Rwanda may be explained by the long and unsuccessful operation in Somalia, in which many UN soldiers were killed. It's also possible that Annan didn't know, at the time, that the conflict would escalate into genocide.

"I believed at that time that I was doing my best," Annan said in 2004, ten years after the genocide, to *BBC News*. "I could have done more to sound the alarm and rally support." Perhaps in an attempt to make up, he reserved April 7 as an international day to reflect upon the Rwandan genocide.

A spokesman for a Bosnian group said, "This award, to me, looks as if it has been commissioned by the UN itself to help them wash their hands of responsibility."[39]

A pile of more than 16,000 shoes collected by German activist Phillip Ruch, each pair representing a victim of the 1995 Srebrenica massacre, was placed in front of the Brandenburg Gate in Berlin, on the fifteenth anniversary of the massacre. This "Pillar of Shame" formed the letters "UN."

The United Nations hasn't always done good. The organization as a whole, is only as good as its constituent parts. With so many different member states that all have a say in the UN's decisions, interests vary widely. The UN Human Rights Council, as an example, is part of the organization that has been blocked by such conflicting interests. The human rights panel was founded by a small group of people, including Eleanor Roosevelt and René Cassin. The idea was noble, but in practice the panel didn't have the effect its founders wished for. For many years, the Sudanese government carried out genocide in Darfur, while that same government was sitting on the UN human rights panel. The UN was unable to do anything about the genocide, probably because Sudan prevented information about what was happening from coming out, or blocked any action to prevent the genocide. Mu'ammar Gaddhafi of Libya was once president of the panel, and other questionable panel members include Zimbabwe's Robert Mugabe, Communist China, Syria, Saudi Arabia, and Cuba.

In 2010, Iran was elected by the other members' representatives to the UN Commission on the Status of Women, a women's rights panel. It's ironic when it's common knowledge that the government of Iran uses rape as means to oppress, punish, and silence women, and stones girls for being gang-raped (yes, being gang-raped is a crime in Iran).[40]

Iran was also "vice chairman" of the UN Disarmament Commission, while violating every nuclear rule itself and pledging to wipe out Israel, another member state. North Korea, another flagrant nuclear violator, chaired the disarmament conference.

Criticism of the UN is not new. Former French president Charles de Gaulle, unconvinced that a global security alliance would help in maintaining world peace, famously referred to it as *le machin*, a disapproving term that, in English, would mean "a contraption."

In 1967, former US president Richard Nixon said that the UN was "obsolete and inadequate" for dealing with the Cold War. Jeane Kirkpatrick, former ambassador to the UN, wrote in a 1983 opinion piece in the *New York Times* that the process of discussions at the Security Council "more closely resembles a mugging than either a political debate or an effort at problem-solving."

Even the late Kofi Annan, years after he received Nobel's medal, seemed to have lost faith in the institution. In 2012, Annan was the UN Arab League Joint Representative for Syria, attempting to find a solution to the conflict in the country. Annan resigned from this position after he became frustrated with the UN's lack of progress, saying, "When the Syrian people desperately need action, there continues to be finger-pointing and name-calling in the Security Council."[41]

Perhaps the Norwegian Nobel Committee will be more careful when considering the United Nations for Nobels in the future.

POLITICAL CURRENCY

When honesty disappears, good relations die . . .
and all that remains is a fight to the finish.
—ALFRED NOBEL

B ECAUSE THE NORWEGIAN Nobel Committee is so tied to the
country's parliament, unlike the other committees in Stockholm for
literature and the sciences, Alfred Nobel's peace prize has become a means
to obtain allies and gain power in world politics.[1] The committee—filled
with politicians—has contributed to maintaining the current power model,
one that has led to many societal dysfunctions, including war. Never was
this more blatantly demonstrated than when the committee awarded the
prize to Henry Kissinger, US secretary of state, and Le Duc Tho, the leader
of North Vietnam, in 1973.

KISSINGER AND THE "NOBEL WAR PRIZE"

Born in Fürth, Germany, in 1923, Heinz Alfred Kissinger, known as Henry Kissinger, was ten years old when the Nazis came to power. Kissinger and his family, who were Jewish, managed to flee Germany in 1938 and settle in New York City when he was fifteen.

A bright young man, Kissinger graduated summa cum laude in political science from Harvard University in 1950. He received his master's and doctorate degrees from Harvard in 1952 and 1954, respectively, before devoting his life to politics.

As early as 1957, it became obvious that Kissinger was no peace champion according to Alfred Nobel's values. In *Nuclear Weapons and Foreign Policy,* Kissinger made it clear that he believed in the deterrent effect of nuclear weapons. Because these weapons would be part of our world, he also wrote that every household should have a bomb shelter.

Kissinger's political career began when he became part of Nelson Rockefeller's campaign for the Republican Party's presidential nomination for the 1968 election. However, Rockefeller lost in the Republican primary to Richard Nixon, and Nixon became the Republican candidate for president, ultimately defeating the sitting vice president Hubert Humphrey.

Nixon, who had anti-Semitic leanings, was an unlikely political ally for Kissinger. The illegal tape recordings that led to the Watergate scandal revealed that Nixon complained to his chief of staff, H. R. Haldeman, that "The Jews are all over the government." Nixon also said that "Most Jews are disloyal," and that the Jews needed to be brought under control by putting someone "in charge who is not Jewish" in key government agencies.

Despite the fact that Kissinger was Jewish, Nixon realized that he could be useful; he was, after all, an expert in international politics who had visited Vietnam three times. Therefore, Nixon asked Kissinger to join his administration if he won the 1968 election. Kissinger, however, despised Nixon. According to Robert Dallek's book *Nixon and Kissinger,* Kissinger referred to Nixon as "that madman," "our drunken friend," and "the meatball mind."

Instead of accepting Nixon's offer, Kissinger chose to serve as a consultant to President Johnson's delegation attempting to negotiate peace with North Vietnam in the months leading up to the 1968 presidential election.

During Johnson's presidency, American involvement in the Vietnam War had escalated. Congress had passed the Gulf of Tonkin Resolution, which gave Johnson the authority to use any degree of military force in Southeast Asia without having to ask for an official declaration of war from Congress.

As a result, the number of American military personnel in Vietnam increased dramatically, from 16,000 soldiers in 1963 to 550,000 in early 1968. At the same time, American casualties soared, and the peace process bogged down. Johnson ordered massive bombing campaigns targeting North Vietnamese cities, and millions of gallons of the herbicide Agent Orange were sprayed on Vietnamese territory.[2] In the United States, riots broke out in most major cities as a reaction to the war, and Johnson's popularity declined dramatically. To save President Johnson's reelection campaign, it was critical to find a peaceful solution fast.

Kissinger, more worried about his career than about peace, sought to hedge his plans to be part of the next administration, no matter who won. A key negotiator in Johnson's delegation and therefore privy to privileged material, Kissinger fed information about the peace negotiations to not only his boss, President Johnson, but also to Nixon with the following strategy: If Johnson went down, he could jump ship over to Nixon.

Kissinger told Nixon that Johnson was close to accomplishing a peace agreement with North Vietnam, knowing that Nixon was worried that such an agreement would cost him the election. As a result, Nixon started communicating in secret with the leader of South Vietnam, Xuan Thuy, with one goal in mind: to prevent that peace agreement.[3] As a result, President Thuy broke off the negotiations for a peace agreement with the Johnson administration—decreasing Johnson's popularity further.

"Certainly one of the reasons was the advice he [President Thuy] got from Nixon's people," said Daniel Davidson, one of Johnson's peace talks delegates. It was clear, according to Davidson, that the Thuy administration was told to hold out on the peace talks.[4]

Because of the failed peace negotiations, Johnson declared that he would not run for reelection. When Nixon won the presidential election in 1968 on the promise to pull US troops out of Vietnam, he appointed Kissinger as national security advisor (in charge of domestic security issues) and secretary of state (in charge of foreign affairs), two jobs that do not always have the same priorities or goals. But with one person, Kissinger, in charge of both, any conflicts between domestic and foreign affairs were eliminated.

Years later, at the National Press Club in 2001, Kissinger jokingly said, "Never before and never since have the relations between the White House and the State Department been as harmonious as they were in those days."[5]

Secrecy and deception were not the only tools Kissinger used to obtain power. He was also a master at cultivating the media before any other politicians knew it was possible to do, according to television journalist Barbara Howar.

Kissinger dated starlets and socialized with film stars, and his very public private life seemed focused on proving that, "Power is the ultimate aphrodisiac."[6] In Howar's opinion, Kissinger used his reputation as a ladies' man as a smoke screen to hide his undercover political work. In one instance, he led the press to believe he was meeting a girlfriend in New York when, instead, he traveled to Paris to negotiate with the North Vietnamese.

Kissinger's style of leadership was divisive instead of unifying, not only in international politics but also within the administration. He endlessly played his staff members against one another and also played them against the president, according to Roger Morris, a Harvard scholar recruited by Kissinger to the Security Council in 1969.

"It was all a game to him, to fortify his position as Nixon's deputy," Morris said.[7]

Although they despised each other, Nixon and Kissinger had more than a little in common, according to Robert Dallek. They both had tumultuous childhoods that left them painfully insecure and a self-serving grandiosity that made them feel they could rationalize dubious means to achieve their ends.

Publicly, President Nixon promised an "honorable end" to the Vietnam War. What the public didn't know, however, was that both Nixon and Kissinger thought that the use of force was the best way to obtain that honorable end. The United States's credibility in foreign policy vis-à-vis the Soviet Union and China was at stake, and Kissinger convinced the president that this was not the time to appear weak or indecisive. Simply pulling back was not an option.

In order to obtain a dignified peace for the United States, Nixon and Kissinger decided to show Hanoi that the newly elected president was willing to do anything, even use extreme force, to end the war. They named their strategy "the madman theory," with the idea to make the hostile leaders of Vietnam and other Communist countries in that region think Nixon was volatile and unpredictable, and thus fear him.

Kissinger started plotting attacks, not only against North Vietnam, but also against Cambodia, a neutral country in the war between North and South Vietnam, which was being used by the North as a base and staging area for its attacks. The idea was that, by destroying these Communist groups outside of North Vietnam, they would prevent the Communists from taking over the region. In addition, without the support from these regions, North Vietnam would be considerably weakened in the conflict with South Vietnam.

According to the US Constitution, the executive branch must ask Congress for an act of war before attacking any country. The US was already at war with Vietnam, so no additional permission was needed there. Cambodia, however, was a different story.

"The motivation behind the secrecy [of the bombing of Cambodia] was because it was illegal. That simple," according to Elisabeth Becker, journalist at the *New York Times*. The last thing Congress wanted at the time was an expansion of the war, so they probably would not have allowed the bombings had they been asked, she said.[8]

With Nixon's permission—although Nixon told him the blame would be his if the plan went wrong—Kissinger designed a plot to bomb Cambodia that was both Machiavellian and brilliant. The fighter pilots would officially be directed to fly over South Vietnam, but midflight they would be redirected to drop the bombs over new targets in Cambodia. According to military records, however, the bombs were dropped on the Vietnamese side of the border, leaving Cambodia out of the official records. Under Kissinger's supervision, the US military flew 3,600 secret missions from March 18, 1969 to May 26, 1970, dropping 100,010 tons of bombs over Cambodia.

Kissinger was intimately involved in the direction and timing of all these missions, according to Colonel Ray Sitton, the reigning expert on B-52 tactics who, together with General Alexander Haig, was part of Kissinger's plan for the secret bombings.

"Not only was Henry carefully screening the raids," Sitton told Hitchens in an interview for *The Trial of Henry Kissinger*, "he was reading the raw intelligence" and he chaired the Washington Special Action Group, the Verification Panel (which dealt with arms control), the Vietnam Special Studies Group (which oversaw the day-to-day conduct of the war), and the Defense Program Review Committee (which supervised the budget of the Defense Department).

"It was therefore impossible for him to claim that he was unaware of the consequences of the bombings of Cambodia and Laos," Hitchens concluded. "He knew more about them, and in more detail, than any other individual."[9]

When information about the secret bombings leaked out to the press, the news caused outrage internationally and in the United States. Kissinger's response to that outrage was—with the help of the FBI—wiretapping aides and employees at the Pentagon, administration staff, and journalists in order to find the leak.[10]

As Nixon promised to remove the military forces from Vietnam, behind the curtain Kissinger was planning another brutal blow against the enemy. For eleven days in December 1972, in what would be known as the "Christmas Bombing," more than one hundred B-52 planes dropped 40,000 tons of bombs on the cities of Hanoi and Haiphong in North Vietnam, hitting a hospital and killing more than 1,600 civilians, according to North Vietnam at that time.

What few people knew was that two months earlier, Kissinger had managed to get North Vietnam to agree to a peace treaty. It was too soon to celebrate publicly, however, because the Thuy government of South Vietnam was not satisfied with the efforts of the United States and would not enforce the agreement. According to Hitchens, the Christmas Bombing was a gesture to South Vietnam as well as a sign of support to the anti-Communist regime of Cambodia. Later, Kissinger would tastelessly brag about the Christmas Bombing, saying it put the Communists "on their knees," according to *BBC News*.[11]

"It was a demonstration bombing," Hitchens said, "a public relations mass murder from the sky."

Hitchens wasn't the only one who believed the Christmas Bombing was unnecessary. Knowing that Le Duc Tho (of North Vietnam) was willing to settle and that the United States could have put pressure on the Thuy government (of South Vietnam) to keep up its part of the agreement, some of Kissinger's aides on the Security Council, including Roger Morris, resigned in protest.

"I felt it was a betrayal to the pledge of an honorable and just end to the war," Morris said. Kissinger and Le Duc Tho had negotiated for and reached a peace agreement, but Kissinger orchestrated and carried out a brutal attack anyway.

Nevertheless, Kissinger's final attack worked. The Christmas Bombing did appease South Vietnam, and Kissinger struck a new agreement—the Paris Accords—with North Vietnam at the end of January 1973. Ironically, this treaty was almost identical to the terms in the treaty President Johnson had tried to implement in 1968 before the US presidential election.

Because of Kissinger's power games, sabotaging Johnson's peace agreement with North Vietnam in order to secure himself a place in the next president's administration, tens of thousands of American lives were lost as well as more than 500,000 Vietnamese and Cambodians in bombing strikes that went on until 1974.

The chaos that followed in Cambodia, with the disruption of agriculture resulting in a massive famine, allowed Pol Pot and the Khmer Rouge to take power. By 1979, more than three million people were dead in the Cambodian civil war and genocide that ensued.

"News of the Paris Agreement," Chair Aase Lionæs said without conviction in her voice, "brought a wave of joy and hope to the entire world."

Perhaps it did. But more important to the committee, according to political experts in Norway and elsewhere, was Norway's wish to strengthen political ties with the United States during the Cold War.[12] After World War II, Norway had chosen to side with the United States over the Soviet Union in the Cold War that followed. Through the Marshall Plan, the United States' financial aid had helped rebuild postwar Norway, and US soldiers are still based in Norway on the Russian border to protect the small country from a possible Russian invasion.

"It is a travesty that Kissinger was awarded the Nobel Peace Prize," Morris said in an interview, "when in fact he was a war-maker, not a war-ender." Morris added that if one were to hold Kissinger to the same standards as other war criminals, such as those prosecuted after World War II, he would be indicted and punished for his actions.[13]

By Alfred Nobel's definition, Kissinger was as far from a peace champion as one could possibly be.[14]

THE "NOBEL WAR PRIZE"

Kissinger was not alone in winning the 1973 Nobel Peace Prize. He shared it with Le Duc Tho, the leader of North Vietnam. Born in October 1911, in the Hà Nam Province in Vietnam, Le Duc Tho—whose real name was Phan Dinh Khai—was a revolutionary, a general, a diplomat, and a politician. A cofounder of the Indochinese Communist Party and an activist for Indochina's (the regions of Vietnam, Cambodia, and Laos) independence, he was imprisoned by French colonial authorities from 1930 to 1936 and again from 1939 to 1944. After he was released in 1945, he lead the Vietnamese independence movement Viet Minh against its French colonizer. This Indochina War lasted until the 1954 Geneva Accords, which dismantled the French colony and ended with the French withdrawing their troops from the area.

During these years, Le Duc Tho moved several times between South and North Vietnam, and in 1956, he led the Communist insurgency against the South Vietnamese government. Most political experts and historians agree that Le Duc Tho was a mass-murdering dictator.

But at least Le Duc Tho was more honest about who he was and the bloodshed he had caused than both Kissinger and the Norwegian Nobel Committee. For the first and only time in Nobel Peace Prize history, a winner turned it down. Le Duc Tho justified his refusal on the grounds that the Paris Agreement was not yet implemented. Not even he could pretend there was peace in Vietnam.

The following is a translation from Le Duc Tho's French letter to Lionæs, the chair of the Nobel Committee, after he learned about the 1973 award, supplied by the Paris office of the Hanoi press agency:

> During the last eighteen years, the United States undertook a war of aggression against Vietnam. The Vietnamese people have waged a tenacious and heroic struggle against the United States' aggression for independence and freedom. All of progressive humanity approves and supports this just cause. . . . However, since the signing of the Paris agreement, the United States and the Saigon administration continue in grave violation of a number of key clauses of this agreement. The Saigon administration, aided and encouraged by the United States, continues its acts of war. Peace has not yet really been established in South Vietnam. In these circumstances it is impossible for me to accept the 1973 Nobel Peace Prize, which the committee has bestowed on me. Once the Paris accord on Vietnam is respected, the arms are silenced, and real peace is established in South Vietnam, I will be able to consider accepting this prize. With my thanks to the Nobel Prize Committee please accept, Madame, my sincere respects [sic].

Kissinger, on the other hand, accepted "with humility" although he didn't travel to Norway to attend the ceremony, aware of the mass demonstrations planned against him. He stated that the award represented "a recognition of the central purpose of the President's foreign policy," giving thanks to Nixon for the conditions that made it possible to bring the negotiations to a "successful conclusion."[15]

The *New York Times* named the 1973 award the "Nobel War Prize."

Bronson P. Clark, of the American Friends Service Committee, wrote the following in a *New York Times* op-ed piece on October 23, 1973:

> "Orwell warned us [in *1984*] that the dreadful day would come when war would be called peace and peace, war. The Nobel Peace Prize committee's homage to the 'talents and goodwill' of Le Duc Tho and Henry Kissinger for their skillful negotiations . . . led us at the American Friends Service Committee to wonder if it should be called the 'Nobel Negotiating Prize.' But Peace Prize?"

According to Clark, the conditions that Kissinger was referring to that led the peace negotiations to a "successful conclusion" included the myth that the president was seeking peace with honor. They also included "the unleashing of one of the most savage bombing raids in the bloody history of war," as well as "the relentless bombing, secretly and then brazenly, of Laos and Cambodia. They included the hidden intent, after the negotiations, to recognize the Thieu *(sic)* government as the sole legitimate government in South Vietnam, even though the accords, which Henry Kissinger helped write and the United States signed, were to recognize two governments in South Vietnam."

What was the "successful conclusion" of the negotiations that Kissinger referred to in his statement?

"Even today," Clark wrote, "although United States soldiers and airmen are out of Vietnam, American technicians, working for American corporations, planes, bombs, guns, and dollars are still there," fueling the war that continued between North and South Vietnam even after the Paris Accords.

Kissinger had the power to make the peace treaty stick, according to Clark. By implementing Article 4, Chapter II of the Paris Accords, which read, "the

United States will not continue its military involvement or intervene in the internal affairs of South Vietnam," Kissinger could have opposed the flow of US dollars that financed President Thuy's war budget. If he had stopped the funding and called for the recognition of the two Vietnamese governments that were party to the Paris Accords, chances are the conflict would have ended there. The problem was that none of the parties honored the agreement.

Chair Lionæs gave a very carefully written presentation speech at the ceremony, which neither Kissinger nor Le Duc Tho attended. The committee, she said, was "fully aware that a ceasefire and not a peace agreement was involved." Although peace had not yet come to Vietnam, she said, the committee—what was left of it after two of its members had resigned in protest of the award—wished to honor the *effort* made by Kissinger and Le Duc Tho.

ABSENCE OF ACCOUNTABILITY

Both Kissinger and Le Duc Tho are responsible for atrocities. When Le Duc Tho conquered South Vietnam in 1975, rendering the Paris Agreement even more meaningless, Kissinger wrote to the Nobel Committee, attempting to return his gold medal, diploma, and prize money. The committee, unwilling to take responsibility for its mistake, refused Kissinger's gesture, explaining that the events in Vietnam in no way reduced its "appreciation of Mr. Kissinger's sincere efforts to get a ceasefire agreement put into force in 1973."

Although Le Duc Tho never accepted the Nobel Peace Prize, the committee did not take his refusal into account, and he is still considered a Nobel laureate. He died on October 13, 1990, in a country that is still a dictatorship. He was never held accountable for his war crimes.

But why has Kissinger not been held responsible for his actions?

The answer leads us to another scandal. The detection of Nixon's and Kissinger's wiretapping eventually led to the discovery of the Watergate cover-up, ending in Nixon's resignation. Because he resigned, the impeachment against

Nixon was dropped. One of the charges of the impeachment concerned Kissinger and the secret bombing of Cambodia. With the resignation, however, in addition to the presidential pardon of Nixon issued by his successor President Gerald Ford, the investigation into the secret war on Cambodia was also dropped. Instead of being punished, Kissinger was appointed secretary of state again, this time by President Ford.

The 1973 award was as ineffective toward peace as applauding a serial killer for promising not to kill any more, rather than punishing him for his former crimes. It is an example of what Alfred Nobel meant when he wrote these lines in his play, *Nemesis*:

> CENCI: *Nothing can be truer than that the end justifies the means.*
> BEATRICE: *Or that abominable acts unjustify the man.*

The 1973 award to Kissinger was surely motivated by something other than the conclusion of the Vietnam War. Norway borders Russia in the northern part of the country, and although it had chosen to side with the United States in the Cold War, the Russian superpower was posing a constant threat because of the geographic vicinity. The Norwegian government—via the Norwegian Nobel Committee—may have felt a need to, once again, prove its loyalty by selecting Kissinger. When selecting Le Duc Tho, however, the Committee was doing its job—honoring both sides in the attempted peace accords.

Politically strategic choices do not justify the actions of the Nobel Peace Prize Committee. On the contrary, they contribute to mistrust in the institution and to leadership in general. Rather than making the world a more peaceful place, the 1973 award has encouraged state leaders to keep a dysfunctional and violent mindset to gain personal power. Little did Nobel know what would become of his last will after he trusted the Norwegian Parliament with his prize, but his words in *Nemesis* are as true today as they were then.

ET SPARK
I LEGGEN

How pitiful to strive to be someone or something in the
motely crowd of 1.4 billion two-legged,
tailless apes running around on our revolving
earth projectile.
—ALFRED NOBEL

THE NOBEL PEACE Prize, in addition to being used for politically strategic purposes, has also sometimes been used with the intent to punish and keep people, especially politicians, in line. Whether or not that tactic works is up for debate.

This was true in the aftermath of the terrorist attacks on American soil on September 11, 2001. All of a sudden, many Western countries felt united against a common enemy—al-Qaeda—and President George W. Bush was able to form an alliance to find and fight the terrorists. As a result, the

United States, through the eyes of the Norwegian government, stood out as too powerful and self-important.

But according to the Norwegian government, there is a solution to avoid one nation standing out too much above the others: the United Nations. The UN is as close to a world government as we have, and the Norwegians see it as a check on the countries with the most power, especially the United States.

As we have seen, the Norwegian Nobel Committee has had a love affair with the United Nations since its inception in 1945. Since then, at least thirteen of the peace prizes have had links to the UN. In 2001, right after the United States declared a "War on Terror" without first checking in with the UN, the Nobel Peace Prize went to the UN and its Secretary–General Kofi Annan.

In his presentation speech at the 2001 peace prize ceremony, Chairman Gunnar Berge complained that the United Nations, in many serious conflicts, including Bosnia between 1992 and 1995 and the genocide during the Rwandan Civil War in 1994, had been sidelined or used as a tool by its member countries, especially by the two superpowers, Russia and the United States. According to Berge, the United States favors an active UN when it sees opportunities to be obtained by it, "but when the UN takes a different stance, they [the United States] seek to limit its influence." For example, when the United States wished to go after the terrorists on its own after the 9/11 attacks.

Chairman Berge went on in his speech to praise Kofi Annan, who had since the assaults on New York and Washington, DC, urged that the UN must be given a leading part to play in the fight against international terrorism.

"The Norwegian Nobel Committee," Berge said, "wishes both to honour the work that the UN and its Secretary-General Kofi Annan have already done, and to encourage them to go ahead along the road to a still more forceful and dynamic United Nations."

According to American journalist Jay Nordlinger, the 2001 award, which was also the centenary celebration of the peace prize, was widely interpreted as a reprimand and warning to George W. Bush: "Don't you dare respond alone; don't you dare form your own coalition; the United Nations must have supremacy in any fight against Islamic terrorism."[1] The 2001 award would be the first of a series of *spark i leggen* (directly translated as kicks in the leg, or slaps in the face) to the US government.

JIMMY CARTER:
TOO LITTLE, TOO LATE

The next reprimand to the Bush administration came in 2002. The winner that year, James Earl Carter, Jr., was born on October 1, 1924, in Plains, Georgia, the oldest of four children of businessman/farmer James Earl Carter, Sr., and nurse Bessie Lillian Gordy.

"He's been a hot candidate every year," secretary of the Nobel Committee Geir Lundestad said in an interview after the 2002 announcement.

What he meant was that US President Carter had been a peace prize candidate since 1978, when he brought Israel and Egypt together to sign the Camp David Accords, which led to a peace agreement between the two countries the following year. Carter would have been a worthy candidate alongside Anwar Sadat (representing Egypt) and Menachem Begin (representing Israel) in 1978, but was excluded because he was nominated to the prize after the February 1 cut-off date.

Finally, in 2002, the Norwegian Nobel Committee had a good reason to give Carter his prize. The previous year, President George W. Bush had launched his War on Terror in Afghanistan and was threatening Saddam Hussein that Iraq would face a US military attack if Hussein didn't comply with the UN resolutions banning weapons of mass destruction.

The committee made its motivation for choosing Carter unquestionably clear. The 2002 award "should be interpreted as a criticism of the line that the current administration has taken," Chairman Berge said at the announcement of the prize in October that year. "It's a kick in the leg to all who follow the same line as the United States," meaning all those nations who engage in conflict without involving the UN.

Berge also made this point in his ceremonial speech in December, although there he was not so blunt. "He (Carter) was, and continues to be, the mediator who seeks peaceful solutions to international conflicts," Berge said. Between the lines, one could almost hear: *Unlike President Bush*.

The 2002 laureate, according to Berge, had done the opposite of what Mark Twain once said about forgetting where you bury the peace pipe, but not where the battle-ax is. "Carter never mislays the peace-pipe," Berge said in his speech. *Unlike President Bush*.

In his speech, Berge emphasized that Carter had broader aims than peace between Israel and Egypt. He wanted peace in the entire Middle East. Carter was the first American president who wished to give the Palestinians their own homeland and stressed that the Israelis had to stop building new settlements on the West Bank. His position on the Palestine-Israel conflict was therefore in line with the Norwegian government's. *Unlike President Bush*.

"Carter only served one term as President of the United States," Berge said as a dig to the United States. "In a country where such importance is attached to outward success, that has cast a shadow. Carter's principal concern was to do what he felt was right, even when it was not the smartest political step to take." *Unlike President Bush* was the subtext.

In justifying Carter's selection, the Norwegian Nobel Committee mentioned that in "a situation marked by threats of the use of power," Carter had stood for resolving conflicts through negotiation and international cooperation. "These are the principles which the Norwegian Nobel Committee hopes that the international community will take as its guidelines in the difficult conflicts the world is facing today and will face in the years to come." When the committee spoke of "threats of the use of power," it pointed its finger, not at terrorists or dictatorships, but at the United States, according to Nordlinger.

Berge said and seemed to enjoy that Carter became more critical of his own country as he grew older. "His criticism of those in power in his own country and abroad has grown sharper."

To Haitian dictator Raoul Cédras, Carter once said, "I'm ashamed of what my country has done to your country."

Carter also expressed sympathy, even support, for some questionable leaders such as Yasser Arafat, Kim Il-sung, Josip Tito, and Fidel Castro.[2]

Lance Morrow, a *Time* magazine essayist, described Carter as "America's anti-president."

By taking a stance against his own country, Carter became the perfect candidate for the Nobel Peace Prize. That is not to say Carter didn't deserve his Nobel medal. In fact, his accomplishments, in addition to bringing Sadat and Begin together in the 1978 Camp David Accords, are numerous.

Carter, through the Carter Center, has observed ninety-six elections in thirty-eight countries to help establish and strengthen democracies. The Carter Center has attempted to find avenues to peace in Ethiopia, Eritrea, Liberia, Sudan, Uganda, the Korean Peninsula, Haiti, Bosnia and Herzegovina, and the Middle East. It has assisted in establishing a village-based health care delivery system in thousands of communities in Africa and has trained health care personnel and volunteers to distribute drugs and provide health education. The center continually works to strengthen international standards for human rights and the voices of individuals defending those rights in their communities worldwide.[3]

The committee also pointed out that Carter averted what could have become a violent crisis in Haiti in 1994. When US warships headed toward the island in September of that year in what was named Operation Uphold Democracy, Carter managed to convince the Haitian military junta to step down and allow the return of the constitutionally elected leader Jean-Bertrand Aristide. It was the Carter Center's seven years of work in Haiti that laid the groundwork for this success.

"He was, and is, engaged in disarmament and arms control," Chairman Berge said. "He has shown, and still shows, an outstanding commitment to democracy and human rights. His humanitarian and social activities have been, and are still, far-reaching."

No one doubts that Carter is a peace champion. However, the timing and motivations of the committee in the awarding of the prize to Carter have been criticized.

"The most prestigious award in the world has been tainted," according to a *New York Daily News* editorial. "By extension, it is a slap in the face of the American people, since our duly elected representatives have just voted to fully support the administration's Iraq policies."

The *Times* editorial regarding Chairman Berge's speech affirmed that, "The point would have been more eloquently made had the committee chairman . . . refrained from explicitly interpreting the prize as a criticism of America's current presidential administration. Jimmy Carter's achievements are big enough to stand on their own."

To the committee, however, Carter served as an instrument of punishment. "Jimmy Carter will probably not go down in American history as the most effective President," Berge said. "But he is certainly the best ex-president the country ever had."[4]

2005:
NUCLEAR WATCH-PUPPY

"This is not a kick in the leg" to President Bush and the United States, Chairman Mjøs said announcing the award. Knowing the committee's past motivations makes it difficult to trust the chairman's assurance. The 2005 award went to the International Atomic Energy Agency (IAEA), a UN agency, and its director Mohamed ElBaradei. ElBaradei, an open foe of President Bush, had been opposing US policy for years, especially in matters concerning Iraq and Iran.

The IAEA—sometimes called the UN's nuclear watchdog—was established in Vienna in 1956, inspired by President Eisenhower's speech "Atoms for Peace," which he delivered before the UN in 1953. Eisenhower wanted nuclear technology used for peaceful, not destructive, purposes.

ElBaradei, like Kofi Annan, fits the classic description of a United Nations darling—a bureaucrat who worked his way up in the system without standing out too much.[5] Born in Egypt in 1942, he had worked for the UN since

1980. In 1984, he began working for the IAEA, and in 1997, he became its director, a post he held for three terms, until 2009.

"If Annan was the 'president of the world,'" Nordlinger wrote, "ElBaradei was a vice president."

Before ElBaradei took over, the IAEA had been a technical agency, politically neutral, mainly known by specialists in the field, giving expert opinions to member states. After 1997, however, the agency became a political body, and as ElBaradei said, "You can't separate security from politics. We cannot be unaware of the political context in which we operate and the political ramifications of our work."

The problem was that ElBaradei took sides in conflicts and hid information from the public in order to protect certain member states. When Iraq invaded Kuwait in 1990, the United States led the coalition forces that expelled the Iraqi forces from Kuwait in what is known as the 1991 Gulf War. The international community was also worried about Iraq possessing nuclear weapons. However, the IAEA claimed that Iraq was in full compliance with the Nuclear Nonproliferation Treaty. This later turned out not to be true. The Iraqis had completed a secret nuclear weapons program right under the UN inspectors' noses.

"It's correct to say," Swedish diplomat and former IAEA Director-General Hans Blix admitted after that war, "that the IAEA was fooled by the Iraqis."[6]

Perhaps the false information from the IAEA had something to do with the fact that Saddam Hussein's regime sat on the IAEA board from 1980 to 1991. In any case, the United States and other countries now had reason to distrust the agency.

When, in 2003, the IAEA again assured the United States that Iraq had no nuclear weapons, the US didn't believe it and went ahead and attacked Iraq. As it turned out, no weapons of mass destruction were found. This time the agency had been correct. This episode, in addition to Bush declaring his War on Terror in 2001, fueled both ElBaradei's and the Nobel Committee's contempt for the US administration.

"I wake up every morning and see 100 Iraqis, innocent civilians, are dying," ElBaradei said to the BBC.

Nevertheless, ElBaradei's history of hiding information from the UN Security Council went beyond the Iraq incident. After his third and last term at the IAEA expired in 2009, it was discovered that ElBaradei had also concealed an unfavorable report about Iran and its nuclear program.

"The agency chief," the Associated Press reported, "has been keen to avoid moves that could harden already massive Iranian intransigence."

ElBaradei's motivations, it seems, were to avoid harsh sanctions against Iran, particularly from the United States.

"I have no brief other than to make sure we don't go into another war or that we go crazy into killing each other," ElBaradei said in his defense. "You do not want to give additional argument to new crazies who say, 'Let's go and bomb Iran.'"[7]

With ElBaradei's help, Iran had the US Security Council fooled for almost twenty years. He went to great lengths to defend and excuse Iran and its oppressive regime and to avoid further sanctions against Iran by the United States and others.

"The danger of a nuclear-armed Iran is overestimated—some even play it up intentionally," he once said.

The idea of an international agency keeping control over the world's atomic energy is commendable, but that is not what the IAEA has done. The IAEA, according to Nordlinger, was not so much of a watchdog under ElBaradei, but more of a watch-puppy.

Iran's secret nuclear program was finally disclosed by an Iranian dissident group in 2002, not by the nuclear watchdog. To make matters worse, it was revealed after ElBaradei was gone that the IAEA knew about the nuclear weapons all along.

Another example of ElBaradei's dishonesty is his misrepresentations about Libya. ElBaradei claimed that the agency was responsible for ending Gaddhafi's nuclear weapons program, when, in reality, the IAEA had no part in it. When the coalition led by the United States made its preparations before going into Iraq in March 2003, Gaddhafi—worried about the consequences of that war for his country—began negotiating with the

United States and Great Britain over Libya's weapons of mass destruction. In May of that year, President Bush established the Proliferation Security Initiative, under which a dozen nations cooperated independently of the UN network. In October 2003, two of those nations, Italy and Germany, detained a ship going to Libya with nuclear weapons from the Abdul Qadeer Kahn network. Toward the end of 2003, when the United States captured Saddam Hussein, Gaddhafi finally gave up his nuclear program and weapons.

Yet another example of ElBaradei's bias is Syria. When Israel attacked and destroyed Syria's nuclear facility in September 2007, a facility supplied and staffed by North Korea, ElBaradei condemned Israel and denied any malfeasance on behalf of Syria. It was only after ElBaradei left office that his successor, Yukiya Amano, confirmed that there had indeed been a nuclear reactor in Syria, and that, thanks to Israel, it had been destroyed.

When ElBaradei left his post in 2009 and Amano took over, the IAEA resumed its original role as a neutral agency, providing technical judgments and reporting facts, leaving political and military decisions to the UN Security Council.

Perhaps time will prove ElBaradei right, and "the threat [of nuclear programs in Iran and Iraq] has been hyped." But in the meanwhile, he did little to promote peace, only pushing his political agenda. The Nobel Committee didn't care so much about ElBaradei's lies and bias.

Although Chairman Mjøs claimed otherwise, the committee's real intentions for the 2005 award were revealed during Mjøs's presentation speech.

"It is hypocritical to go on developing one's own nuclear weapons while doing everything in one's power to prevent others from acquiring such weapons," he said, criticizing the United States for not wanting its enemies to obtain nuclear weapons. "As ElBaradei himself has put it, it is like 'some who have . . . continued to dangle a cigarette from their mouth and tell everybody else not to smoke.'"[8]

The 2005 Nobel Peace Prize can hardly be explained other than as another *spark i leggen.*

2007:
"GORE V. BUSH"

"This year's award decision was not especially difficult," Chairman Mjøs said about the 2007 award that went to the Intergovernmental Panel on Climate Change and Al Gore. It is rare, he continued, "for the world to be so concerned with a particular phenomenon or for that phenomenon to have such a decisive impact on our existence on earth."[9]

Was the 2007 award politically motivated? Chairman Mjøs denied that it was.

"These denials," the *Washington Post* reported, "are hard to take seriously from a group that has handed the peace prize to adversaries of President Bush."

Three Norwegian historians and authors of *The Nobel Peace Prize* had this to say: "The Committee hoped the prestige that comes with the Peace Prize would give Gore an even greater standing in the media and strengthen the Democrats' fight for a new, eco-friendly USA."

Born in Tennessee in 1948, Albert Gore, Jr., was brought up in Washington, DC, where his father served in the US Senate for eighteen years. Gore was vice president under Bill Clinton for eight years, and as the Democratic presidential nominee in 2000 he won the popular vote over George W. Bush, but lost the Electoral College.

"This was probably the most disputed and bitterest election in American history," Nordlinger wrote.

Battered but not broken, Gore could now devote his time to his passion: the environment and global warming. Governments and societies, Gore said, must change their ways drastically in order to counter the threat. Gore stated a point that is still valid today. However, the manner in which he tried to prove this point was unworthy of him as a leader. He compared skeptics and critics to Holocaust deniers and to "people who believe that the earth is flat" or who "believe the moon landing was staged on a movie lot in Arizona."

IPCC's chairman, Rajendra Pachauri, joined in and said that skeptics "are people who deny the link between smoking and cancer. They are people who say that asbestos is as good as talcum powder. I hope that they apply it to their faces every day."

The IPCC is a subdivision of the UN, just like the IAEA. It is supposed to be a technical agency, giving neutral information and facts to the member states. With Pachauri's involvement and comments to the press, the IPCC stepped out of its neutral role and became more of a political body, even trying to dictate what the UN member states must do.[10]

In 2004, Pachauri verbally attacked Bjørn Lomborg, the Danish scientist who—without denying global warming—warned against radical measures to counteract it. "What's the difference," Pachauri said to *Jyllands-Posten*, "between Lomborg's way and Hitler's way of viewing humanity? If you follow Lomborg's way of thinking, it might be right, what Hitler did."

Gore's global-warming movement reached its peak in 2007 at the World Economic Forum in Davos, which was almost entirely devoted to the environment and climate change. In this movement, the United States was judged the black sheep of pollution, as it was by Gore in his movie *An Inconvenient Truth*.

In February 2007, the film won the Academy Award for Best Documentary Feature. Gore is the only person who has won the world's two most prestigious prizes—the Oscar and the Nobel—and he did both in the same year.

The Nobel Committee's 2007 choice was most certainly motivated by a genuine wish to avoid a climate crisis. And Al Gore did a phenomenal job creating awareness about the threat of global warming. However, as the former vice president of the United States, he already had a platform for his message, and he didn't really need Nobel's prize. For the committee, however, Gore was an easy and safe choice because he and his cause were already recognized by many. And it certainly didn't hurt that he was also a foe of George W. Bush.

Gore may have lost the election to Bush, but as the *New York Times* put it in its headline, "With Prize, Gore Is Vindicated Without Having to Add President to Résumé."

The *Washington Post* editorial was titled "Gore v. Bush: The Nobel Peace Prize Committee Hands a Victory to Al Gore."

BARACK OBAMA IN 2009:
"A SIGNAL TO THE WORLD"

"If the Norwegian Nobel Committee—if Scandinavian political elites—could design an American president, he would look a lot like Obama." Nordlinger's quote is fitting for the 2009 laureate. Barack Obama shares much of the same worldview as the Norwegian government and was a welcome successor—and a relief—after George W. Bush. Obama's campaign speeches were indeed like music to the Nobel Committee's ears.

"I truly believe that the day I'm inaugurated," he said in 2007, "not only does the country look at itself differently, but the world looks at America differently. . . . The world will have confidence that I am listening to them, and that our future and our security is tied up with our ability to work with other countries in the world."

French president Nicolas Sarkozy said about Obama becoming president that, "It confirms . . . America's return to the hearts of the people of the world."

According to the committee, the 2009 award was given to Barack H. Obama "for his extraordinary efforts to strengthen international diplomacy and cooperation between peoples." Never mind that Obama had been in office for fewer than two weeks when he was nominated on February 1, 2009, and that he had served as president for roughly eight-and-a-half months when he was announced the winner in October of that year.

Jagland said at the announcement that Obama's "diplomacy is founded in the concept that those who are to lead the world must do so on the basis of values and attitudes that are shared by the majority of the world's population." When asked by an American journalist present at the announcement what he had to say about Obama increasing the number of armed forces sent to fight in Afghanistan, Jagland responded evasively that the committee was hoping that the peace prize would help in some way to find a resolution in that conflict. Another journalist asked Jagland—after Jagland said that the prize was given to Obama for his preceding year's achievements—to name three things Obama actually had done in the past year to deserve Nobel's prize.

"I could list many, many things," Jagland said. He was not able to answer in any detailed manner, however. He did mention that Obama reached out to the Muslim world when he visited Egypt in an attempt to find a resolution to the problems in the Middle East, that Obama wished to cooperate with the UN, and that he pledged to work toward a world free of nuclear weapons. When the audience at the press conference still wanted more specific reasons, he finally said, "We want to send a signal to the world."[11]

Contrary to Bush, Obama was willing to work with the UN and try to make the world a better place in a way the Norwegian government approved of. During his presidency, he supported finding national and international solutions to deal with global climate change and opposed the war in Iraq. He also talked about closing the Guantánamo Bay prison and pulling US troops out of Afghanistan. He cancelled antimissile defenses in Eastern Europe, to the relief of the Russian government (but to the discomfort of Poland and the Czech Republic). He reduced the antimissile defense program in the United States.

In addition, Obama's stance on the Israeli-Palestinian conflict was pleasing to the Nobel Committee. Later in his presidency, Obama even created a distance between the US administration and Israel when he gave the Medal of Freedom to Mary Robinson, the former president of Ireland who, on numerous occasions, had sided with the Palestinians. After Israel's attack on Gaza in 2014, Robinson joined former US president Carter to call for an end to Israel's military operations against Gaza and siege and blockade of the narrow coastal strip. As head of the UN Human Rights Commission, she adopted a strong stance on the Israeli occupation and settlement of territory Palestinians wanted for their state.[12]

Committee Chairman Jagland also hailed Obama's conciliatory attitude toward China, but that gesture was more to please China than to praise Obama. The Norwegian government has been trying to soothe the new superpower since it gave the Nobel Peace Prize to Liu Xiaobo, a declared enemy of the Chinese state.

Despite the committee's aspirations, the Obama presidency wasn't perfect. He has been criticized for encouraging friendly relations with the regime in Iran—while ignoring the democratic protesters in Iranian streets.

"Obama, Obama!" the people of Iran chanted. "Either you are with *them* [meaning the regime], or you're with *us*." Nathan Sharansky, in an interview with *The Wall Street Journal*, called Obama's position during the Iranian uproar, "maybe one of the biggest betrayals of people's freedom in modern history."[13]

Contrary to the committee's hopes, Obama did not decrease the U.S. involvement in Afghanistan at the beginning of his presidency. Instead, he sent 30,000 additional troops less than two weeks before traveling to Oslo to accept the prize. The Obama administration's use of drones in the Middle East and the resulting massive civilian casualties is hardly a qualification for the peace prize. Although claiming that Guantánamo was a disgrace while Bush was in office, Obama did not close the prison during his terms.

He did say he was "surprised and deeply humbled" by the decision of the Nobel Committee, even undeserving, and in his acceptance speech he did not promise to end the wars.

"Still, we are at war, and I'm responsible for the deployment of thousands of young Americans to battle in a distant land," he said. "Some will kill, and some will be killed." He also said that "the instruments of war do have a role to play in preserving the peace," and that we must acknowledge the hard truth that "We will not eradicate violent conflict in our lifetimes. There will be times when nations—acting individually or in concert—will find the use of force not only necessary but morally justified."

Even Obama supporters were surprised by that year's award.

"Let's face it," Joe Klein wrote in *Time* magazine, "this prize is premature to the point of ridiculous."

Ruth Marcus of the *Washington Post* wrote, "I admire President Obama. I like President Obama. I voted for President Obama. But the peace prize? This is supposed to be for doing, not being—and it's no disrespect to the president to suggest he has not done much yet. Certainly not enough to justify this prize." After all, he had only been president for a couple of months.

At the Nobel banquet after the ceremony, Obama himself had this to say, referring to Jagland and his presentation speech. "I told him afterwards that I thought it was an excellent speech—and that I was almost convinced that I deserved it."

As it turned out, Obama didn't deserve Nobel's medal. His award was based on the hope he articulated, beginning with his keynote speech as an Illinois State Senator at the 2004 Democratic Convention. He spoke of a unified America: "There's not a Black America and White America and Latino America and Asian America; there's the United States of America."

Before he took office in 2008, Obama promised to end America's grueling conflicts in Iraq and Afghanistan, according to a January 2017 article in the *LA Times*.[14] During his second term, he pledged to take the country off what he called a permanent war footing. He did neither.

Obama did not work to further peace in accordance with Nobel's intentions, let alone fulfill the committee's aspirations for him. US military forces were at war for all eight years of Obama's presidency. He launched airstrikes or military raids in at least seven countries: Afghanistan, Iraq, Syria, Libya, Yemen, Somalia, and Pakistan.

While Obama reduced the number of US troops in war zones from 150,000 to 14,000 and stopped the flow of American soldiers coming home in body bags, he vastly expanded the role of elite commando units and the use of new technology, including armed drones and cyber weapons.

"The Obama administration's response to the military interventions of the Bush years was to gradually replace boots on the ground with drones in the air," author and director of Foreign Policy in Focus at the Institute for Policy Studies John Feffer wrote. "But this drone campaign has not reinforced the rule of law, has not established fair principles of justice, and has certainly not endeared people in the targeted regions to the United States."[15]

As such, Obama's military efforts did not improve the United States' relationship with these countries. Neither did he work toward disarmament.

"The whole concept of war has changed under Obama," said Jon Alterman, Middle East specialist at the Center for Strategic and International Studies, a nonprofit think tank in Washington.[16] According to Alterman, because of Obama's new war tactics, "We're now wrapped up in all these different conflicts, at a low level and with no end in sight."

When Donald Trump took over the presidency in 2017, the United States faced more threats in more places than at any time since the Cold War, according to US intelligence. For the first time in decades, there was at least the potential of an armed clash with America's largest adversaries, Russia and China.[17]

Despite the early hopes, Obama's was not a peaceful presidency and the committee's aspirations for him to turn into a peace champion were a disappointment.

The truth is that the Nobel Committee didn't care so much whether Obama deserved the prize or not. It was more focused on its message to the United States: Get back in line. Stop acting on your own and thinking you are anything special.

You can almost hear the echo of the Law of Jante (Scandinavian unwritten rules to keep anybody from standing out) which really is *et spark i leggen*, or a slap in the face, to someone trying to be different or important, to anyone who feels that they are entitled to be more than a cog in the wheel. That is what the kick in the leg is really about. Nobel's peace prize seems to have become both the carrot and the stick, a political weapon and reward.

Time after time, recipients either excel in a field far removed from Nobel's ideals, or they are just amazingly poor choices for the prize. Awarding these laureates betrays not only Nobel, but the citizens of this earth whom Nobel wanted to honor. One of the most flagrant of these choices, Muhammad Yunus, probably destroyed more people than many warriors, and he did it with the most unlikely of weapons—money.

11

BANKER TO THE POOR

The truthful man is usually a liar.
—ALFRED NOBEL

———

T HE 2006 NOBEL Peace Prize was awarded jointly to Muhammad Yunus and Grameen Bank "for their efforts to create economic and social development from below." This choice is so egregious that it deserves its own chapter.

The first issue with the 2006 prize has to do with the scope of the peace prize. According to Alfred Nobel's will, the winner shall be a champion of peace, having done the "the best work for fraternity between nations, the abolition or reduction of standing armies," and finally for the "holding and promotion of peace congresses."

Microcredit, which is what Yunus does through Grameen Bank, is the business of lending small amounts of money at supposedly low interest to new businesses in the developing world.

It's difficult to see how this lending practice directly brings nations closer together or reduces the military. This book has already taken to task the awarding of the prize to humanitarian and environmental recipients who, though being of good intentions and noble aims, do not fall within Nobel's explicit scope of the peace prize.

"The purpose of the prize has become muddled," *The Economist* reported in connection with the 2006 award. " . . . The Nobel committee could have made a braver, more difficult choice by declaring that there would be no recipient at all."

As mentioned in Chapter Two, the committee can skip giving out the prize for up to five years if there are no suitable candidates on its list of nominees. Most likely, there were several qualified candidates that year. But, instead of picking someone who matched Nobel's criteria, the Norwegian Nobel Committee created, yet again, its own definition of peace.

Even if microfinance did participate in creating a more peaceful world by reducing poverty and thus conflict over resources, Muhammad Yunus might not be the peace champion the committee wanted him to be.

Yunus, who was born in Bangladesh in 1940, was appointed professor of economics at the University of Chittagong in 1972, following his studies in Bangladesh and the United States. When Bangladesh suffered a famine in 1974, he decided to start a business giving long-term loans to people who wished to start their own businesses.[1]

"I found it difficult," Yunus said in his Nobel lecture, "to teach elegant theories of economics in the university classroom, in the backdrop of a terrible famine."[2]

This initiative was extended on a larger scale when he founded Grameen (or "Village") Bank with the objective to grant poor people small loans on easy terms, so-called microcredit. Poverty, Yunus said, means being deprived of all human value. According to him, microcredit is both a human right and an effective means of emerging from poverty.

"Lend the poor money in amounts which suit them," he said, "teach them a few sound financial principles, and they manage on their own."

Yunus has written several books on the subject. Best known is his 2003 autobiography *Banker to the Poor*, the title of which became his nickname.

A GOOD CAUSE?

"Lasting peace cannot be achieved," the committee wrote in its announcement of the 2006 Nobel Peace Prize, "unless large population groups find ways in which to break out of poverty. Micro-credit is one such means. Development from below also serves to advance democracy and human rights."

The so-called grassroots movement underscores basic Norwegian beliefs regarding human nature and economics. Everyone loves the underdog who accomplishes despite his or her circumstances. That belief is the basis of the American Dream. The Norwegian Dream, although not stated as such, is that everybody should have a little, and no one should have a lot. In practice, the realities are always far more complex. To the Nobel Committee, Yunus helped even out financial inequalities, which was a worthy endeavor. But did he really accomplish that goal?

Thomas Dichter has many years of experience battling poverty from his work at the UN and the World Bank. "It almost has an irresistible magic to it," he said about microcredit. "The magic is that a poor person gets a small loan, invests that money, makes a little money, and gives the money back. What could be better than that? A low-cost—if not, no-cost—investment, and BOOM, poverty is solved."

Unfortunately, the real story is not that simple.

NRK's *Brennpunkt* aired a documentary in November 2010 on Norwegian television about Yunus and Grameen Bank, and about the effect microfinance has on poverty. Over a period of two years, *Brennpunkt* and the Danish journalist Tom Heinemann traveled around the world, interviewing experts and people in villages who had received microloans.[3]

Brennpunkt began its investigation in the small village of Jobra in Bangladesh, the place where Yunus started his operations in 1976 when he lent

$27 to forty-two women in the village. In that same village, *Brennpunkt* met Narunnahar Begum, the daughter of Sufiya Begum, one of the original loan-takers, who was used as a star example of those Yunus helped. Narunnahar Begum, who met Yunus once after he had won Nobel's prize, told the Norwegian journalist that Yunus had promised her a house at that meeting. Since then, she has gone to Grameen Bank numerous times to ask about the house, but, to this day, nothing has happened. Under what conditions Yunus promised Begum a house is uncertain. Nevertheless, he hasn't always proven to be trustworthy.

According to local press, Sufiya Begum died in poverty in 1998. Still, Grameen Bank continued to use Begum as a success story of microcredit, showing a house she supposedly bought with a loan from Grameen. Interestingly, a neighbor of Sufiya Begum, Abdus Salam, claims that the house Grameen used in its marketing material wasn't Begum's, it was his.

"Grameen bank," Salam said, "claims that they have built this house for her, that my house belongs to Sufiya Begum. They have been showing my house and earned millions on the publicity."

According to both Salam and Narunnahar Begum, Grameen's marketing material about the success of microcredit was misleading. The Norwegian Nobel Committee, at least partly, based its decision on these success stories.

"My parents gave me my birth, but Grameen gave me a life," Chairman Mjøs said at the prize ceremony, referring to something Sufiya Begum had allegedly said.

Showing success is Yunus's strong suit. In 1995, First Lady Hillary Clinton visited a small village southeast of Jobra to see the success of Yunus's microcredit. He proudly showed her his accomplishments.

"The word," she said to Yunus, "about what you have achieved has traveled all the way to the United States."

Brennpunkt visited the village—which since then has been called Hillary Village—thirteen years later to see how life had evolved for the people there. Among many, they met with a man named Kartik and his family.

"When Hillary Clinton was here," Kartik said, "they promised to help us build a house. They don't keep their promises. There are sixty families here they were supposed to help. Five or six received help. The rest, nothing."

Although microloans are supposed to help people get on their feet and create businesses that will sustain them in the future, Grameen Bank also offers other types of microloans, for example to buy a house, mobile phone, or for education.

Khude and his family were one of these families who received a loan from Grameen bank.

"Apart from four new houses, there is no development in this village," Khude told the Norwegian journalist. He also said that between fifty and eighty people had been granted loans. Of those, only four families have gotten a better life. The other families, because of the debt they couldn't pay back, either sold their houses or left the village.

More than 100 million people around the world have microloans today, thanks to success stories of poor people who have gotten a better life with microcredit. These showcases, however, just like with Sufiya Begum, were not always accurate. Jude Fernando, who holds a PhD in development studies at Clark University, went to Hillary Village the year after Clinton's visit to see for himself what microcredit had accomplished to empower poor women. Fernando was told that most of the women who had spoken during Clinton's visit to showcase how their lives had been transformed, were not even from that village. But Yunus's showcases worked, and since then, many had taken up such loans. To be clear, Hillary Clinton had nothing to do with Yunus's marketing campaign. However, as a role model for women worldwide, her presence added value to Yunus's sales pitch to empower women. The women from Hillary Village who bought into the success stories, and whose lives had not been improved by signing up for loans, later felt betrayed.

Milford Bateman, in his book *Why Doesn't Microfinance Work?* wrote that "Microfinance institutions publish the tiny number of successes, but what they don't tell us is the much, much larger number of failures."[4] Failure meaning those people who are not able to pay off the debt, thus ending up even poorer than before.

Despite the miscommunication about microloans to potential customers, the question remains: Is microcredit an effective means to reduce poverty? Alex Counts is one who believes it does. The president and CEO of Grameen Foundation in Washington, DC, is a big supporter of Yunus and microcredit. Counts first went to Bangladesh as a Fulbright Scholar and spent six years working under Professor Yunus at Grameen Bank. He started the foundation in 1997, wishing to help other organizations use the Grameen method. Counts reported that the savings and loan business is growing every day, and that they are contributing to eliminating poverty in Bangladesh, Indonesia, and elsewhere.

From a small enterprise in the 1970s, Grameen Bank has grown to an enormous machine with nearly ten million Bangladeshi clients in 2019. According to Grameen Bank's own website, ninety-seven percent of these customers are women. The bank's success is partly due to its cooperation with other companies. In addition to the lending business, Grameen is cooperating with many multinational companies, including Adidas and BASF in Germany. More than fifty Grameen companies produce everything from water, textiles, yogurt, health insurance, telephone networks, mobile phones, and solar panels. Poor people can buy all these products once they get microcredit from Grameen Bank. It's a brilliant business idea for the owners of Grameen and their affiliates.

"Today, six billion mobile phones are being used throughout the world, with approximately 75 percent of users living in developing countries," Counts wrote in a *Huffington Post* blog on September 13, 2012. "Mobile technology provides unparalleled opportunities to break the cycle of poverty by providing access to markets, information, financial services, and viable business opportunities that were previously unavailable."

According to Counts, 80 percent of the population in Indonesia uses a cell phone, and 96 percent of those users text regularly.

"Farmers are now able to access information about weather conditions and market pricing for their cash crops, the unemployed can search for job opportunities electronically, and the unbanked can engage in secure financial transactions," Counts wrote.

Mobile phones, according to him, are empowering users to gain control of often volatile financial conditions, particularly in informal markets.

"If the microfinance institutions weren't succeeding, people wouldn't borrow from them," Counts said. "That's the best evidence we have that they are working."

Yet, it remains to be seen if microcredit makes poor people's lives any better, or if such loans empower women. What good is a mobile phone if one cannot afford to eat? And while Indonesia's economy is growing and the poverty rate has decreased from 15 percent in 2008 to just under 10 percent in 2018, one third of the population still lives on less than US $3.20 per day, which is the poverty threshold, according to the World Bank.[5] The question remains, however, if the reduction in poverty was caused by microcredit or by the government-led poverty reduction programs.

"There is no evidence," Bateman said, "that you get out of poverty through Grameen Bank or any of the Grameen companies."

In 2007, Bangladesh financial experts published a report on microcredit, which included a survey of 2,500 poor people who had received such loans. More than one third had loans with Grameen Bank. One of the experts of the report, Q. K. Ahmad, PhD in economics, said that these people's assets have not grown. On the contrary, about one-third have less than they did before receiving loans. Ahmad also found that neither the people's sanitary situations nor their food intake had improved, and the children who started school would soon drop out. The reason, he said, was that they had to pay installments on their loans every week. Finding money to pay the installments became the main concern for these people, which meant they had to disregard other family needs.

According to Ahmad, the first time he saw the results from the survey, he didn't believe them.

"Micro-credit has been praised all over the world, and I thought it was a good thing," he said. "But the numbers don't lie. The poor people stay where they are or become poorer. Only a few do better with the loans."

Microcredit, instead of helping people to sustain themselves, seems to have done the opposite by pushing Western consumer practices onto the poor people in developing countries. Many of the borrowers also said that "These banks are not good for us."

Microcredit is very good for the banks, their owners, and the consumer goods manufacturers. One of the shareholders of GrameenPhone, the Norwegian phone company Telenor, made a profit of approximately US $130 million in eight years.[6] And Yunus has been ranked among Forbes's 400 billionaires in the United States.

Let's take a look at how microcredit actually works.

GROUP PRESSURE AND SKY-HIGH INTEREST RATES

For a majority of people who sign up for microloans, part of the problem lies in the business model of the bank, including Grameen's. Because everyone qualifies, and no training is given as to how to create a viable business, many of the borrowers are not able to pay back the loan.

"I bought a piece of land," a woman said to *Brennpunkt*'s journalist, "but the profit from it was not enough to pay the interest, so I had to take up another loan. Now I have many different loans." This woman, along with many others, was caught in a debt trap.

Also, because the banks don't look at an individual's ability to service the loan, they group applicants together. The rule is that the people in the group will guarantee for one another. If one member of the group can't pay, the other group members are all responsible to pay for them. That is why there is no need for a guarantee in order to obtain a microloan. The bank doesn't care which member pays, as long as the payment is made.

"They use the group as collateral," Khushi Kabir, Director of Nijera Kori, a women's rights institution in Bangladesh, said. "When one person in the group cannot make a payment, it has grave consequences for the other members, and the pressure is immense. One person's default is the entire group's default. Many people commit suicide or are on the run as a result."

One reason the borrowers of microcredit end up in debt traps is the interest rate. According to Grameen Bank's website, the interest rate for all loans is 16 percent. Except it's not that simple. On another webpage of Grameen Bank it says that the rate is 10 percent on a "flat" basis, which, according to David Roodman, senior fellow at the Center for Global Development in Washington, DC, means that when someone borrows 1000 taka (the currency in Bangladesh) and repays in weekly installments over the course of a year, she pays 100 taka total in interest. However, according to Roodman, "Since she pays that 100 taka on an average balance of 500 (the balance falls steadily from 1000 to 0 over the year), her effective interest rate is more like 100/500 = 20%."[7]

So, the interest rate on microloans is now at 20 percent. It gets even more complicated. The true cost of credit includes more than the interest rate. Clients are often required to put some of their borrowings into creditor-run savings accounts (or forced savings) as a kind of collateral, which, Roodman says, reduces available credit without proportionally reducing interest payments and thus effectively raises the rate. There may be upfront fees, too. In the case of Grameen, each member of a microcredit loan group must buy a 100 taka share of the bank once their forced savings balance is high enough to pay for it. Often, the clients must buy insurance as well. When Roodman took all these factors into account, the true interest rate was closer to 25 percent.

In comparison, regular consumer loans may have an interest rate between 12–13 percent, but microloans are considered high risk for the bank. In other developing countries, interest rates on microcredit are much higher. In Africa, *Brennpunkt* asserts, interest rates around 100 percent are not unusual. In Mexico, they often surpass 200 percent. Many end up with the local loan sharks to repay Grameen and other similar institutions.

This is how, according to Milford Bateman, "The poor are gradually getting caught in a web of micro-debt." The well-known Korean economist Ha-Joon Chang at Cambridge University confirmed that microloans lead people into a debt trap.

"The whole thing has to be re-examined," he said. "What kind of business makes 30 to 100 percent profit? Micro-credit does not help the poor."

In the last few years, more people have become critical of this type of business.

"If microfinance was so good for people," Khushi Kabir said, "why is it that money institutions exist in the villages, and that the interest rates have not gone down? The high interest rate makes it almost impossible to pay the weekly installments." She pointed out that very few of the poor who sign the loan documents can read or write, and therefore most don't know what they are signing.

Hazera, a woman from the northern part of Bangladesh, in an interview with *Brennpunkt*, said she struggles with making the payments.

"I've had a loan with Grameen for fifteen years. I pay the installments on time. One time I had problems paying. The employees of the bank yelled at me, called me names. They said they would sell the metal plates that make the roof on my house. That they would put me on the street."

Afraid, she sold everything she owned and paid the installment. During the interview, Hazera started crying and showed *Brennpunkt* the holes in the roof.

"The house is falling apart," she said. "The rain pours through the roof. If only I had money to repair it. I have no one to help me."

In Bangladesh, more than 80 percent of the population still lives on less than two US dollars per day. Whatever Grameen Bank is doing, it seems insufficient to help reduce poverty.

"Most people are not entrepreneurs," Dichter said. "Most of us will not become Bill Gates. Why do we expect poor people to be different?" If you ask them what they really want, he continued, they will say that they want a stable economy and security. "They do not want to go out in the hot sun, selling a bag of rice, standing next to twenty other guys selling the same thing, earning pennies."

MICRODEBT AND SUICIDE

For the poor, microcredit can have tragic consequences.

"Thirty-five years into it," Roodman said, "we don't have any evidence that micro-credit—microfinance more generally—actually reduces poverty."

According to Jonathan Morduch, professor at New York University, there is more evidence of the contrary, of people who are getting into trouble over their loans. Families sink financially because they have too many loans and are unable to handle the money effectively. *Brennpunkt* reported that many people leave their villages to go to Dakha and other cities in Bangladesh to seek work there, in order to pay off their microloans. In the big cities, because they are unable to find a job, they sink even deeper into poverty.

Kartik has a loan with Grameen Bank, and he has difficulties making the group installments.

"Some men in the group want to beat me," he said. "They yell at me and tell me I will get no more loans. I have to go to private lenders to be able to pay. I want to end my life."

He is not alone. A report from February 24, 2012, in *Business Insider*, connected hundreds of suicides in India to microfinance organizations.

"First, they were stripped of their utensils, furniture, mobile phones, televisions, ration cards, and heirloom gold jewelry," the article stated. "Then, some of them drank pesticide. One woman threw herself in a pond. Another jumped into a well with her children. Sometimes, the debt collectors watched nearby."[8]

According to *Business Insider*, more than two hundred poor, debt-ridden residents of Andhra Pradesh killed themselves in late 2010. The Indian government blamed microfinance companies "for fueling a frenzy of over-indebtedness and then pressuring borrowers so relentlessly that some took their own lives." The article also confirms that sometimes employees of the lending institutions were pushing their clients to commit suicide.

BBC News has also reported on this suicide epidemic as a result of microloans. "Multiple lending, over-indebtedness, coercive recovery practices, and unseemly enrichment by promoters and senior executives [of micro-credit companies] has led to this situation," Vijay Mahajan, chairman of India's Microfinance Institutions Network, said to *BBC News* on December 16, 2010.

The article compared India's microfinance crisis to the 2008 subprime mortgage meltdown in the United States, where finance companies threw cheap and easy loans at homebuyers until prices crashed, and borrowers were unable to sell their homes or pay their debts. The difference, however, is that in India the borrowers are even poorer, with no social security.

"Micro-credit has become 'Walmartized' by unrestrained selling of cheap products to the poor," Malcom Harper, chairman of the ratings company Micro-Credit Ratings International Ltd. in Gurgaon, India, said to *Bloomberg News* in an article published on December 28, 2010. "Selling debt is like selling drugs," Harper said. "Selling debt to illiterate women in Andhra Pradesh, you've got to be a lot more responsible."

K. Venkat Narayana, an economics professor at Kakatiya University in Warangal has studied how microfinance lenders persuaded groups of women to borrow.

"Microfinance was supposed to empower women," he said to *Bloomberg*. Instead, "Microfinance guys reversed the social and economic progress, and these women ended up becoming slaves."

The link between microcredit and suicide wasn't known to the Nobel Committee when it chose Yunu's and Grameen Bank in 2006. Nevertheless, the committee should have waited to see if such loans actually alleviated poverty or done more research into the true effects of microfinance before bestowing the world's most prestigious prize to Yunus. The hasty decision to honor Yunus and Grameen makes one wonder if the committee, in lieu of sufficient research before making its selection, was swayed by Yunus' popularity.

THE COMMITTEE'S MOTIVATIONS

For more than thirty-five years, Yunus has been celebrated for the idea of lending small loans to poor people.

"Hillary Clinton got on the bandwagon, Hollywood celebrities got on the bandwagon, Bono got on the bandwagon," Thomas W. Dichter said. "Then Yunus received the Nobel Peace Prize. This [microfinance] must be good!"[9]

Clinton wasn't the only one. Actresses Sharon Stone, Anjelica Huston, and other celebrities shared Clinton's exuberance. In addition to the Nobel

Peace Prize in 2006, Yunus received the United States Presidential Medal of Freedom in 2009 and the Congressional Gold Medal in 2010. President Obama praised Yunus and his bank for having dispersed more than eight billion dollars in microloans to poor people all over the world.

"We felt it was a good cause," Nobel Committee Chairman Mjøs said in an interview with a journalist from NRK. "The battle against poverty is the best type of work toward peace."

One might ask if the committee felt pressured into giving the prize to Yunus. Among Yunus's many admirers, President Bill Clinton strongly supported him as a Nobel choice. In a speech given at the University of California, Berkeley in 2002, President Clinton described Yunus as "a man who long ago should have won the Nobel Prize [and] I'll keep saying that until they finally give it to him."[10] At his presentation speech in 2006, Chairman Mjøs said, "Now Clinton will no longer need to remind us."

In his presentation speech, Mjøs also managed to mix the demonization of Islam in with his tribute to Yunus, perhaps as another kick in the leg to the United States.

"Since the 11th of September 2001," he said, "we have seen a widespread tendency to demonize Islam."

What Islam has to do with microlending is unclear, except for the fact that Islam is the official religion in Yunus's home country Bangladesh. Nevertheless, Mjøs continued his rant about how the West has something to learn from the Muslim part of the world and not the other way around.

"The peace prize to Yunus and Grameen Bank is also support for the Muslim country of Bangladesh and for the Muslim environments in the world that are working for dialogue and collaboration," he said.

SUBSIDIES FROM WESTERN COUNTRIES

Microcredit has proven to be a profitable business for lending institutions. However, these banks, including Grameen, owe their success in part to

Western countries, such as Norway, donating large amounts of money to these banks' development. Morduch says that more than US $170 billion was poured into the industry in the form of subsidies between 1990 and 1995. Norway is one of the countries that has contributed the most to Grameen Bank, through the Norwegian Agency for Development Cooperation, or NORAD. Knowing how closely tied the Nobel Committee is with Norwegian politics, perhaps the Nobel Peace Prize was an attempt at justifying Norway's investment. There is, however, one incident involving Muhammad Yunus the committee may not have known about.

For almost fifteen years, from 1996 until 2010 when NRK *Brennpunkt* released its documentary, NORAD kept secret a dispute they had with Yunus regarding the use of these funds. Part of the dispute concerned the money Yunus used to start up GrameenPhone, in direct breach with the agreement the bank had with the Norwegian institution.

"Microfinance is a fantastic remedy against poverty," Prime Minister Jens Stoltenberg said in an interview with NRK. What he probably didn't know was that NORAD was sitting on documents they had kept away from the public eye about another side to Grameen Bank and Yunus. Already in 1993, NORAD internally warned against the risk of poor people ending up in a debt trap. Their research showed that almost all the women with microloans had to get private loans for repayment. NORAD calls them "pyramid loans." But even though they knew about this risk, NORAD—perhaps in an attempt cover up its mistake and to avoid criticism from the Norwegian public—continued to pour money into Grameen Bank.

Subsidies, in themselves, are not necessarily problematic. What Yunus did with the money he received is. Here's a brief account of what happened. Grameen had an agreement with the government of Bangladesh, exempting the bank from paying taxes, and this agreement was about to expire. In 1996, Yunus set up a new company that he controlled himself, called Grameen Kalyan. Yunus transferred more than $80 million—according to documents *Brennpunkt* managed to obtain—from Grameen Bank to the new company to avoid paying taxes. Kalyan then loaned the money back to the bank, and the new company received interest on the loan. Yunus's actions might have been fine under different circumstances. Not here. The money had been given specifically to Grameen Bank—not to any other entities of Yunus—by Norway, Sweden, and other donor countries for the cause of eradicating poverty, not to enrich Yunus himself.

The Norwegian embassy in Bangladesh discovered the scheme by coincidence in 1998 and protested. Ambassador Hans Frederik Lehne wrote a confidential letter informing NORAD about what Yunus had done, which constituted a breach of the agreement Norway had with Bangladesh and Grameen. When NORAD and the Norwegian embassy put pressure on Yunus to transfer the money back to the bank, Yunus responded on January 8, 1998 that he had made the transfer to gain a more responsible handling of the money and to avoid paying taxes. He later denied having attempted tax evasion.

To avoid a scandal, Yunus wrote a letter in April 1998 asking for a meeting with head of NORAD, Tove Strand.

"Dear Tove," he wrote, "I need your help. If people within and outside of the government who don't support Grameen learn about this letter, we will have serious problems in Bangladesh."[11]

He certainly didn't want to give any ammunition to the critics of microcredit. NORAD didn't want the public to know how Norwegian taxpayers' money had been misused. Shortly after, Yunus visited Oslo and reached a compromise with Strand. *Brennpunkt* was not successful in speaking with Strand about what was said at the meeting. But only part of the money was transferred back, and NORAD agreed to keep quiet about what had happened. All the documents regarding the case were stamped confidential, and Parliament, the press, and likely also the Norwegian Nobel Committee, were kept out of the loop.

David Roodman of the Center for Global Development said in an interview that Western countries have been lured to believe in the storytelling about microcredit eradicating poverty.

"On the other hand," he said, "it is also our fault. We decide who gets our money based on who has the best story that makes us feel good about ourselves. We usually don't give our money to the ones who have the best scientific evidence that the idea will actually work."

Ha-Joon Chang at Cambridge University also believes that the donating countries were duped into believing that microfinance is the ideal solution to reduce poverty.

"Microfinance as an industry," Dichter said, "wants everyone to believe that their work is important, and that it needs the subsidies and generous support from the public. The public isn't interested in hearing about the details of this thing; they want to see the smiling face. And that's why the smiling face will continue to be there."

After the release of *Brennpunkt*'s 2010 documentary "*Caught in Micro Debt*," Norwegian authorities investigated the allegations that Yunus and Grameen had misappropriated funds donated by Norway. The authorities cleared both Yunus and Grameen Bank due to insufficient evidence.

Microfinance has brought Yunus fame, wealth, and many prizes, including Nobel's. That doesn't qualify him or his bank as peace champions. A great leader—or peace champion—inspires confidence and trust. They think holistically and put the needs of the people before their own personal wealth. A peace champion certainly doesn't lie about the success of the people they tried to help or lure others into debt traps and unnecessary consumption. Nor does a true leader transfer donations meant to reduce poverty into different company entities, so as to make a personal profit.

While I agree with the committee that poverty reduction is important to create a more stable and peaceful world, the Norwegian Nobel Committee has, in this case, either not done its homework in researching Yunus or was too blinded by the lobbying efforts of celebrities. Or, most distressing, perhaps they knew all along but did not feel like they would have to have any accountability or repercussions to face once the flaws and disastrous effects of Yunus' program came to light.

GANDHI:
OVERLOOKED AND
DISREGARDED

It is said that the dynamite and the explosive gelatin have,
by accelerating the completion of the railway,
saved millions in interest alone. But that has to be wrong.
Had that been the case, not even the most
ill-mannered churl would have neglected to send
me an invitation to the occasion.

—ALFRED NOBEL

MAHATMA GANDHI WAS a lawyer, politician, and social activist who, through nonviolent civil disobedience, led India to independence from British rule and inspired movements for civil rights and freedom across the world. Yet he did *not* win a Nobel. It's a staggering thought considering bankers, environmentalists, and warmongers have received the award, but the global face of nonviolent resistance did not.

Gandhi didn't work toward the fraternity between nations, as Alfred Nobel wrote in his last will. Perhaps the committee got caught up in this criterion with Gandhi, unlike with so many other laurates. However, Gandhi did promote brotherhood and peace between groups of people with different religions within India. His mission was about standing up to the oppressive rule of the British in India, demanding equal rights for Indians and eventually freeing India from its British colonizer. He took a firm stance on nonviolence and the reduction of standing armies. As leader of the Indian people, he also held gatherings that qualify as peace conferences, preaching peace and equality for all people.

As we have seen examples of in previous chapters, the Norwegian Nobel Committee has extended Nobel's definition and handed the prize to people who did not fill Nobel's criteria of peace champions numerous times. From day one, the committee has taken Nobel's final words lightly.[1] The first peace prize in 1901 was awarded to Henry Dunant, the founder of the Red Cross, "not for the prevention of war but for the alleviation of suffering," according to Heffermehl. As you may recall from Chapter Seven, Mother Teresa won the Nobel Peace Prize in 1979, despite the fact that her work as a humanitarian didn't, with a strict interpretation of Nobel's will, qualify her as a peace champion.

In previous chapters, we have seen how the committee considers itself entitled to design its own prize regardless of Nobel's final words. Sometimes the prize is more a pat on the back or kick in the leg depending on the Norwegian government's foreign policy than an outstretched hand to those in the peace movement.

Instead of following Nobel's instructions, the committee has widened the scope to all kinds of different work that, in its opinion, has "conferred the greatest benefit on mankind."[2]

"Thus the Nobel Peace Prize," committee chairman Egil Aarvik said, "can never be more—or less—than a hand stretched out to individuals or groups who give expression to the longing for peace and freedom felt by all the peoples of the world, wherever they live."[3]

Few individuals have given such an expression to the longing for peace and freedom as Mahatma Gandhi.

A TRUE CHAMPION OF PEACE

"The greatest omission in our 106-year history is undoubtedly that Mahatma Gandhi never received the Nobel Peace Prize," Secretary Lundestad said in 2006. He was, however, nominated five times between 1937 and 1948.[4]

Born on October 2, 1869 in Porbandar, a coastal town in the Kathiawar Agency of the British Indian Empire, Mohandas Karamchand Gandhi was raised in a Hindu merchant caste family. He was the youngest of four siblings. The name Mahatma, meaning "high souled" or "venerable" in the ancient Indian language Sanskrit, was first given to him in 1914 in South Africa.[5, 6, 7]

The classic Indian stories of Shravana and King Harishchandra had great impact on Gandhi's childhood and provided him with values of love and truth. Following local customs and Hindu tradition, Gandhi entered into an arranged marriage when he was only thirteen years old.

"As we didn't know much about marriage," Gandhi later recalled, "for us it meant only wearing new clothes, eating sweets, and playing with relatives." The couple's first child, who lived only a few days, was born when Gandhi was fifteen. Later, they had four more children, all boys.

In school, Gandhi was a mediocre student. One of the reports rated him as "good at English, fair in Arithmetic and weak in Geography; conduct very good, bad handwriting." He was reserved due to lack of confidence, and "shone neither in the classroom nor on the playing field," according to the Encyclopedia Britannica. When he was not attending to his then-ailing father or helping his mother with her household chores, he loved to go out on long solitary walks.[8]

He passed the matriculation exam at Samaldas College in Bhavnagar, but left for London instead, to study law. Left to himself, he probably would have become a doctor. However, if he were to continue his family's tradition of holding high office in one of the states of Gujarat, he had to become a barrister.

After three years in England, he returned to India in 1891. His law practice in Bombay failed because the legal field was overcrowded, and because he was much too reserved to elbow his way forward. He was also terribly shy. In his very first case, he lost because he was not aggressive enough to cross-examine the witnesses. Because he couldn't get another job, he was left with making a modest living drafting petitions for litigants. That's why, in 1893, at twenty-four years old, when Gandhi was offered a job at Dada Abdulla & Co., an Indian law firm in the colony of Natal, South Africa, he gladly accepted. South Africa was, at the time, part of the British Empire and many Indians worked there. India has several different religious groups, including Muslims and Hindus. The Indians in South Africa were led by wealthy Indian Muslims. Gandhi, while representing Indian Muslim traders at the law firm, noticed the historic differences between Indians of different castes and religions and believed he could bridge these differences and unify the groups. It was during his twenty-one years in South Africa that Gandhi developed his political views and leadership skills, which would later qualify him for Nobel's prize.

In South Africa, Gandhi also experienced the discrimination that was directed at all people of color, including the different Indian groups. Once he was thrown off a train at Pietermaritzburg after refusing to move from the first-class wagon. Continuing his travel by stagecoach, he was beaten by a driver for refusing to move to make room for a white passenger. On that same journey, he was also barred from hotels. In another incident, the magistrate of a Durban court ordered Gandhi to remove his turban, which he refused to do. These events of injustice—turning points in Gandhi's life—shaped his social activism and changed him. Gandhi, who had never been the self-assertive type, suddenly decided he would no longer accept being denigrated. He would defend his dignity as an Indian and as a human. Because the British administration was behind the injustices, he also began to question his people's place in the British Empire as second-class citizens, in South Africa but also in India.

Instead of immediately returning to India with his mission, Gandhi extended his stay in South Africa to assist Indians opposing a bill that denied them the right to vote. All of a sudden, at twenty-five years old, Gandhi, who had suffered from terrible stage fright, became a proficient political campaigner. It was as if he just needed the right motivation to push him out of his shyness. He asked Joseph Chamberlain, the British colonial secretary, to reconsider his position on this bill but was unable to stop it. Nevertheless, his campaign was successful in drawing attention to the grievances of Indians in South Africa.[9]

In 1894, he unified his people despite religious differences by founding the political organization Natal Indian Congress. As secretary of this congress, he flooded the South African government, the legislature, and the press with documented statements of Indian grievances.[10] He even managed to expose the British discrimination practices against Queen Victoria's Indian subjects in one of her own colonies in Africa.[11]

However, his efforts for people of color were not well viewed by South Africa's ruling class. In January 1897, when Gandhi returned to Durban after he had been to India to bring his wife and children back with him to South Africa, a mob of white settlers attacked him. He barely managed to escape with the help of the Durban police chief's wife, who happened to be passing by at the time and, using her parasol, protected Gandhi from the mob until police officers arrived. Refusing to press charges against any member of the mob, Gandhi applied one of his famous principles: "An eye for an eye only ends up making the whole world blind."

When the South African Boer War broke out in 1899, Gandhi argued that the Indians, who claimed the full rights of citizenship in the British crown colony of Natal, had a duty to defend it.[12] However, he refused to take an active part in the battle. Instead, he volunteered to form a group of Indian ambulance drivers to participate. He wanted to prove the British wrong in their belief that Hindus were not fit for dangerous activities. He was also convinced that their support would enhance the Indians' chances of obtaining full citizenship in South Africa. Gandhi enrolled eleven hundred

Indian volunteers, who were trained and medically certified to serve on the front lines.

On one occasion, General Redvers Buller praised the Indians who—despite the heat and lack of food or water—carried wounded soldiers for miles to a field hospital because the terrain was too rough for the ambulances. For this, Gandhi and thirty-seven other Indians received the War Medal. The conflict ended with British victory, but that didn't improve the situation for the Indians in South Africa.

In 1906, the government of the province of Transvaal announced a new law requiring the Indian population in South Africa to register with the government. Gandhi, disappointed that the Indians' effort during the Second Boer War had not granted them full citizenship, saw the new law as an insult. At a mass protest meeting held in Johannesburg on September 11 that year, Gandhi adopted his methodology of *satyagrahis* (meaning devotion to the truth in Sanskrit), or nonviolent protest, for the first time. Sanskrit is the primary holy language of Hinduism and the predominant language of most works of Hindu philosophy, as well as some of the principal texts of Buddhism and Jainism. With the Sanskrit philosophy in mind, Gandhi's method consisted of redressing wrongs through inviting, rather than inflicting, suffering, and resisting adversaries without rancor and fighting them without violence. In other words, he urged Indians to defy the new law and to suffer the punishments for doing so. The community adopted the plan, and during the ensuing seven-year struggle, thousands of Indians were imprisoned, beaten, or shot for refusing to register, for burning their registration cards, or engaging in other forms of nonviolent resistance.

The government successfully repressed the Indians, but the public outcry over the harsh treatment of peaceful protesters forced South African leader Jan Christian Smuts to negotiate a compromise with Gandhi. The essence of the compromise was that the government would repeal Act 2 of the 1907 law, which made registration compulsory, upon which the Indians would register voluntarily.[10] Although not the ideal result that Gandhi had hoped for, it ended the persecutions of the Indians. Gandhi, however, bore no hatred or ill-feelings toward Smuts during the struggle. Once, during his not-infrequent stays in jail, Gandhi made a pair of sandals for Smuts. Much later, Smuts recalled that when the fight was over "there was the atmosphere in which a decent peace could be concluded."[13]

In the end, Gandhi's efforts didn't provide an enduring solution for the Indians in South Africa. More importantly, perhaps, his experiences of injustice in South Africa had prepared Gandhi for his work back home in India. During his last years in South Africa, as of 1904, Gandhi moved to live on a farm outside of Durban with his family and friends, in pursuit of a simple life of manual labor and austerity. In 1910, he established an idealistic community that he named Tolstoy Farm near Johannesburg, where he nurtured his policy of peaceful resistance.

South Africa had not only inspired Gandhi "to evolve a new and nonviolent technique for political action but also transformed him into a leader" who cared more for the well-being of his people than his own personal needs.[14] In 1918, the British Classical scholar Gilbert Murray wrote the following about Gandhi in the Hibbert Journal, which, in hindsight, reads like a premonition.

"Persons in power," he wrote, "should be very careful how they deal with a man who cares nothing for sensual pleasure, nothing for riches, nothing for comfort or praise, or promotion, but is simply determined to do what he believes to be right. He is a dangerous and uncomfortable enemy, because his body which you can always conquer gives you so little purchase upon his soul."[15]

BACK TO INDIA WITH A CAUSE

In 1914, just before the outbreak of World War I, Gandhi decided to leave South Africa. After six months in London, he and his family returned to Bombay in January 1915 at the request of Gopal Krishna Gokhale, a key leader of the Congress Party, who was known for making change from within the system. Having built an international reputation as a leading Indian nationalist, Gandhi joined Gokhale at the Indian National Congress that same year.

A couple of major achievements marked the period before Gandhi took leadership of Congress in 1920. The first came in 1917 when local farmers in the Champaran region were forced to grow indigo (opium), even though its demand had been declining over the last two decades. They were also forced to sell their crops at a fixed price. Unhappy, the farmers appealed to Gandhi, who responded by encouraging a nonviolent protest by refusing to cooperate. The administration, who backed the British landlords, were taken by surprise and gave into the protesters request.[16]

The following year, floods and famine hit Kheda, and the farmers demanded tax relief. Gandhi moved his headquarters to the area and organized scores of supporters and volunteers from the region, the most notable being Vallabhbhai Patel (also known as Sardar Patel), the Indian politician who became the first deputy prime minister after India obtained its independence. To help the farmers, Gandhi's strategy of noncooperation entailed a signature campaign where the farmers pledged that they wouldn't pay taxes even under the threat of land confiscation. A boycott of *Mamlatdars* and *Talatdars* (revenue officials within the district) accompanied the campaign. The administration resisted for five months, but finally, in May 1918, it gave way on important provisions and relaxed the conditions of payment of revenue taxes during the famine.[17]

Toward the end of World War I, in 1918, the viceroy—or the governor-general of India, who represented the British monarch—invited Gandhi to a war conference in Delhi. The viceroy must have seen Gandhi as an influential leader that could convince the Indian population to fight in the British army. In return, the viceroy promised to assist Gandhi's quest for independence. Gandhi believed the viceroy and agreed to recruit Indians to assist in the war, this time as combatants, in contrast to the Boer War in South Africa and at the outbreak of World War I in 1914.

"If we want to learn the use of arms with the greatest possible dispatch, it is our duty to enlist ourselves in the army." Gandhi wrote in a June 1918 leaflet, *Appeal for Enlistment*. His appeal went against his own principles of nonviolence. In a letter to the viceroy's private secretary, he wrote that he "personally will not kill or injure anybody, friend or foe."[18]

Gandhi's war recruitment campaign brought into question his stance on nonviolence, and, for the purpose of this book, his qualifications as a Nobel peace champion.

"The question of the consistency," his private secretary, Mahadev Haribhai Desai, noted in his diary, "between his creed of 'Ahimsa' (nonviolence) and his recruiting campaign was raised not only then but has been discussed ever since."[19]

Not only did he betray his own values, the British only offered minor reforms in return for India's participation in the war, and the country was no closer to independence. He certainly wasn't perfect, but Gandhi realized his mistake and learned from it (as we shall see later in this chapter, when the British wanted the Indians to fight in World War II).

In February 1919, the British pushed through the Rowlatt Acts, despite fierce Indian opposition, which gave the authorities power to imprison without trial those suspected of sedition, meaning those who incited resistance of the British authorities. Gandhi responded by announcing a satyagrahis nonviolent struggle, which shook the country. Violent outbreaks followed—notably the Jallianwala Bagh massacre (also known as the Amritsar massacre) in April 13, 1919, where British troops in Punjab killed nearly four hundred peaceful civilians who were gathered in an open space in Amritsar. The massacre led to a national protest and riots. In return, the British administration enacted martial law.[20]

Despite these violent confrontations, Gandhi kept his principles of peace and reconciliation. Gandhi criticized both the actions of the British Raj and the retaliatory violence of Indians. True to his nonviolent and conciliatory principles, he wrote a resolution offering condolences to British civilian victims and also condemning the Indian riots. The resolution, in form of a letter stating Gandhi's beliefs, was first met with opposition in the Indian congress. However, after an emotional speech advocating his principle that all violence was evil and unjustified, congress accepted Gandhi's resolution.[21]

Despite his conciliatory acts, Gandhi was not afraid to voice his disapproval of the British insensitivity to the Amritsar massacre. He also took sides with the Indian Muslims who felt resentment toward the British with regards to the peace terms offered to Turkey after World War I. The Ottoman Empire had been dismembered as a result of World War I, and Muslims feared for the safety of their holy places and the prestige of their religion. Convinced that the British government was unfair in its dealings with Muslims, Gandhi returned the medals bestowed on him by the British government, including for his accomplishments in the Boer War, as a mark of solidarity.[22]

In 1919, Gandhi decided to support the Muslims in the Khilafat movement, a worldwide protest by Muslims against the collapsing status of the caliph, the leader of their religion.[23] This strengthened his position in congress. Gandhi, soon the most prominent spokesperson for the All-India Muslim Conference, attracted a strong base of Muslim support with local chapters in all Muslim centers in India. Because of his wide popularity among both Hindus and Muslims, Gandhi took leadership of the Indian congress in 1920. He even convinced the extreme faction of Muslims to support the peaceful movement.

Although Gandhi was a Hindu, he didn't look upon Hinduism as the only true religion.

"The one religion is beyond all speech," he once said. "Imperfect men put it into such language as they can command, and their words are interpreted by other men equally imperfect. Hence the necessity for tolerance, which does not mean indifference towards one's own faith, but a more intelligent and pure love for it."

A unifier of people with different religious beliefs, Gandhi was India's first national leader with a multicultural base. With the necessary support in congress to employ noncooperation, nonviolence, and peaceful resistance as weapons in the struggle against the British Raj, Gandhi began a steady escalation of demands toward independence. He also continued to focus on uniting different religious groups, and, under his leadership, congress was reorganized with a new constitution, and membership in the party was opened to anyone prepared to pay a token fee, transforming it from an elite organization to one of national appeal.

As he stepped up his efforts toward complete Indian self-government, Gandhi expanded his nonviolence platform to include boycotting British educational institutions and courts of law, encouraging people to resign from government employment, and to forsake British titles and honors. Gandhi urged people, including women, to boycott British and other foreign-made goods, and encouraged all Indians to wear *Khadi*, or homespun cloth, instead of British-made textiles. Gandhi even invented a small, portable spinning wheel that could be folded into the size of a small typewriter, in a strategy to include women in the movement at a time when many thought they should not take part in political activities.[24] Hence, Gandhi became an early women's rights activist who strongly encouraged the emancipation of women.

"The women have come to look upon me as one of themselves," he once said.

He opposed child marriage and the extreme oppression of Hindu widows. On rare occasions, these widows (who were married off at a young age and not allowed to remarry once their husbands died) were forced to sit on their husband's dead body in the funeral pyre, to be burned alive.

A human rights activist, Gandhi also took a stance against untouchability, or people outside the caste system who were considered "untouchable," or dirty. Having experienced grave injustices himself in South Africa, Gandhi felt no one should be excluded from society.[25]

Because of the widespread participation, including women and untouchables, the noncooperation movement electrified the country, breaking the spell of fear of British rule, and led to the arrests of thousands of *satyagrahi*s, who defied the law and—sometimes—cheerfully lined up for prison. But just as the movement reached its peak, it ended abruptly as a result of a violent outbreak in the town of Chauri Chaura on February 5, 1922, when a large group of protesters, participating in the noncooperation movement, clashed with the police, who opened fire. In retaliation, the demonstrators attacked and set fire to a police station, killing all of its occupants. Three civilians and twenty-two policemen died that day. Fearing that the movement of mass civil disobedience was about to take an even more violent turn, Gandhi called it off a few days later, on February 12.[26]

In his autobiography, Jawaharlal Nehru, who was an Indian independence activist and first prime minister of India, describes Gandhi's decision as a setback and extremely demoralizing for all members of congress who were in prison when Gandhi took this decision.

Despite calling off the noncooperation campaign, Gandhi was arrested on March 10, 1922 for sedition and, as the man behind the uprising, sentenced to six years in prison. He was, however, released for an appendicitis operation in February 1924 after serving two years, and never finished his sentence.[27]

FIRST ATTEMPT AT INDEPENDENCE

Without Gandhi's unifying personality during the two years he was in prison, the Indian National Congress began to unravel. It split into two factions, one favoring party participation in the legislatures, and the other opposing such participation. Furthermore, cooperation between Hindus and Muslims, which had been strong at the height of the nonviolence campaign, was breaking down. Freed from prison, Gandhi attempted to bridge these differences through negotiations and reasoning with fanatics. He also undertook a three-week fast in the fall of 1924 in an attempt to unify the different political factions in congress, but with limited success. Still, he was elected president of the congress party in December 1924, and he served for one year. After this, Gandhi remained in congress but seemed to have lost his motivation to fight for independence. Instead, he focused on resolving the differences between the Swaraj Party and the Indian National Congress. He also continued his work to improve the situation for the untouchables, and made efforts to eliminate alcoholism, illiteracy, and poverty.[28]

Gandhi's fire was renewed in 1927 when the British government appointed a constitutional reform commission under Sir John Simon, a prominent

English lawyer and politician, which excluded Indian members. The Indian political parties, despite their differences, responded with a boycott, and Gandhi called on the British government to grant India autonomy within the British Empire. If the government refused, Gandhi threatened to launch a new noncooperation campaign demanding complete independence. When the British did not respond, the Indians raised their flag in Lahore and celebrated this first attempt at independence on January 26, 1930. None-theless, the silence didn't mean the British were ready to give in and grant India its freedom from colonial reign.[29]

That same year in March, Gandhi launched a new satyagrahis against the tax on salt, which mostly affected the poor, culminating in the famous Salt March from March 12 to April 6. Joined by thousands of Indians, including the women Gandhi had encouraged to participate, he walked 388 kilometers (241 miles) from Ahmedabad, which is situated inland, to the coastal village of Dandi, to symbolize that the Indians were being taxed on their own salt that came from their own ocean. When they arrived in Dandi, they were met by the British who responded by imprisoning more than 60,000 people. Still, the Salt March was a success in that the Indian people stood up for themselves against their oppressor.[30]

In 1934, Gandhi resigned from the Congress Party. In his opinion, its leading members had adopted nonviolence out of political expediency and not as the fundamental creed it was for him. In place of political activity, he focused on building the nation from the bottom up by educating rural India, which accounted for 85 percent of the population. He promoted hand spinning and weaving to supplement farmers' incomes, especially women's, and continued his fight against untouchability.[31]

When Jawaharlal Nehru became president of the Indian Congress in 1936, Gandhi tutored him in his work toward independence.[32] But Gandhi's nonviolent approach was again disrupted when Subhas Chandra Bose replaced Nehru in 1938. Despite Gandhi's opposition, Bose won a second term, but was forced to resign after a massive protest by the All-India leaders objecting to Bose's abandonment of Gandhi's principles.

INDIA AND WORLD WAR II:
QUIT INDIA

With the outbreak of World War II in 1939, the nationalist struggle in India entered its last crucial phase. Again, the British wanted the Indians to fight in the British army. The Indian National Congress was prepared to support the British war effort if Indian self-government was assured. Gandhi spoke up against it. Gandhi detested Fascism and all it stood for, but he was also fundamentally against war.[33] Perhaps more important, he had learned his lesson from World War I when he had made the terrible mistake of encouraging Indian participation in return for independence.

After long deliberations in congress, Gandhi's view prevailed, and he declared that India could not be party to a war that was fought for democratic freedom while that freedom was denied India itself.

Tensions between the British and the Indians reached a high in 1942 when Gandhi, in a speech at Gowalia Tank Maidan, demanded that the British immediately quit India. The Allied Forces were at a critical phase against the Axis Powers—consisting of Germany, Italy, and Japan—and the British, having their hands full, reacted sharply to Gandhi's revolt. They responded by imprisoning thousands of people, including Gandhi and the other congressional leaders, for the duration of the war.[34]

In 1945, at the end of World War II, the Labor Party won the elections in Britain, which opened up the dialogue with India about the country's independence. When the British government finally gave clear indications that power would be transferred to Indian hands, Gandhi called off the Quit India protest, and approximately 100,000 political prisoners, including the leaders of congress—who were detained solely for their noncooperation—were released.[35]

During the next two years, there were protracted negotiations between leaders of the Congress, the Muslim League under Muhammad Ali Jinnah, and the British. Gandhi had a vision of a united India despite the religious differences in the country. What he didn't know was that, in 1943, while the Indian National Congress and Gandhi were busy protesting for independence, the Muslim League had passed a resolution asking the British to divide India before leaving. When Gandhi learned of this, he suggested a compromise that required congress and the Muslim League to cooperate and attain independence under a temporary government. In his mind, the question of partition could be resolved later.[36]

When Jinnah called for Direct Action on August 16, 1946, meaning the Muslim League went directly to the British to obtain its goal of a separate Muslim state, Gandhi was infuriated. A year later, as the negotiations between the three parties culminated in the Mountbatten Plan of June 3, 1947 and the Indian Independence Act was passed, the Muslim part of India became Pakistan.

As Gandhi had feared, the partition of India didn't go smoothly. In border areas, between ten and twelve million people moved from one side to the other, and one-half million were killed in riots where Hindus, Muslims, and Sikhs were fighting each other. Gandhi visited the most riot-prone areas to stop the massacres, but to no avail. He did, however, prevent the conflict in these areas from getting worse. According to Norwegian historian Jens Arup Seip, had it not been for Gandhi's presence, there would probably have been much more bloodshed during the partition.

The "plan to carve up British India was never approved of or accepted by Gandhi," Stanley Wolpert wrote. His dream had been a free and united India, where everyone, no matter their religious beliefs, could live in harmony. He didn't see the need to split up a country and upheave groups of people.

"The golden rule of conduct," Gandhi said, "is mutual toleration, seeing that we will never all think alike and we shall always see truth in fragment and from different angles of vision. Even amongst the most conscientious persons, there will be room enough for honest differences of opinion. The only possible rule of conduct in any civilised society is, therefore, mutual toleration."

According to Wolpert, Gandhi "realised too late that his closest comrades and disciples were more interested in power than principle, and that his own vision had long been clouded by the illusion that the struggle he led for India's independence was a nonviolent one."

* * *

GANDHI HAD ALL the qualities a Nobel peace champion should have. He worked toward peace, freedom, and equality for all people; he wished to abolish standing armies; and he made efforts to unify all people despite their differences. He was also an important influence for others, including Martin Luther King, Jr. and Nelson Mandela, who won the Nobel Peace Prize in 1964 and 1993, respectively. Albert Einstein was right when, in 1931, he called Gandhi "a role model for the generations to come."

We will never know why Gandhi didn't win the Nobel Peace Prize before he was assassinated in 1948. Perhaps the committee didn't want to alienate Great Britain—an important ally to Norway—so soon after World War II. We only know that the Nobel Committee in later years has shown remorse for the omission.

"Gandhi could do without the Nobel Peace prize," former Secretary Lundestad said in 2006. "Whether the Nobel Committee can do without Gandhi is the question."

However, regret was not so prevalent in 1948, the year of Gandhi's death, when the committee stated that, "there was no suitable living candidate," and therefore didn't give out the prize that year. The committee has proven that when it really wants to, it can give the prize to anyone, dead or alive. Dag Hammarskjöld, the Swedish diplomat, received the prize posthumously in 1961, even though he had died before the announcement day.

One of Gandhi's best-known quotations goes like this:

> First they ignore you,
> then they laugh at you,
> then they fight you,
> then you win.

Ultimately Mahatma Gandhi did win, even though he was denied the one prize that he so clearly deserved.

OVERLOOKED
PEACE CHAMPIONS

Justice is to be found only in imagination.
—ALFRED NOBEL

—⁂—

ALTHOUGH GANDHI MIGHT have been the most flagrant example of disrespect by the Nobel Committee, he wasn't the only worthy contender they ignored. Alfred Nobel was adamant that the winner of his prize should be a champion of peace, having a) done the best work for fraternity between nations, b) worked toward the "abolition or reduction of standing armies," and finally c) worked to hold and promote "peace congresses."

The Nobel Peace Prize was not intended to award humanitarian work or caring for victims of battle. Maybe it should, but that is not for the committee to decide alone. It was meant to reward *profound change* in society and prevention of war. Organizers of peace congresses have been ignored by the committee, despite the fact that Nobel specifically mentioned them in his will.[1] In this chapter, we will take a look at some of these people who, involved in peace congresses or not, would qualify as true peace champions. While we can't know why the committee never selected them, because the list of nominees and selection process is kept secret, we can guess. One reason might be that the committee was unaware of a certain candidate because he or she was never nominated. What we know about the selection process, as written in Chapter Two, is that the committee meets every March to make a shortlist of the candidates received by the February 1 deadline. Then the committee sends the shortlist of candidates to the Nobel Institute to be considered by the institute's four permanent advisers. The committee may also ask Norwegian and foreign experts for additional research of the candidates, but because of the secrecy there is no way of knowing whether this was done. The final decision, no matter the opinions of the advisers or experts, lies with the five members of the Nobel Peace Prize Committee.

Apart from lack of awareness of worthy candidates, another reason the peace champions in this chapter never won Nobel's prize might be that the committee had a different agenda—political or otherwise—and a different candidate filled that political need at the time.

DAISAKU IKEDA:
FORGING BONDS OF TRUST BETWEEN PEOPLE

One who qualifies is Daisaku Ikeda.[2] A Japanese Buddhist leader, peace builder, prolific writer, poet, and educator, Ikeda is president of the Soka Gakkai (meaning "value-creating society") and founder of the Soka Gakkai International, a movement based on a 700-year-old Buddhist tradition characterized by its emphasis on individual empowerment and social engagement to advance culture, education, and peace. With this movement, Ikeda qualifies as an organizer of peace congresses.[3]

Ikeda has also founded a number of cultural, educational, and peace research institutions around the world. The Boston Research Center for the 21st Century (renamed the Ikeda Center for Peace, Learning, and Dialogue in 2009), the Toda Institute for Global Peace and Policy Research, and the Institute of Oriental Philosophy, are examples. The goal behind all of these is to promote fraternity between nations through nonmilitary means. In addition, Ikeda is connected to the Min-On Concert Association and the Tokyo Fuji Art Museum, both of which promote mutual understanding and friendship between different cultures through the arts.[4]

Ikeda's commitment to peace started when he was a teenager. Born in Tokyo, Japan, on January 2, 1928, to a family of seaweed farmers, he witnessed the devastation and senseless horror of World War II. He shares Alfred Nobel's love of mankind and believes that lasting peace is possible to obtain when people develop connection with each other, mutual trust, and compassion for themselves and others.

"World peace is not something that can be realized simply by politicians signing treaties, or by business leaders creating economic cooperation," Ikeda said. "True and lasting peace will be realized only by forging bonds of trust between people at the deepest level, in the depths of their very lives."[5]

For Ikeda, peace is far more than the mere absence of war. Peace, according to him, is about embracing and appreciating cultural differences and communicating to resolve conflict and build trust.[6] "With love and patience, nothing is impossible," he said. To Ikeda, peace is not obtained by the threat of standing armies, missiles, or drones, because that peace lives in fear. Today's leadership worldwide is driven by fear and distrust, which we see examples of in politics, in corporations, and even in the Norwegian Nobel Peace Prize Committee. When there are no values in place and our leaders make decisions in secrecy, there can be no predictability and therefore no trust. Since the 1970s, Ikeda has pursued dialogue with a wide range of leaders around the world, including Mikhail Gorbachev, Norwegian American Quaker sociologist Elise Boulding, Joseph Rotblat—the Polish physicist who won the Nobel Peace Prize in 1995—and the French author and statesman André Malraux, about the importance of trust.[7]

Contrary to many peace prize laureates, his work is not about signing peace treaties that may or may not hold. It's to create profound change in our societies to prevent war, which may not be visible enough for a committee driven by a need to prove to the world that it's exceptional. Ikeda, on the other hand, is not motivated by insecurity or fear. As the true peace champion that he is, his work is driven by a wish for unity and a love of mankind.

SARI NUSSEIBEH:
PROVIDING HOPE OF PEACE IN THE MIDDLE EAST

"Isn't this inability to imagine the lives of the 'other' at the heart of the Israeli-Palestinian conflict?" Sari Nusseibeh asked in his 2007 book *Once Upon a Country: A Palestinian Life*.[8] If anyone understands the conflict, it is Nusseibeh.

Born in 1949 in Damascus, Syria, Nusseibeh is a Palestinian professor of philosophy and former president of Al-Quds University in Jerusalem. Until December 2002, he was the representative of the Palestinian National Authority in that city. Nusseibeh comes from an old Jerusalem family who descends from legendary leaders of the early Islamic tribes. Still today, the Nusseibeh family members are trustees and key-holders of the Temple Mount, one of the most important religious sites in the old town of Jerusalem that is venerated as a holy site in Judaism, Christianity, and Islam alike.

Nusseibeh's family has also been involved in the conflict between the Palestinians and the Israelis. His mother, who was from a wealthy aristocratic Palestinian family and the daughter of political leader Yaqub al-Ghusayn, was a lifelong political and women's rights activist who helped establish many of the women's institutions in the West Bank and Jerusalem. She also organized the very first civilian protests against Israeli occupation after the June 1967 war. Nusseibeh's father was a distinguished statesman in Palestinian-Jordanian politics and diplomacy.

After the 1967 war, when he was eighteen years old, Nusseibeh took "the most astounding trek of my life," into Israeli Jerusalem, where he volunteered for

Kibbutz HaZore'a. This experience formed his values of education, connection, and compassion as underlying drivers to obtain peace. A kibbutz, or communal settlement of mostly Jewish members, is a unique rural community dedicated to mutual aid and social justice. It is a socioeconomic system based on the principle of joint ownership of property, equality, cooperation of production, consumption, and education. Admiring the ideological commitment of the kibbutz members, Nusseibeh wondered if what he had learned there could be used to unite the two parallel cities of Jerusalem. His vision of peace would later give him stature as a Palestinian leader, although, by his own admission, he is a reluctant politician. Probably because he has never been interested in power games or fighting the Israelis, whom he doesn't look upon as an enemy.

Unlike most leaders in any conflict, Nusseibeh understands and empathizes with both sides. He has witnessed the immense injustice and outrage of the Israeli occupation, from the confiscation of lands that belonged to his family for generations, to the daily degradations, imprisonments, deportations, threats, and violence his people have suffered. But he also sees the suffering on the Israeli side.

After finishing his studies from Christ Church, Oxford, and his PhD in Islamic philosophy from Harvard University, Nusseibeh returned to the West Bank in 1978 to teach at Birzeit University and remained a professor of philosophy there until the university closed from 1988 to 1990 during the first Intifada. As you may recall from Chapter Six, the Intifada was a civilian, mostly nonviolent, Palestinian uprising against Israel. In return, Israel closed all Palestinian schools. An important leader during this Intifada, and thus an organizer of peace congresses, Nusseibeh authored the Palestinian Declaration of Principles and worked to strengthen the Fatah movement in the West Bank toward Palestinian independence in nonviolent ways. He drafted leaflets guiding the uprising and gave it its moral and political objectives. Nusseibeh also helped create the political and technical committees that were intended for a future Palestinian administration.

Just as Nobel would have wanted for his peace champions, Nusseibeh strongly opposes violence and guerrilla tactics. In the 1980s, he suggested that Israel either annex the territories and offer Palestinians equal rights within the Israeli democratic system, or give them independence. His stance drew him into a series of negotiations, covert and overt, with Israeli politicians. In July 1987, Nusseibeh and Faisal Husseini met with Moshe Amirav, a member of Israel's Likud Party, in an attempt to make a pact between the Israeli government, PLO, and Fatah. In doing so, they were the first prominent Palestinians to meet with a member of the right-wing Israeli party.

His work of conciliation between Palestine and Israel has not been without danger, and he is viewed as a threat by extremists on both sides of the conflict. Once he was attacked outside his Birzeit classroom by local Tanzim militants associated with Yasser Arafat's Fatah. Still, he believed that the solution was to create a sense of brotherhood between the two peoples, so he continued.

"It was worth the risk if I could help avert the brewing war between our peoples," he wrote. "They can't beat that out of me," he said, while still in his cast and bandages.

According to Rabbi John Rosove's March 1, 2012, *Jewish Journal* article, Nusseibeh was arrested a number of times and imprisoned for his consistently peaceful and moderate advocacy of a negotiated two-state solution to the Israeli-Palestinian conflict. Once, during the First Gulf War between 1990 and 1991, he was arrested by the Israelis, who accused him of being an Iraqi agent. The reason was that Iraq had fired seven Scud missiles on Tel Aviv during the war, and Nusseibeh had discussed these attacks with the Iraqi ambassador in Tunis. Palestinians saw the arrest as a political warning that Israel did not intend to negotiate with any Palestinian leader, regardless of their willingness to make peace.

"This is a message to us Palestinian moderates," Professor Saeb Erekat of An-Najah University said. "The message is, 'You can forget about negotiations after the war because we are going to make sure there is no one to talk to.'"

British and American officials questioned the arrest, and the US administration urged that Nusseibeh should either be charged with a crime, or the arrest would be considered political. Following suit, Amnesty International adopted him as a prisoner of conscience. After ninety days of imprisonment in Ramle Prison shortly after the end of the war, Nusseibeh was finally released.

Arrests or threats by extremists didn't discourage him from working with the opposition or impede his willingness to compromise. During the First Gulf War, Nusseibeh began working with the Israeli group Peace Now on a common approach to condemn the killing of civilians. In 2001, during the beginning of the negotiations that led to the Oslo Accords, Nusseibeh began to promote the controversial idea that the Palestinians give up their right of return in exchange for a Palestinian state in the West Bank and Gaza Strip. The Palestinian right of return is a political position asserting that Palestinian refugees, both first generation and their descendants, have a right to return and to retrieve the property they left behind or were forced to leave as part of the exodus resulting from the 1948 war and the 1967 Six-Day War.

Nusseibeh was all for peaceful demonstrations, as he had promoted during the Intifada in the late 1980s, and he was deeply disturbed by the militarization of the second Intifada in January 2002. Therefore, he called for the renunciation of Palestinian suicide bombings. Then he took his non-violence stance one step further.

"A Palestinian state should be demilitarized," he said, "not because that's what Israel demands, but in our own interest."

Both his speech and actions are in line with a true Nobel peace champion working toward brotherhood between nations and demilitarization. On June 25, 2002, Nusseibeh and more than fifty leading Palestinians, including Hanan Ashrawi, signed the communiqué Against Martyrdom Attacks calling for the end of military operations targeting Israeli civilians. According to the document, these attacks only increased hatred and undermined the possibility of coexisting peacefully. In interviews in the Arab-Israeli press, Nusseibeh said that the attacks were not only counterproductive but that "Palestinians must not sacrifice their moral values."

Also in 2002, Nusseibeh and former Shin Bet (Israel's internal security service) director, Ami Ayalon, started The People's Voice campaign, an

Israeli-Palestinian initiative that aimed to advance the process of achieving peace between Israel and the Palestinians. The campaign included a
draft peace agreement calling for a Palestinian state based on Israel's 1967
borders, and for a compromise on the Palestinian right of return.

Nusseibeh has not given up his work toward peace in the Middle East.
He writes about his vision of peace and he gives lectures internationally. In
2008, in an open online poll, he was voted one of the most influential intel-
lectuals in the world by *Prospect Magazine* and *Foreign Policy*.

After years of working toward the establishment of a functioning Palestinian state alongside Israel, Nusseibeh showed how far he is willing to go to
obtain peace. In his 2011 Harvard University Press article *What's A Palestinian
State Worth?* he called for a "thought experiment" of a single state in which
Israel annexed all the territories, and Palestinians would be "second-class
citizens." By that he meant that Palestinians would have "civil but not political rights," and that the Israelis would run the country. His optimal solution
would be two states; however, Nusseibeh feared that this might no longer be
possible. A single state granting citizenship to all living in Israel and in those
Palestinian territories Israel conquered in 1967, seemed equally unlikely.

"Simply put, in this scenario the Jews could run the country while the
Arabs could at last enjoy living in it." This Israeli state, in his view, is not an
end in itself but a means to a good life. The idea of a "second-class citizenship" for Palestinians, he added, could possibly be just an "interim step."[9]

Nusseibeh's strengths lies in that he recognizes the fears and hopes of the
Israelis as well as the Palestinians, and he works toward profound change in
the mentality of both of them. He has a strong vision of peace between the
two people, and an infallible faith in humankind. Nusseibeh's true constitu-
ency is ordinary people from two nations which, he insists, are not enemies
but "natural allies."[10] As a courageous leader, he is willing to risk his freedom,
even his life, to promote his vision and to work together with the Israelis
toward peace. Nusseibeh also has the humility to compromise and to put
his own and his people's egos aside, if that means they can be safe and well.
Above all, he stresses the importance of nonviolence.

Nusseibeh's conciliatory approach is refreshing, especially in a time when the Islamic State and other extremists fill the news with violence and terror. He fulfills all of Nobel's criteria of having worked towards fraternity between nations, the "abolition or reduction of standing armies," and finally the "holding and promotion of peace congresses."

Perhaps the only thing missing to attract the Nobel Peace Prize Committee is that his work does not promote Norway as a peace negotiator in the Middle East, unlike when the prize was awarded to Arafat, Rabin, and Peres in 1994. Nevertheless, Nusseibeh is a peace champion of people everywhere, regardless of the committee's decision. That being said, Nobel's prize might give him the necessary voice and platform to make more of a difference.

Both Nusseibeh and Ikeda can still receive the prize. For other overlooked candidates, however, it is too late.

U THANT:
AVERTED WAR WITH CUBA

Born on January 22, 1909, U Thant was a Burmese diplomat and secretary-general to the United Nations from 1961 to 1971. Known as Pantanaw U Thant, in reference to his hometown, he was a devout Buddhist and had a calm and humble manner that won people's respect in his home country as well as abroad. As a public servant, U Thant was admired so much by the Burmese population that when the military government refused to honor him after his death in 1974, riots broke out in Rangoon.

U Thant was appointed to the position of UN secretary-general in 1961 when his predecessor, Dag Hammarskjöld, died in a plane crash in Northern Rhodesia (now Zambia).

After finishing Hammarskjöld's term, he was unanimously reelected in 1962 for another five-year period. Most of U Thant's work to promote peace was done while he was working at the United Nations. In his first term as secretary-general, he facilitated negotiations between President John F.

Kennedy and Soviet leader Nikita Khrushchev during the Cuban Missile Crisis in October 1962, and averted what could have become a nuclear war.

U Thant got involved in the Cuban missile crisis on October 20, 1962, when President Kennedy showed U Thant aerial reconnaissance photographs of Soviet missile installations in Cuba. The president ordered a naval quarantine to remove all offensive weapons from Soviet ships bound for Cuba. Meanwhile, Soviet ships were approaching the quarantine zone. To avoid a naval confrontation, U Thant proposed that the United States should make guarantees not to invade in exchange for Soviet missile withdrawal. President Khrushchev welcomed the proposal and agreed to suspend missile shipments while the negotiations were ongoing.

On October 27, 1962, the crisis was intensified when an American U-2 plane was shot down over Cuba. Joint Chiefs of Staff and the Executive Committee pressured President Kennedy to retaliate by invasion. According to Walter A. Dorn and Robert Pauk's 2009 *Diplomatic History* article "Unsung Mediator: U Thant and the Cuban Missile Crisis," Kennedy responded that, "On the other hand we have U Thant, and we don't want to sink a ship . . . right in the middle of when U Thant is supposedly arranging for the Russians to stay out."

Because of U Thant's work, the negotiations continued, and the crisis was resolved. The United States agreed to dismantle missiles in Turkey and guaranteed never to invade Cuba in exchange for the removal of Soviet missiles there. U Thant then convinced Fidel Castro to return the body of the U-2 pilot to the United States. But Castro, furious that the Soviets agreed to remove missiles without his approval, refused to allow any UN missile inspectors on the island. In the end, the inspection was done from the sea by US reconnaissance aircraft and warships.

"At a critical moment—when the nuclear powers seemed set on a collision course—the Secretary-General's intervention led to the diversion of the Soviet ships headed for Cuba and interception by our Navy," Adlai Stevenson declared to the Senate Foreign Relations Committee on March 13, 1963. "This was the indispensable first step in the peaceful resolution of the Cuban crisis."[11]

For his role in defusing the Cuban crisis, the Norwegian ambassador to the United Nations informed U Thant that he would be awarded the 1965 Nobel Peace Prize. However, that didn't happen. The 1965 Nobel Peace Prize was instead awarded to the United Nations Children's Fund, or UNICEF, for its humanitarian efforts for women and children in the developing world.

Why didn't U Thant win Nobel's prize? The answer remains a mystery.

Although most members of the Nobel committee wished to honor U Thant, Chairman Gunnar Jahn lobbied heavily against it. Why Jahn lobbied against U Thant is unknown, other than comments he made about U Thant just doing his job. For some unknown reason, UNICEF—which was also just doing its job—was an acceptable prize winner to Jahn. The disagreement in the committee about U Thant lasted three years, and no prize was given in 1966 and 1967. While the committee chairman does not have official veto power (a simple majority of the committee members suffices to elect a winner) Jahn managed to pressure the other members during those three years from selecting U Thant.[12] This incident shows another way in which the selection process is flawed and the committee has gone against Nobel's intent.

U Thant was not upset about not being awarded Nobel's prize.

"Is not the Secretary-General merely doing his job when he works for peace?" he said.

Perhaps U Thant was right. According to Dorn, U Thant was pleased when UNICEF was announced as the winner. However, Ralph Bunche, U Thant's undersecretary who won the Nobel Peace Prize in 1950, complained that the committee had shown a "gross injustice to U Thant."

To Bunche, U Thant used his position as leader of the UN to do the best work for fraternity between nations, and work toward the reduction of standing armies when he averted what could have become nuclear war between the United States and the Soviet Union in 1962. But it wasn't just his position as UN Secretary-General that made U Thant accomplish what he did. U Thant had a vision for peace between nations and his goal was to be of service to this mission. It was his humility and ability to connect with the leaders on both sides of a conflict that inspired the trust he needed in order to settle differences and avoid war. If the Nobel Peace Prize would have been awarded to U Thant, it wouldn't have been an award to the United Nations, it would have been an acknowledgment of the man and peace champion U Thant truly was.

Although he wasn't awarded Nobel's medal, U Thant was recognized by numerous others. True to his humble nature, however, U Thant was generally reluctant to accept prizes as well as the publicity associated with them. He declined Burma's second highest honor awarded to him by U Nu's government in 1961. However, he did accept the Jawaharlal Nehru Award for International Understanding in 1965, the Gandhi Peace Award in 1972, and several other honorary degrees. U Thant even has his own award, the U Thant Peace Award, established in his memory by Sri Chinmoy, the leader of the UN Meditation Group, which gives out the award. Another honor and fun fact: there is a tiny island between the UN headquarters in New York City and Long Island that is named "U Thant Island."

POPE JOHN PAUL II:
FRATERNITY AMONG RELIGIONS

Karol Józef Wojtyła has since his canonization in 2014 been referred to as Pope Saint John Paul II or Saint John Paul the Great. Born in Poland on May 18, 1920, he was the first non-Italian pope since the Dutch Pope Adrian VI, who served from 1522 to 1523. He held this position for twenty-seven years, from 1978 until his death in 2005.

Pope John Paul II worked persistently on reconciliation between people and nations through apology and dialogue across religious borders. His wish was to place the Catholic Church "at the heart of a new religious alliance that would bring together Jews, Muslims, and Christians in a great religious armada." Through his work, he significantly improved the Catholic Church's relations with Judaism, Islam, the Eastern Orthodox Church, and the Anglican Communion.

In addition to working toward fraternity between nations and religious groups, he opposed any military intervention or armed conflict, and he used his platform as head of the Catholic Church to gather large groups of people and inspiring them to take positive action toward brotherhood and peace. He was as close to a peace champion as one can get, meeting all of Nobel's criteria. Let's take a look at some of his accomplishments that would have qualified him for Nobel's prize.

One of the most traveled world leaders in history, John Paul II visited 129 countries during his pontificate and held peace congresses. He was a fresh face for the Catholic Church and attracted large crowds at events such as the Manila World Youth Day in the Philippines on January 15, 1995, where he offered mass to between five and seven million people, the largest single gathering in Christian history.

Pope John Paul II had a gift of connecting with people everywhere he went, and he wasn't afraid to speak up to power. When traveling to Haiti in 1983, he spoke in Creole to thousands of impoverished people gathered to greet him at the airport. "Things must change in Haiti," he declared, referring to the disparity between the wealthy and the poor. "All those who have power, wealth, culture," he said, should "understand their serious and urgent responsibility with respect to their brothers and sisters."[13] He was met with roaring applause. Shortly after, in 1984, the Haitians rose up and started a series of demonstrations against the dictator Jean-Claude "Baby-Doc" Duvalier. Two years later, in 1986, Duvalier was overthrown and driven out of the country.

Although religious differences still make for violent conflicts around the world, John Paul II made many attempts at unifying people of different beliefs. He was the first reigning pope who traveled to Protestant countries, including the United Kingdom in 1982, where he met Queen Elizabeth II. In 1985, he spoke to a gathering of 50,000 young Muslims in Morocco, at the invitation of the king. In 1986 at Assisi, he organized a day of prayer for world peace that was attended by more than 150 representatives of the world's major religions including the Dalai Lama, the Archbishop of Canterbury, American Indians smoking a pipe of peace, and African spirit worshippers.

In 2000, he was the first modern pope to visit Egypt and, in March 2000, while visiting Jerusalem, John Paul II became the first pope in history to visit and pray at the Western Wall, a holy site for Jews, Christians, and Muslims. He was also the first Catholic pope to pray in an Islamic mosque, in Damascus, Syria, in 2001. When visiting the Umayyad Mosque, a former Christian church where John the Baptist is believed to be interred, he made a speech calling for Muslims, Christians, and Jews to live peacefully together. This visit broke new ground as a symbol of harmony between Christianity and Islam. Muslims and Christians should be in "respectful dialogue, nevermore as communities in conflict," the pope said. And he added, "for all the times that Muslims and Christians have offended one another, we need to seek forgiveness from the Almighty and offer each other forgiveness."

John Paul II showed courage when, in September 2001, just days after the September 11 terrorist attacks on the United States, he traveled to Kazakhstan with an audience largely consisting of Muslims. The pope said that Kazakhstan had the mission of being a bridge between religions, nations, and continents. According to Tomasz Peta, the leader of the Catholic community in Kazakhstan, President Nursultan Nazarbayev was deeply impressed by the pope's visit to his country in such dramatic international circumstances. As a result, Nazarbayev founded the first Congress of Leaders of World and Traditional Religions in 2003 for the purpose of peace and reconciliation. Nazarbayev's initiative received the support of international politicians and leaders, including Kofi Annan, George W. Bush, Margaret Thatcher, Jiang Zemin, Nelson Mandela, Valéry Giscard d'Estaing, and Mikhail Gorbachev. This peace congress has taken place every three years since. In 2018, at the sixth Congress of Leaders of World and Traditional Religions, many of the participants praised the ethnic harmony and religious tolerance in Kazakhstan, a majority Muslim country with strong secular traditions, citing it as an example for others to follow.[14]

For the late John Paul II, his love of humanity was at the core of all his work. He was determined to restore respect for life, which made him a human rights activist, taking a stand against any oppressive governments, such as President Duvalier's in Haiti. It should also be noted that the pope was vehemently opposed to abortion and birth control, as was laureate Mother Teresa, stating that under no circumstances should contraception or terminating a pregnancy be considered a moral choice.

In the context of Nobel's peace prize, by being the spiritual inspiration and catalyst, John Paul II helped end Communist rule in his native Poland and eventually Eastern Europe. For the pope, according to BBC, "communism was a tyranny that chopped down human freedom and saw people as mere resources to be used as the state saw fit; an attitude utterly intolerable to a man to whom each and every human being was an image of God."[15]

The pope was essential to the creation of the Solidarity labor movement, which again was critical in the fall of Poland's totalitarian government, according to the *New York Times* and Timothy Garton Ash, a historian at Oxford who has written extensively on the fall of Communism in Eastern Europe.[16]

"Before his pontificate, the world was divided into blocs," Lech Wałęsa, the founder of Solidarity, said. "Nobody knew how to get rid of communism. In Warsaw, in 1979, he [Pope John Paul II] simply said: 'Do not be afraid,' and later prayed: 'Let your Spirit descend and change the image of the land . . . this land.'"

For Bronislaw Geremek, who is both a former Solidarity activist and foreign minister of Poland, the pope's visit was a crucial event in history.

"The Communist regime had to collapse and it would have happened without John Paul II," he said. "But I do believe that the time matters in human life, and we could have had the continuation of the Communist regime for one more generation, without John Paul II."

According to Geremek, there had been uprisings before this in Poland, in 1970 and 1976, but these had been violently crushed by the authorities. "But in 1979 the pope's message was that a Communist regime cannot work without social approval and he was saying, 'Don't approve.'"[17]

John Paul II may have been more than just a spiritual catalyst. It has been alleged that the Institute for Religious Work, or the Vatican bank whose sole purpose is to promote the Catholic religion, covertly funded Solidarity.[18] In a 1996 book, *His Holiness,* authors Marco Politi and Carl Bernstein claim that Pope John Paul II systemically sent money to Solidarity through a papal discretionary account in an effort to defeat Communism in Eastern Europe.[19] British historian and scholar Tony Judt backs this up. According to his book *Postwar: A History of Europe Since 1945,* Solidarity received as much as $50 million from both the Vatican and the United States.

"No one can prove conclusively that he was a primary cause of the end of communism," Timothy Garton Ash said shortly after John Paul II's death. "However, the major figures on all sides . . . now agree that he was. I would argue the historical case in three steps: without the Polish Pope, no Solidarity revolution in Poland in 1980; without Solidarity, no dramatic change in Soviet policy towards eastern Europe under Gorbachev; without that change, no velvet revolutions in 1989."[20]

Among those major figures were Wojciech Jaruzelski, who—even though he was the head of the Communist government in 1981 and attempted to crush the Solidarity freedom movement—credited the pope with a crucial role in ending communism in Poland.[21]

Soviet leader Mikhail Gorbachev was another such major figure. "The collapse of the Iron Curtain would have been impossible without John Paul II," Gorbachev said. Aleksander Kwaśniewski, who was president of Poland from 1995 to 2005, said on the night John Paul II died, "We wouldn't have had a free Poland without him."[22]

A peace champion working for fraternity between nations, John Paul II wished to tear down the Iron Curtain—and the Berlin Wall—and unite Europe. As Gorbachev said upon the pope's death, "I will never forget [the pope's] words about Europe. 'Europe,' he said, 'must breathe with both its lungs.'"[23]

John Paul II also opposed any violent conflict, including the Gulf War of 1990 to 1991.

"No, never again war," he declared in his 1991 encyclical *Centesimus Annus,* "which destroys the lives of innocent people, teaches how to kill, throws into upheaval even the lives of those who do the killing, and leaves behind a trail of resentment and hatred, thus making it all the more difficult to find a just solution of the very problems which provoked the war."

His opposition to the Iraq War resulted in his nomination for the 2003 Nobel Peace Prize the same year the Iranian attorney Shirin Ebadi won. Why didn't John Paul II win in 2003 or before, for his work to free Poland and Eastern Europe from Communist oppression?

According to his 2008 book *Norge sett utenfra* (*Norway Seen From Outside*), Johan Galtung, a pioneer of modern peace research, is convinced that the reason John Paul II wasn't awarded Nobel's prize is because he, as a religious leader who inspired people to stand up to their oppressors, was incompatible with Norwegian foreign policy. The pope didn't negotiate peace accords with state leaders like so many other peace prize winners had. Neither did he shine a light on the Norwegian government's peace efforts. Galtung also mentioned the Leipzig churches, and especially the Nikolaikirche (St. Nicholas's Church), which led the Monday demonstrations in 1989 that eventually resulted in the tearing down of the Berlin wall and ending the Cold War on November 9, 1989. Although the result was aligned with Nobel's last words, the churches and John Paul II didn't fit because of their method.

"Why should we be members of NATO," Galtung asked, "if such a dissolution from within could happen?"[24]

Instead of the pope, the Nobel Committee selected Solidarity's leader, Lech Wałęsa for the Nobel Peace Prize in 1983, for his and the worker union's role in ending Communist rule in Poland.

And in 2003? As I wrote in Chapter Ten, after al-Qaeda's terrorist attacks on September 11, 2001, the committee was on a mission to send a message of disapproval to the US government about its war on Iraq. Although John Paul II sent Cardinal Pio Laghi to Washington, DC, in an attempt to dissuade President Bush from going to war—arguing it was up to the United Nations to solve the international conflict, and that a US unilateral aggression was a violation of international law—the Nobel Committee must have felt that Shirin Ebadi presented a more efficient kick in the leg to the Bush administration.

The 2003 award shows the Nobel Committee's loyalty to the Norwegian government, which was confirmed by then-Nobel secretary Geir Lundestad.

"The Norwegian government did not determine the choices of the Norwegian Nobel committee," Lundestad wrote in the article *Peace Prizes 1901–2000*, "but these choices reflected the same mixture of idealism and realism that characterized Norwegian and Scandinavian foreign policy in general."

Idealism and realism. These euphemisms are attempts to explain away political choices. It is not as if the committee didn't have more deserving candidates than the ones it selected. It had outstanding choices. But more important to the committee, it also had an agenda to stay loyal to the Norwegian government.

"A Nobel committee loyal to narrow Norwegian foreign policy interests cannot do much to rescue mankind from the yoke of militarism and war," Heffermehl wrote. "By failing to respect his will, his great vision for mankind, Parliament has wronged Nobel, to the detriment of humanity."

THE FASCIST, THE DICTATOR, THE ASSASSIN, & THE HEIR APPARENT

The savants will write excellent volumes. There will
be laureates. But wars will continue just the same until the
forces of the circumstances render them impossible.

—ALFRED NOBEL

BENITO MUSSOLINI. ADOLF HITLER. Joseph Stalin. Vladimir
Putin. All have been nominees for the Nobel Peace Prize.

Every year, the Norwegian Nobel Committee sends out thousands
of letters inviting those eligible to submit their nominations for the
prize. Although the names of the nominees and nominators must
remain confidential until fifty years have elapsed, leaks do occur, and
the committee does reveal the *number* of contenders each year. [1] For the
2019 Nobel Peace Prize, 301 valid nominations—seventy-eight of them
organizations and the rest individuals—were received. In 2016, there

was a record 376 candidates, perhaps a result of the prize becoming more about rock star status and less about peace.

As you may recall from Chapter Two, nominations can be made by a large number of people, including politicians, university professors, present and past members of the Norwegian Nobel Committee, members of national assemblies and governments, university chancellors, and university professors of social science, history, philosophy, law, and theology.[2] This means that the committee has little control over who gets nominated, unless someone on the committee nominates someone themselves. Still, the committee has to consider every nominated candidate. One should think the committee has numerous worthy candidates to choose from every year. As this chapter will show, that's not always the case.

BENITO MUSSOLINI:
FASCIST AND DICTATOR

It is difficult to fathom why Mussolini would be considered a peace champion, but nonetheless, he was nominated in 1935.[3] Born on July 29, 1883, the Italian politician, journalist, and leader of the National Fascist Party, Benito Amilcare Andrea Mussolini was prime minister of his country from 1922 until his ousting in 1943. Ruling constitutionally until 1925, Mussolini then dropped all pretense of democracy and set up a full dictatorship. Known as Il Duce or "the leader," Mussolini was one of the key figures in the creation of Fascism. To understand why the Italian people would choose him to lead them, we have to go back and look at the history.

Not even as a child was Mussolini close to a peace champion. Unruly and aggressive, he assaulted fellow students with his penknife and was expelled from several schools. As a young man, he was a ferocious reader and had a big mouth, and eventually Mussolini became a political journalist, intellectual, and one of Italy's most prominent socialists. He was imprisoned several times for inciting trade union strikes and violence. He also had remarkable rhetorical talents and a striking presence, which drew people to him. As the editor of the socialist newspaper *Avanti!*, he doubled the paper's readership with his antimilitarist, antinationalist, and anti-imperialist articles.[4] He thunderously opposed Italy's intervention in World War I. Then he changed his mind. Convinced by Karl Marx's principle that social revolution usually follows war and persuaded that "the defeat of France would be a deathblow to liberty in Europe," he began writing articles and making speeches in favor of war. He resigned from *Avanti!* and was expelled from the Socialist Party PSI. He then became the editor of *Il Popolo d'Italia* ("The People of Italy"), which was financed by the French government and Italian industrialists, both of whom favored war against Austria. His new philosophy, "From today onward we are all Italians and nothing but Italians—*Viva l'Italia!* [Long live Italy!]," was the birth cry of Fascism. Mussolini then went to fight in the war as a sharpshooter.[5]

When he returned a wounded soldier, he had a mission. Italy was in a state of economic and political crisis, and Mussolini, in February 1918, began "advocating the emergence of a dictator—a man who is ruthless and energetic enough to make a clean sweep"—to confront the crisis. Three months later, in a speech in Bologna, he hinted that he himself might be that dictator.[6] "Mussolini gathered groups of restless revolutionaries, anarchists, discontented socialists, and republicans—who began wearing black shirts to show their allegiance—calling them "fighting bands."

He had an impressive physique, "and his style of oratory, staccato and repetitive, was superb."[7] He was theatrical, his words dramatic, his opinions contradictory, his facts were often wrong, and his attacks were often malicious and misdirected. But to the Italians who were disillusioned by the current leadership and desperate to improve their livelihood, he was the solution. Fascist militias inspired by Mussolini swept through the Italian countryside, terrorized the local population, rounded up socialists, beat them, and burned down union and party offices.[8] In 1920, the Blackshirt squads, often with help from local landowners and encouraged by Mussolini, began to attack local government institutions. The government, headed by the liberal Luigi Facta, did little to combat the militias or to protect the local population. By late 1921, the Fascists controlled large parts of Italy.

In the summer of 1922, an opportunity for Mussolini to claim power presented itself. The remnants of the trade-union movement called a general strike. Mussolini declared that unless the government prevented the strike, the Fascists would. And they did. Later that year, on October 24, at a gathering of 40,000 Fascists in Naples, Mussolini threatened, "Either the government will be given to us, or we will seize it by marching on Rome."[9]

Prime Minister Luigi Facta asked King Victor Emmanuel III, who according to the Albertine Statute held the supreme military power, to declare martial law as an emergency response to Mussolini's threat, but the king refused. Following the March on Rome on October 28, 1922, when about 30,000 Fascist Blackshirts gathered to demand the resignation of Prime Minister Facta, the king handed Facta's position over to Mussolini.

Mussolini, who became prime minister at the age of thirty-nine, didn't win an election. He won by terrorizing the population and the king. Mussolini had certainly been helped by a combination of circumstances, both political and economic, but his success also owed something to his personality and to his unique gifts as an agitator. Imagine if he had used his gifts for the cause of peace instead of power.

Why did the king give in? He and the conservative establishment feared a possible civil war, and Mussolini enjoyed wide support in the military and among the industrial and agrarian elites. The king also thought Mussolini could restore law and order in the country. Mussolini did, but not in the way the king had hoped.

Through a series of laws, Mussolini and his Fascist followers consolidated their power and transformed the nation into a one-party dictatorship. Mussolini's political strategy consisted of destroying all political opposition through secret police and outlawing labor strikes. Free speech was crushed. Within five years, he had created a totalitarian state.

Ruling Italy, however, wasn't enough for Mussolini. In 1935, the same year he was nominated for the Nobel Peace Prize, he invaded Ethiopia, fulfilling his dream of leading an empire. While Europe expressed its horror at Mussolini's brutal conquest, dropping gas bombs on the Ethiopian people, Germany encouraged Italy's invasion. Hitler, Germany's leader at the time, had his own dream of an empire and the two sympathized. Following the German example, in 1938 Mussolini's government passed anti-Semitic laws in Italy that discriminated against Jews in all sectors of public and private life and prepared the way for the deportation of some 20 percent of Italy's Jews to German concentration camps during World War II.

In 1939, Mussolini was hesitant about Italy becoming a part of the European war. Italy lacked the military capacity to carry out a war with France and the United Kingdom, and he realized that a long-lasting war would take a toll on the country. At the same time, he wished to maintain a good relationship with Germany. As he watched Germany's victories and saw that France was on the verge of collapse, Mussolini, thinking that Germany was likely to win the war, quickly sided with Germany on June 10, 1940. Mussolini believed that, as Germany's ally, Italy would gain new territories in Europe. In his strategy, while Germany focused on Europe, Italian forces could concentrate on a major offensive in Egypt, where British and Commonwealth (which included overseas territories, protectorates, India, and the semi-independent Canada, Australia, South Africa, and New Zealand) forces were outnumbered by Italian troops. Mussolini didn't count on the fact that the United Kingdom would not surrender to Germany's victories in Eastern, Western, and Northern Europe, and that the war would continue. Hitler, considering Mussolini as a junior partner in the alliance, never discussed any war plans with him. The Italian troops were ill-equipped and not much help to the Germans. On the contrary, Germany had to help out the Italians in their unsuccessful invasions of Greece in 1941 and in North Africa in 1943. By then it was clear that Mussolini had failed his country by joining the war, and he realized that he had lost support in Italy.

On July 24, 1943, around the same time as the Western Allies invaded Sicily, the Fascist Grand Council—the supreme authority of Italy—passed a resolution with an overwhelming majority that dismissed Mussolini from office. Nonetheless, Mussolini went to his office the next day as if nothing had happened. King Victor Emmanuel III had to arrest him to remove him from power, in accordance with the Grand Council's decision. Again, Hitler came to Mussolini's aid. On September 12, 1943, German Special Forces rescued Mussolini from prison in the Gran Sasso raid, and he became the leader of the Italian Social Republic, a region under German rule in northern Italy. Mussolini held this post until his death on April 28, 1945, when Hitler was defeated. After a desperate attempt to escape north, Mussolini was captured and executed near Lake Como by Italian partisans. His body was brought to Milan, where it was hung upside down at a service station for public viewing.

Mussolini was hardly a peace champion. He did not work toward brotherhood between nations nor did he promote disarmament. He was a bully and a warmonger until the end.

However, at the time he was nominated, in 1935, Mussolini's achievements were considered miraculous outside of Italy. "Well, at least Mussolini made the trains run on time," is a saying that developed in the late 1920s by a British tourist in Italy. He had transformed and reinvigorated his divided and demoralized country, and he had carried out his social reforms and public works without losing the support of the industrialists and landowners.[10] Abroad, many people believed Mussolini's propaganda. Perhaps that explains his nomination to the peace prize by two different people. One nomination came from a German law professor, and the other was from a professor in France. However, the letters are missing and the reasons behind the nominations remain unknown.

At the time of the nominations, it was public knowledge that Italy had invaded Ethiopia and brutally massacred Ethiopians. The Norwegian Nobel Committee must have known that, because Mussolini was not considered for the shortlist by the Nobel Committee. That year, the committee did its job and gave the prize to German dissident Carl von Ossietzky. It quickly saw Mussolini for who he was, and he was certainly no peace champion.

ADOLF HITLER:
NOMINATED AS A JOKE

Even more shocking than Mussolini, Adolf Hitler was nominated in 1939.[11] The infamous Hitler doesn't need an introduction. Instead, I'll summarize the main points that made this man the antithesis of a peace champion.

Hitler, or Der Führer (the Leader), rose to power in the aftermath of World War I, when the Western Allies forced the German government—the Weimar Republic—to sign the Versailles Treaty. This treaty, as you might recall from Chapter Four, left Germany in pieces in several ways. First, it divided territories, displaced people, and created unnatural borders. Second, the punitive damages Germany had to pay according to the treaty left the country broken for an unforeseeable future. Third, the German people were demoralized. Hitler spoke to peoples' feelings of betrayal and shame, and he promised them that he would make Germany great again. Which he did, creating jobs for an impoverished population. He also used tactics of blame. In his book *Mein Kampf*, Hitler denounced international capitalism and Communism as being part of a Jewish conspiracy against the Germans. Blame and conspiracy theories were well received by a disheartened German population in the midst of a financial depression. He was also a charismatic orator. To the German population, he was a hero and a savior, and most followed him until the end.

Despite what the Germans thought of him back then, Hitler was the opposite of a Nobel peace champion. He almost singlehandedly started World War II in 1939. At his defeat in 1945, most of Europe was destroyed. In German-occupied Europe, some six million Jews were killed during the war, exterminated in concentration camps, as were millions of other victims whom he and his followers deemed inferior.

Instead of facing his defeat, Hitler committed suicide on April 30, 1945, to avoid capture by the Red Army after the Soviets had seized Berlin. The German people had to face what they would later call "Year Zero," 1945.

Hitler was clearly no peace champion. How did his name end up on the Nobel Committee's list in 1939? E. G. C. Brandt, then a member of the Swedish parliament, nominated Hitler to the Nobel Peace Prize. Brandt later claimed that he didn't intend the nomination to be taken seriously, and that he did not actually believe in what the Führer stood for. A dedicated anti-Fascist, Brandt said his nomination was a "satiric criticism" of the current political debate in Sweden. The nomination, he said, was a protest against the British Prime Minister Neville Chamberlain who had also been nominated that year for his role in the Munich Agreement. The Munich Agreement was a treaty between Nazi Germany, Italy, France, and Britain that allowed Germany to annex parts of Czechoslovakia. However, Czechoslovakia was not part of the agreement. By recommending Hitler alongside Chamberlain, Brandt wanted to point out the flaws in the agreement and to demonstrate that Chamberlain was no more a peace champion than Hitler. However, those satirical intentions were not well received, and the Nobel Committee didn't shortlist Hitler. Brandt soon withdrew his nomination, but it would forever be part of the Nobel records.[12]

JOSEPH STALIN:
20 MILLION DEAD

Another outrageous Nobel Peace Prize candidate was Iosif Vissarionovich— or Joseph Stalin, the secretary general of the Soviet Union Communist Party from 1922 to 1953. Stalin was nominated for the Nobel Peace Prize in 1945 and 1948 for his efforts to end World War II.[13] The first nomination was sent in by Halvdan Koht, Norwegian Labor Party politician and former foreign minister. The official reason behind Koht's recommendation is unknown. However, by taking a look at the historical events, we might be able to guess. But first, let's take a quick look at what kind of man Stalin was.

Stalin was one of the revolutionaries during the Russian Revolution in 1917, who organized labor strikes and demonstrations against the tsar. Prior to 1917, Stalin was imprisoned several times, but managed to escape.

Standing up to the oppressing tsar didn't make him a bad person. However, his methods were questionable. As an outlaw, he continued his work in hiding, raising money for the revolutionary cause through robberies, kidnappings, and extortion. It was during this time that he was nicknamed Stalin, meaning "steel" in Russian. Perhaps he wanted to be perceived as a "man of steel," because he kept the name.

Stalin didn't have the same appeal as his comrades Vladimir Lenin or Leon Trotsky. He was neither a strong orator like Lenin nor an intellectual like Trotsky. But Stalin had something else. He excelled in the mundane operations of the revolution, calling meetings, publishing leaflets, and organizing strikes and demonstrations. When the Bolsheviks—the members of the Russian Communist Party who were committed to the ideas of Karl Marx—won the revolution in 1917 and the tsar abdicated, Lenin became the head of the country. In 1922, Lenin appointed Stalin to the newly created office of general secretary of the Communist Party. Although not a significant post at the time, it gave Stalin control over all party member appointments, which allowed him to build his base. With Lenin as a front figure, Stalin operated in the background, making shrewd appointments and consolidating his power so that eventually nearly all members of the central command owed their position to him.[14] By the time anyone realized what he had done, it was too late. Even Lenin, who was gravely ill, was helpless in regaining control from Stalin. After Lenin's death in 1924, Stalin set out to destroy the old party leadership and take complete control. Between 1934 and 1939, Stalin organized and led the so-called Great Purge of the party, government, armed forces, and intelligentsia, in which millions of enemies of the Soviet people were imprisoned, exiled, or executed. Major figures in the Communist Party, such as the old Bolsheviks, Trotsky, and most of the Red Army generals were killed with the justification that they were plotting to overthrow the government.

After he had finished with his purge, Stalin could direct his attention outwards. In August 1939, after failed attempts to conclude anti-Hitler pacts with other major European powers, Stalin entered into a nonaggression pact with Nazi Germany, also called the Molotov-Ribbentrop Pact, which divided their influence and territory within Eastern Europe. Did Stalin have peace in mind when he signed the pact with Hitler? According to Yale history professor Timothy Snyder, he did not. Stalin wanted to expand Soviet territory, just like Hitler wanted to expand German territory. In a 2014 blog on The *New York Review of Books*, Snyder wrote that the Molotov-Ribbentrop Pact led directly to the German-Soviet invasion of Poland, which instigated World War II.

"For five years," Snyder wrote, "the Soviet leader had been seeking an occasion to destroy Poland."

When Germany, in June 1941, violated the Molotov-Ribbentrop Pact and launched a massive invasion of the Soviet Union, Soviet forces managed, despite heavy human and territorial losses, to halt the German attack. It was Soviet forces that defeated the Nazis on the Eastern Front, and in May 1945 the Red Army seized Berlin, ending the war.

It was also the Russian Red Army who liberated Northern Norway from Nazi occupation in the fall of 1944, which might explain Halvdan Koht's nomination. Foreign Minister Koht came from Tromsø, a town located in the very north of Norway. To the people in that part of the country, the Russians were looked upon as saviors. Still, that didn't change the fact that Stalin also played a part in starting the entire conflict.

Whether the Nobel Committee seriously considered Stalin for the prize is uncertain. What we do know, as you may remember from Chapter Four, is that the committee post World War II had another agenda of strengthening ties with the United States, and that the 1945 prize would be presented to US Secretary of State Cordell Hull instead.

While the 1945 nomination might have been for sentimental reasons, the second nomination of Stalin in 1948 was probably motivated by politics. This nomination was sent to the committee by Czechoslovakian professor Władysław Rieger. In 1948, the Soviet Union's contribution to end the war was still fondly remembered. Perhaps more importantly, the Russians were increasing their power in Eastern Europe—including Czechoslovakia—at the beginning of the Cold War. Rieger's nomination might have been a way to pay respect to the Soviet leader, and to buy Stalin's goodwill. Again, Stalin would be passed over by the committee. In fact, the prize would not be awarded at all that year. The reason, the committee stated, was for a lack of suitable living candidates.

It's reassuring that the committee didn't find Stalin suitable. During Stalin's governance, the Soviet state was responsible for killing at least twenty million people, according to historian Robert Conquest. Professor Rudolph J. Rummel contends that while the exact numbers may never be known with complete certainty, they are even higher if one includes those killed by the Soviet government in Eastern Europe.

A true dictator, Stalin was not used to being denied anything, so when he was nominated for Nobel's prize, he expected to win. Disappointed and furious at having been passed over, he created his own prize—the Stalin Prize for Strengthening Peace among Peoples—in 1949 as part of his seventieth birthday celebration. A few years later, when the Kremlin removed the name "Stalin" from buildings and places after having condemned many of his actions, the prize was renamed after Lenin. Obviously, neither Stalin nor Lenin were men of peace by Nobel's definition. However, according to Jay Nordlinger, the author of *Peace, They Say*, both men stood for a certain kind of peace, the kind of peace "that comes from an individual's absolute submission to the party and state."

The nominations of Mussolini, Hitler, and Stalin are all in the past, but they show a troubling trend of the ability to even put forward in the formal process some of the worst examples of humanity. To that end, as the nomination process has not changed, the following nominees might still have a chance of winning Nobel's prize.

VLADIMIR PUTIN:
WEAPONS SUPPLIER AND KGB AGENT

Much to the dismay of many, Russian president Vladimir Putin was nominated for the Nobel Peace Prize in 2014 for his efforts in the Syrian conflict, despite his role as the main supplier of weapons to Bashar al-Assad's regime.[15]

Nominated by the International Academy of Spiritual Unity and Cooperation of Peoples of the World, which is one of the groups eligible according to the Nobel Peace Prize Committee, the former KGB agent "actively promotes settlement of all conflicts arising on the planet," the Russian advocacy group stated, conveniently omitting *how* Putin settled those conflicts. Nor did it mention Putin's violent campaign against the separatists in Chechnya or the war he waged on Georgia. Instead, the group pointed to his efforts to prevent an air strike by the United States on the Syrian regime following a chemical gas attack in August 2013.

A Nobel Peace Prize winner is supposed to work toward brotherhood between nations, disarmament of armies, and hold peace conferences. In 2013, he prevented an airstrike on Syria, which is good. But is that act alone enough? Let's take a closer look at Putin's leadership.

Vladimir Vladimirovich Putin was born on October 7, 1952, in Leningrad (today Saint Petersburg). For sixteen years, he was an officer in the KGB, rising to the rank of lieutenant colonel before retiring in 1991 to enter politics in his native Saint Petersburg. In politics, Putin was known to be extremely loyal and efficient. According to British journalist Ben Judah, Putin worked mostly behind the scenes and kept a low profile. He reportedly was "the man to see if things needed to get done."[16] Ambitious, he moved to Moscow in 1996 to join President Boris Yeltsin's administration, where he rose quickly, probably because of his proven loyalty and efficiency. He became acting president on December 31, 1999, when Yeltsin resigned.

Putin won the 2000 presidential election and was reelected in 2004, because he pulled his country out of the financial crisis that his predecessor had left him. Real incomes increased by a factor of 2.5, real wages more than tripled, and unemployment and poverty decreased by more than 50 percent. Overall, the quality of life of the Russian population rose significantly.[17, 18] Putin also reformed the military and the police, reduced taxes, supported high-tech industries, and helped make Russia an energy superpower. A rise in foreign investment contributed to a boom in many sectors including the automotive industry. None of this, however, qualifies him for the Nobel Peace Prize.

To Putin, power seems to be an end in itself, not a means to confer the greatest benefit on mankind. Putin has had creative ways of keeping political power even when the law forbids it. Because the Russian constitution limited a president from serving more than two consecutive terms, Putin was ineligible to run again in 2008. Instead, Dmitry Medvedev, at Putin's recommendation, was elected president.

It has been suggested that Putin and Medvedev represented a modern Russian duumvirate, sometimes referred to as "tandemocracy." In a survey of the 2007–2008 election called *Russians and the Putin-Medvedev "Tandemocracy,"* Henry E. Hale of George Washington University and Timothy J. Colton of Harvard University wrote that, "Putin, the incumbent president since 2000, did honor the Constitution and left office upon the expiration of his second term. But he also personally led the candidate list of the ruling United Russia party to a landslide win in the 2007 parliamentary elections, orchestrated the election of his younger protégé Medvedev as presidential successor, and then assumed the formal leadership of United Russia."

According to Hale and Colton, Medvedev closed the circle by nominating Putin to be prime minister, a choice quickly ratified by the United Russia majority in parliament.

"Most observers," Hale and Colton wrote, "contend that Putin continues to call the shots in Russian politics but acknowledge that Medvedev wields important powers which may enable him eventually to move out from under the shadow of his patron."

Medvedev never did. In September 2011, following a change in the law extending the presidential term from four to six years, Putin announced that he would run again for election and won in March 2012. Medvedev regained his post as prime minister. Again, in 2018, Putin won the election with a 77 percent vote in his favor and is now serving his fourth term as president. In March 2020, he signed off on changes to the constitution proposed by parliament that will allow Putin to stay in power beyond his fourth term as president. The constitutional reform was put to to a vote in June 2020, and nearly 78 percent of the Russian population backed the proposed changes that will reset Putin's term limits to zero in 2024, allowing him to serve two more six-year terms.[19] Other than staying in power, what else has Putin accomplished? In 2014, the same year he was nominated for Nobel's prize, he invaded Ukraine, annexed Crimea, and justified the invasion by arguing that the Russian ethnic population needed protection. It's the same type of argument Hitler used when Germany seized Austria and part of Czechoslovakia in 1938, and Stalin's rationale for attacking Poland in 1939. By September 2015, the United Nations estimated that some 8,000 people had been killed and 1.5 million people had been displaced as a result of the fighting in Ukraine. Because of Putin's handling of the situation in Ukraine and annexation of Crimea, Russia was excluded from the G8 group.[20]

Also, in the fall of 2015, Russia became an active participant in the Syrian Civil War, when Russian aircraft struck targets near the cities of Homs and Hama. Although Russian defense officials stated that the air strikes were intended to target troops and materials belonging to the Islamic State, the actual focus of the attacks seemed to have been on opponents of Syrian president and Russian ally Bashar al-Assad. With these attacks, the justification for his nomination for the Nobel Peace Prize by the Russian advocacy group became meaningless.

In addition, Putin has been labeled undemocratic by his opposition and foreign observers. The 2011 Democracy Index, in view of Putin's candidacy for president and flawed parliamentary elections, stated that Russia was in "a long process of regression [that] culminated in a move from a hybrid to an authoritarian regime." The constitutional changes in 2020 reinforces this conclusion. Putin's administration is also overtly anti-gay, anti-women, and religiously conservative. His administration has tightened abortion laws and passed anti-gay laws, justifying these changes on so-called moral grounds, but also out of concerns over the reduced population.[21]

"The Europeans are dying out . . . and gay marriages don't produce children," Putin said at the Valdai International Discussion Club in September

2013, according to *PinkNews* on September 20, 2013. "Do you want to survive by accepting immigrants? Society can't absorb such a number of immigrants. Let us make our own choice, as we see it for our country."

Putin's hostility toward immigration and even greater hostility toward foreign oversight has been demonstrated by the increased burden Russia has placed on foreign NGOs.[22] The NGOs that received funding from abroad were labeled as "foreign agents" and banned from the country.

During his last two terms in office, democracy has been threatened further. Opposition leaders have been silenced, jailed, and killed. On February 27, 2015, opposition leader Boris Nemtsov was gunned down within sight of the Kremlin, just days after he had spoken out against Russian intervention in Ukraine. In January 2016, a British public inquiry officially implicated Putin in the 2006 murder of former Federal Security Service (the successor to the KGB) officer Alexander Litvinenko. Litvinenko, who had spoken out against Russian government ties to organized crime both before and after his defection to the United Kingdom, was poisoned with polonium-210 while drinking tea in a London hotel bar.

Putin has also meddled with democracy abroad. In the months prior to the 2016 US presidential election, a series of hacking attacks targeted the Democratic Party and its presidential candidate Hillary Clinton. Computer security experts tied these attacks to Russian intelligence services, and an FBI investigation later confirmed that Russia did try to influence the presidential election. According to a 2019 article by Abigail Abrams in *Time* magazine, Russia went all out in its meddling. "Over the course of the election, a wide-ranging group of Russians probed state voter databases for insecurities; hacked the Hillary Clinton campaign, the Democratic Congressional Campaign Committee and the Democratic National Committee; tried to hack the campaign of Senator Marco Rubio and the Republican National Committee; released politically damaging information on the internet; spread propaganda on Twitter, Facebook, YouTube, and Instagram; staged rallies in Florida and Pennsylvania; set up meetings with members of the Trump campaign and its associates; and floated a business proposition for a skyscraper in Moscow to the Trump Organization."[23]

The goal, according to Abrams, as determined by the US intelligence community and backed up by evidence gathered by FBI Special Counsel Robert Mueller, was to damage the Clinton campaign, boost Trump's chances, and sow distrust in American democracy.

The International Academy of Spiritual Unity and Cooperation of Peoples of the World, who recommended Putin for the peace prize, might have come to regret its nomination. Unless, of course, it's a puppet on Putin's string. Perhaps Putin's nomination for Nobel's prize in 2014 has something to do with him being named the most powerful man of 2013 by *Forbes* magazine. Sometimes, fame and honor lead to more fame and honor, as was the case with Ellen Johnson Sirleaf, former president of Liberia, who won Nobel's prize in 2011 after she had been on the cover of *Time* magazine. As was the case of Nobel laureates Muhammad Yunus, Al Gore, and Malala Yousafzai.

"We took some heat last year when we named the Russian President as the most powerful man in the world," wrote *Forbes* in 2014, "but after a year when Putin annexed Crimea, staged a proxy war in the Ukraine, and inked a deal to build a more than $70 billion gas pipeline with China (the planet's largest construction project), our choice simply seems prescient. Russia looks more and more like an energy-rich, nuclear-tipped rogue state with an undisputed, unpredictable, and unaccountable head unconstrained by world opinion in pursuit of its goals."

Putin has indeed created an image of himself as a tough guy and super-hero, to a point that he is sometimes referred to as "Superputin." That may well qualify him as the most powerful man in the world. It does not, however, make him a peace champion according to Nobel.

EDWARD SNOWDEN:
"THE ONE TRUE HOOHA"

In 2014, the same year Putin was nominated, so was Edward Joseph Snowden. The two Norwegian politicians who nominated him said he "contributed to a more stable and peaceful world order."[24] Snowden leaked classified information from the National Security Agency (NSA) while working there in 2013. He did not work toward brotherhood between nations, disarmament, or hold peace conferences. Let's take a look at why Snowden's nominators thought he was qualified.

Born on June 21, 1983, in Elizabeth City, North Carolina, Snowden moved as a child with his parents to Maryland where he attended public schools in Anne Arundel County, south of Baltimore, before dropping out of high school in his sophomore year. While in high school, Matthew Cole and Mike Brunker of *NBC News* reported, Snowden developed a fascination with computers and technology. He also registered on the Ars Technica website, a hacking and technology forum, and over a two-year period posted as "The One True Hooha" or just "Hooha."

In 2004, Snowden passed a General Educational Development test to receive credentials equivalent to a high school diploma, and enlisted in an Army Reserve Special Forces training program to fight to help free people from oppression in Iraq, Cole and Brunker reported. But after he broke his legs in a training accident later that year, the army discharged him. Snowden then got a job as a security guard at the Center for Advanced Study of Language at the University of Maryland, which has a close relationship with the NSA, according to *NBC News*.

Because of his computer skills, he was hired by the CIA as a system administrator—responsible for the upkeep, configuration, and operation of computer systems. Still working for the CIA, he was sent to Geneva, Switzerland, from 2007 to 2009 under diplomatic cover as an IT and cyber security expert. This position gave him access to a wide array of classified documents, Cole and Brunker wrote, and during this period, Snowden became disillusioned "about how my government functions and what its impact is in the world. I realized that I was part of something that was doing far more harm than good."

In March 2013, he joined the consulting firm Booz Allan Hamilton inside the NSA center in Hawaii, with a plan to obtain the necessary information to leak to the press. Having retrieved the information he needed, Snowden left the United States for Hong Kong in May that year. He had already contacted journalist Glenn Greenwald and film director Laura Poitras in December 2012, and now he asked them to meet him in Hong Kong.

"I hope you understand that contacting you was extremely high risk," Snowden said to Poitras according to her 2014 documentary, *CitizenFour*, as he handed over classified documents providing evidence of mass indiscriminate and illegal invasion of privacy by the NSA. "From now know that every border you cross, every purchase you make, every call you dial, every cell phone tower you pass, friend you keep, site you visit, subject you type, is in the hands of a system whose reach is unlimited, but whose safeguards are not. In the end, if you publish this source material I will likely be immediately implicated. I ask only you ensure this information makes it home to the American public. Thank you and be careful."

According to the *Washington Post*, based on information from Snowden, the NSA collects more than 250 million email inbox views and contact lists every year from online services such as Yahoo, Gmail, and Facebook.

While Snowden's revelations were shocking, and important for the public to know, the question remains: How do they make him a Nobel peace champion? His nominators, left-wing politicians Baard Vegar Solhjell and Snorre Valen said in 2014 that the public debate and policy changes "in the wake of Snowden's whistleblowing has contributed to a more stable and peaceful world order."[25] But has it really? Rather, his revelations may have created a deeper rift between the US and some of the nations they have been spying on. The French government was furious when it found out that the NSA had been spying on three of their presidents.

The fact that countries spy on each other is nothing new. Even friendly countries do that in order to keep a competitive edge. Snowden was not so concerned with international relations, what bothered him was the individual's right to privacy, which is part of the reason Snowden's nominators felt he would be a suitable candidate for Nobel's prize. His disclosures in 2013 have definitely fueled much-needed debates over mass surveillance, government secrecy, and the balance between national security and the individual's right for privacy. As such, he may be responsible for a profound change in our societies, just not the kind of change Alfred Nobel intended.

Snowden has been called many things, including a hero, patriot, dissident, and traitor. He is certainly brave. On June 9, 2013, four days after Greenwald and Poitras first exposed the secret NSA program based on his leaks, Snowden made his identity public, believing that the US government probably already knew he was the source of the leak. On June 14, the US Department of Justice charged him with two counts of violating the Espionage Act and theft of government property, punishable by up to thirty years in prison. Facing prosecution in the United States, Snowden was given temporary asylum in 2013 in Russia, where he still lives, now as a permanent resident, unable to go home to the United States. A prize for bravery may be suitable. But Snowden is no champion of peace according to Nobel's definition.

* * *

BEING NOMINATED IS no guarantee for winning the Nobel medal. It just means the committee has to consider the nominee's candidacy. Some of the nominees in this chapter are shocking, but at least none of them won. However, when candidates who may not be worthy of Nobel's prize are presented to the committee, and the committee doesn't do its homework, we're in trouble. Some nominees, including President Donald Trump, are overtly campaigning for the Nobel Peace Prize, even though they don't share the values or intentions of Alfred Nobel. So far, the committee hasn't been swayed by Trump's self-promotion. Nevertheless, his and the cases presented in this chapter show the need for a transparent selection process and guidelines the committee must follow. If the names of the nominees were public, more information about them might come forward before the committee makes its final choice. As it stands today, the whole process is secret, and the committee does as it pleases—often without taking Nobel's last words seriously. That doesn't create trust. Perhaps we, you and I, also have a responsibility to restore trust in the world's most prestigious prize. We can, and maybe we must, make sure to bring forward names of worthy candidates to the committee's attention. If we are not eligible ourselves, it shouldn't be too difficult to find someone who is.

15

LIFE AFTER THE PRIZE

A heart can no more be forced to love than a stomach can
be forced to digest food by persuasion.
—ALFRED NOBEL

—m—

THE NOBEL PEACE prize is no magic wand. It cannot transform a war
monger or a con artist into a champion for peace. Because so many of
the committee's selections were based on political expediency, the recipients
failed to live up to Nobel's expectations after the award just as they had failed
to before it. They could not do anything else because they had never been
peace champions.

Sometimes, a peace champion—who was worthy at the time of the
award—regressed in the years following the award. No one in peace prize
history has proven to be a greater disappointment than the winner of the 1991
Nobel medal.

1991:
AUNG SAN SUU KYI, FALLEN FROM GRACE

Winner of the 1991 Nobel Peace Prize, Aung San Suu Kyi has fallen from grace.

Born in 1945, Suu Kyi was the modern symbol of freedom in Burma (renamed Myanmar by the military regime in 1989). The daughter of the legendary liberation movement leader, Aung San Suu Kyi left Burma to study abroad before she returned home in 1988. From then on, she led the opposition to the military junta that had ruled the country since 1962. She was one of the founders of the National League for Democracy (NLD) and was elected secretary general of the party in 1988. Like Mahatma Gandhi, she opposed all use of violence and called on the military leaders to hand over power to a civilian government. The aim was to establish a democratic society in which the country's ethnic groups could cooperate in harmony.

In the 1990 election, NLD won a clear victory, but the generals prevented the legislative assembly from convening, and continued arresting members of the opposition. Suu Kyi had already been placed under arrest in 1989. The 1991 Peace Prize had a significant impact in mobilizing world opinion in favor of Suu Kyi's cause, and for her as a political prisoner, but she remained under house arrest in Rangoon and could not travel to Oslo to receive the prize herself. Still, she had the world on her side. In addition to Nobel's prize, she won numerous other awards, including the European Union's Sakharov Prize given for peaceful struggle for human rights, the US Congressional Medal given for significant achievements that will have an impact on American history and culture, Amnesty International Ambassador of Conscience Award, and the US Holocaust Museum's Elie Wiesel Award, which promotes human dignity.

She was finally released from house arrest in 2010 as Myanmar's military regime embarked on reforms, trying to soften its image. Suu Kyi and NLD could begin to rebuild a hold on the country, and in 2012, she was able to travel to Oslo to meet the Nobel Committee and be honored as a peace champion.

"The prize we were working for was a free, secure and just society where our people might be able to realize their full potential," Suu Kyi told an ecstatic crowd in Oslo's City Hall. "The honor lay in our endeavor. History had given us the opportunity to give our best for a cause in which we believed."

In the 2015 elections, NLD won a landslide victory, taking 86 percent of the seats of the Assembly of the Union. As leader of her country, however, Suu Kyi has not established a society in which the country's ethnic groups could live in harmony. Close to a million Rohingya Muslims have fled a bloody military crackdown in western Myanmar to refugee camps in Bangladesh. Hundreds of Rohingya villages have been burned to the ground since 2017, and the UN's expert group has stated that, in December 2019, there was still a threat of genocide of the Rohingyas in Myanmar.

Since becoming the leader of Myanmar, Suu Kyi has showed shocking indifference to the atrocities committed by the Myanmar military and increasing intolerance of freedom of expression. Ten years after her release from house arrest, she had not used her political and moral authority to safeguard human rights, justice, or equality in Myanmar. The reason is political. In a country that is 90 percent Buddhist, there is little sympathy to be found for the predominantly Muslim Rohingya people. Expressing support could mean political suicide for Suu Kyi and the military-backed ruling party, especially so close to the next parliamentary elections, likely to be held in November 2020.

On December 10, 2019, the same day as the Nobel Peace Prize was handed to Abiy Ahmed, the prime minster of Ethiopia, Aung San Suu Kyi took the stand as Myanmar's top civilian leader before a hearing on war crimes at the International Court of Justice in The Hague. She is the first national leader to appear directly before the court while genocide in Myanmar is still allegedly unfolding.

International press has numerous times expressed its outrage and called for the revocation of the 1991 Nobel medal to Suu Kyi, just as revocation was called for in 1973 (Kissinger and Le Duc Tho), in 1978 (Menachem Begin), and in 1992 (Rigoberta Menchú).

"Suu Kyi stood back until now," editor of the *San Francisco Chronicle* Marshall Kilduff wrote about the hearing before the ICJ. "This week she mouthed the military line, defending the suppression in an appearance that stunned human rights groups and Muslim countries clamoring for better treatment of the Rohingya. Her performance suggests it's time to retrieve the peace prize and find another heroine who deserves it."[1]

Some of Suu Kyi's other awards have already been rescinded. The Elie Wiesel award was rescinded in March 2018. In November 2018, Amnesty International revoked its 2009 award to Suu Kyi.

"As an Amnesty International Ambassador of Conscience, our expectation was that you would continue to use your moral authority to speak out against injustice wherever you saw it, not least within Myanmar itself," Amnesty International president Kumi Naidoo wrote. "Today, we are profoundly dismayed that you no longer represent a symbol of hope, courage, and the undying defense of human rights. Amnesty International cannot justify your continued status as a recipient of the Ambassador of Conscience award and so with great sadness we are hereby withdrawing it from you."[2]

The Nobel Peace Prize Committee has been silent. Until now, the committee has never revoked any prizes, despite public outcry that it should. On the one hand, Suu Kyi was worthy of the Nobel medal when she received it in 1991, and the committee cannot be expected to predict what the laureate does in the years following the award. On the other hand, the Nobel Peace Prize is supposed to be an inspiration and a beacon of hope for generations to come. Aung San Suu Kyi, by allowing genocide to unfold in her country, has proven that she is no longer a role model or peace champion. Allowing her to keep Nobel's prize is an insult, not only to Alfred Nobel, but to the world.

2000:
KIM DAE-JUNG, "THE NELSON MANDELA OF ASIA"

Kim Dae-jung, who was president of South Korea from 1998 to 2003, won the Nobel Peace Prize in 2000 for promoting democracy and human rights in South Korea and Asia, and for his Sunshine Policy. This Sunshine Policy encouraged interaction with and economic assistance for North Korea, thus promoting brotherhood between the two states. The problem with the Sunshine Policy, however, was that it only looked good on paper.

Kim Dae-jung was born on December 3, 1925 during the time when Korea was under Japanese colonial rule. In 1943, he graduated at the top of his class from Mokpo Commercial High School and began working as a clerk for a Japanese-owned shipping company, which he eventually owned. A self-made man, Kim entered politics in 1954 during the administration of Korea's first president, Syngman Rhee. He gained unwavering loyalty among his supporters, probably in part because he was a talented orator and in part because of his courage opposing President Rhee and his successors' authoritarian regimes. Because of his bravery, Kim was sometimes called the "Nelson Mandela of Asia."[3] Just like with Mandela, opposing the regime in his country did not come without risk. He was kidnapped, imprisoned, and sentenced to death more than once.

"In August of 1973, while exiled in Japan, I was kidnapped from my hotel room in Tokyo by intelligence agents of the then military government of South Korea," Kim said in his Nobel lecture. "The agents took me to their boat at anchor along the seashore. They tied me up, blinded me, and stuffed my mouth. Just when they were about to throw me overboard, Jesus Christ appeared before me with such clarity. I clung to him and begged him to save me. At that very moment, an airplane came down from the sky to rescue me from the moment of death."

Rumors have it that the CIA sent the airplane.[4]

The news of his troubles startled the world, and when he was imprisoned again in 1976, Amnesty International adopted him as a prisoner of conscience. When he again was sentenced to death on charges of sedition and conspiracy in November 1980 by then-South Korean President Chun Doo-hwan, Pope John Paul II sent a letter to the South Korean president asking for clemency. The United States government also intervened, and when his sentence was stayed, Kim was given exile in the United States. Settling temporarily in Boston in 1983, he taught as a visiting professor at Harvard University Center for International Affairs.

During his two years abroad, Kim wrote a number of opinion pieces that were critical of the South Korean government in leading western newspapers, before, in 1985, he returned to his homeland. His first act after becoming president in 1998 was to pardon the generals who had sentenced him to death. "Only the truly magnanimous and strong," he wrote to his son from prison, "are capable of forgiving and loving."

Kim's Sunshine Policy culminated in an historic summit meeting in 2000 in Pyongyang with North Korean leader Kim Jong-il. The summit marked a critical moment in inter-Korean relations, and the world witnessed emotional reunions of families who had been split up in the conflict, which must have touched the Nobel Peace Prize Committee. Kim appeared to be a real peace champion. But what happened after he was awarded Nobel's prize?

As it turns out, his post-Nobel leadership and Sunshine Policy were polluted by greed and a hunger for power.

"Eager to thaw Cold War tensions," *The Village Voice* reported in 2003, "Kim implemented a gradualist strategy for reconciling with North Korea, propping up and befriending the struggling nation with humanitarian aid and increased trade. His plan, though, also included covering up North Korea's appalling human rights record and secretly funneling hundreds of millions in government money into Kim's coffers."

In fact, Kim paid money to North Korea just before the summit in 2000 so the North Korean leader Kim Jong-il would play along pretending to be brothers to the outside world. According to Nordlinger, the "Nobel Peace Prize was purchased for the sum of $500 million."

The Nobel Committee, however, couldn't have known about this bribe when it awarded the South Korean leader. But Nobel's prize didn't make Kim into more of a peace champion either. Shortly after the 2000 summit, negotiations between the two states stalled and Kim Dae-jung was never able to lessen the gap between North and South Korea. When the United States declared North Korea part of the Axis of Evil after the terrorist attacks on September 11, 2001, the North cut off talks with the South.

In November 2010, the South Korean Unification Ministry officially brought the Sunshine Policy—which was the reason behind the Nobel Peace Prize—to an end, declaring it a failure. The relationship between North and South Korea was still tense at the time of this writing in 2020.[5]

2014:
MALALA, "THE MOST FAMOUS TEENAGER IN THE WORLD"

Born on July 12, 1997, Malala Yousafzai is the youngest-ever Nobel Peace Prize winner. She was only seventeen years old when she won Nobel's prize in 2014. A human rights activist, Malala didn't work toward the brotherhood between nations or to demilitarize armies. Her mission is to fight for girls' right to education. Again, the committee widened the scope of Nobel's will.

Malala, who comes from Pakistan, began blogging about girls' right to education for the BBC under a pseudonym in early 2009, at only eleven years old. In this blog, she described her life under Taliban occupation, the group's attempts to take control of the valley where she lived, and her views on promoting education for girls. In that same year, journalist Adam B. Ellick made a *New York Times* documentary—*Class Dismissed: The Death of Female Education*—about her life after the Taliban military took over the Swat region of Pakistan and forbade education for girls. The Yousafzai family owned several private schools in the region, and they were forced to close many. When they didn't comply with the Taliban's demand to close down, the school buildings were blown up. The documentary featured young Malala, who broke down in tears when explaining that her dream to become a doctor had been shattered. The film also explained how the family lived in constant fear of being killed by the Taliban because Malala's father, Ziauddin, was a known social activist in Swat.

The young woman's courage touched many.

"They cannot stop me," she said in the documentary. "I will get my education, if it is at home, in school, or anyplace."

In May 2009, the Yousafzai family, along with more than one million others, was forced to leave Swat, fleeing for their lives as a war broke out between the Taliban and the Pakistani government forces, who fought for control of the region.

At the end of the documentary, Malala declared that her new dream was to become a politician and to save her country from Taliban rule. The Yousafzai family was able to return to Swat a few months later, and although the Pakistani army had won this particular battle, the Taliban was still present and more than two hundred schools remained closed.

Ellick's documentary, as well as interviews with international media, made Malala a target for the Taliban. In addition, South African activist Desmond Tutu nominated her for the International Children's Peace Prize. In the afternoon of October 9, 2012, when Malala boarded her school bus, a gunman asked for her by name and fired three shots at her. One bullet hit the left side of Malala's forehead, traveled under her skin through the length of her face, and went into her shoulder. In the days immediately following the attack, she remained unconscious and in critical condition. On October 12, a group of fifty Islamic clerics in Pakistan issued a fatwa against those who tried to kill her, but the Taliban reiterated their intent to murder Malala and her father Ziauddin. As soon as her condition improved, Malala was sent to the safety of Queen Elizabeth Hospital in Birmingham, England, for intensive rehabilitation.

The assassination attempt sparked a national and international outpouring of support for Malala, and her advocacy grew into an international movement. Malala may have become "the most famous teenager in the world," *Deutsche Welle* wrote in January 2013. Gordon Brown, the UN's Special Envoy for Global Education launched a petition in her name, using the slogan "I am Malala," and demanding that all children worldwide be in school by the end of 2015. Pakistan's Right to Education Bill was ratified shortly after.

On April 29, 2013, *Time* magazine featured Malala on the magazine's front cover and as one of "The 100 Most Influential People in the World." In July that year, she spoke at the UN headquarters calling for worldwide access to education. Now a celebrity, she was nominated for the 2013 Nobel Peace Prize, and when she didn't receive it, many were disappointed.

Because of her touching story and cause, she was awarded the Sakharov Prize for 2013. On October 16, 2013, Canada gave her honorary citizenship. On May 15, 2014, Malala was granted an honorary doctorate degree by the University of King's College in Halifax, and in October 2014, she won the World Children's Prize in Sweden.

Perhaps the committee members thought her too young at age seventeen to receive the prize, so Malala had to share the 2014 Nobel Peace Prize with Kailash Satyarthi, a children's rights activist from India who has won numerous international awards.

Both Malala and Satyarthi had received so much attention already that Nobel's prize may not make much of a difference in their future efforts. But that's alright because the committee likes celebrities who make the Nobel Peace Prize look good.

Although Malala's mission is commendable, she does not promote brotherhood between nations, or focus on the disarmament of armies. She is no champion of peace according to Nobel's criteria in his last will. But the attention Malala has received is undeniable. German prime minster Angela Merkel even called Malala "the identity of Pakistan." She was a safe bet for a committee eager to please the public.

What has Malala accomplished since? By speaking out about what had happened to her and her village, Malala raised international awareness to a problem and a place it seemed the world had forgotten. As a famous young woman, Malala continues to travel the world, advocating education for girls. Whether Nobel's prize has made any difference is difficult to determine because she already had a platform when she won in 2014.

"Another empty Nobel Peace Prize," Akhilesh Pillalamarri called the 2014 award. "Malala, while being an important symbol, has hardly done anything noteworthy in the past few years other than making speeches," he wrote on October 11, 2014, in *The Diplomat*. "Unfortunately she seems to be rapidly on her way to becoming another commercialized symbol who makes a lot of speeches from exile and is disassociated with the situation on the ground in her home country."

As with the award to Obama in 2009, the 2014 Nobel Peace Prize to Malala seems to have been awarded on potential and not upon actual deeds, which sets the recipients up for likely failure in the case they don't live up to the expectations of the committee.

In addition to pleasing public opinion by giving Nobel's medal to the popular Malala, it would appear as if the 2014 award was the committee's creative attempt at being a peace champion on its own.

"What we are saying is that we have awarded two people with the same cause, coming from India and Pakistan, a Muslim and a Hindu," the committee chairman said. "It is in itself a strong signal." Especially at a time when military tensions between India and Pakistan are at its deadliest in more than a decade.

* * *

IN SELECTING ITS laureates, former committee chairman Gunnar Berge once said that there is always a risk of "reverses," meaning the winner might end up disappointing. But the Nobel Committee, according to Berge, "adheres to the principle, 'Nothing ventured, nothing gained.'"

While that is true, and the committee cannot know how a Nobel laureate evolves, it is responsible for ensuring Nobel's vision and the public's trust in the peace prize. That's why the committee has to stop rewarding candidates on their potential. And when a laureate takes a disappointing turn, it has to sometimes step up and rescind the award, as it should in the case of Aung San Suu Kyi.

THE OTHER SIDE
OF THE MEDAL

In nature's great work, there is no mercy, no profit for
virtue, no punishment for crime. Everything is corrosive or
being corroded, torturing or being tortured,
and God's reward, like that of the State,
goes to the strongest.

— ALFRED NOBEL

N OBEL'S WORDS FROM his play *Nemesis*, Act I, scene VI shows us
that he understood the dark side of human nature. Nevertheless, he
wrongly idolized Norway and he gave the Norwegian Nobel Committee too
much freedom. It wouldn't be the first time he was too trusting. From the
numerous letters Alfred Nobel wrote to his girlfriend Sofie Hess, it's clear
that he felt she was exploiting his generosity.

"Though I have a generous nature, I have no desire to be used," he wrote. "Be good and observe this little word!"

Nobel was indeed generous, and he had great compassion for people in need, especially if he saw potential in them and he felt that his money could help them reach their goals. Sofie, however, spent his money irresponsibly, as if there would be no end to his charity. She was right. He supported her even when she was unfaithful to him and after they had broken up. When she became pregnant by another man and told her friends and acquaintances in Austria that she was, "Mrs. Nobel," pretending the baby was his, Nobel continued sending her money from Paris. He did so even after she married another man. Nobel's compassion and generosity toward Sofie is admirable, but it didn't have any consequences beyond the money he spent on her. With the Nobel Peace Prize, however, it's a different story. He cared about his legacy.

With great power comes great responsibility. Nobel had worked hard for his money, and—by rewarding men and women who created something in the same idealistic spirit as his own—he wanted to make a difference in the world. Peace, he had decided, would be his cause. His name would be synonymous with it. Little did he know then that the Norwegians would also betray him.

When Nobel bestowed his prize upon Norway, the country was still governed by Sweden and was politically insignificant. Nobel had hoped that the Norwegian parliament would be less inclined to use the prize as political currency than his own Sweden. He was wrong.

In his will, Alfred Nobel used three concepts to clarify his approach toward a more peaceful world and which type of work he wished to support. He wanted to award those people committed to breaking the military tradition and building an international community of disarmed nations. The three expressions he used—*the best work for fraternity between nations, for the abolition or reduction of standing armies, and for the holding and promotion of peace congresses*—were clear references to the ideas of Bertha von Suttner, the love of his life and fifth recipient of his prize in 1905.

Nobel made a choice between two alternatives, two directly opposite views of the roads toward peace. Instead of conventional ideas of national security based on military strength, he wished to support efforts for disarmament. In his mind, the only way nations and their people would be safe was by cooperating and obeying international law, not by threatening each other with deadly arms.

Nobel entrusted the Norwegian parliament, then a supporter of Suttner and her ideas, with selecting the five-member Nobel Committee. Over time, the committee's ideas of peace in Norway have changed, but Nobel's last words remain the same. By ignoring Nobel's last will and testament, and therefore ignoring vital security interests of the world population, the committee has disconnected from Nobel and transformed his prize for global disarmament into a general prize for whatever it defines as "peace" at the moment. What would Nobel have done if he were alive to see what has become of his prize? Would he take it away from the Norwegian parliament?

LEGALLY BINDING—AND IGNORED NEVERTHELESS

The legally binding obligation of the awarders is to make the prize the challenge to militarism that Nobel intended. If they don't, some argue, the task should be placed in the hands of others who will. According to former Norwegian supreme court judge and author Fredrik S. Heffermehl, the specific intention of Nobel has systematically been ignored since the committee seats have been filled with old political party-liners who hold an approach to peace far from Nobel's. Instead of a committee consisting of friends of peace and disarmament, according to Heffermehl, the world has been handed a committee believing in the military and the use of weapons, in line with the Norwegian government. The Swedish Law of Foundations, however, is clear. The Norwegian committee members are obligated to follow Nobel's instructions, not pursue their own purposes.

"The basis for Nobel's Peace Prize is in his will from 1895," Michael Nobel wrote. According to him, "The rules concerning wills—including Alfred Nobel's—are crystal clear." The prize should be awarded to champions of

peace, meaning persons who work to prevent war through global cooperation and disarmament based on international law and global institutions.
"Nothing more and nothing less," he wrote.

That hasn't happened. "Champions for human rights, the environment,
and many others have received the prize despite the fact that their efforts in
no regard fulfill Nobel's specific vision of peace," Michael Nobel wrote. "I
don't wish to undermine their efforts—most of these prize winners have done
much for humanity. But they should never have gotten Nobel's Peace Prize."[1]

There have been several claims challenging the Norwegian Nobel
Committee on the grounds that it's not following Alfred Nobel's instructions
in his last will, including a 2014 request for criminal investigation of the
Nobel Committee by Heffermehl and sixteen others sent to ØKOKRIM,
Norway's national prosecutor for economic crime. ØKOKRIM, however,
decided that the matter was too peripheral to its special field of authority
and priorities.

Even though the committee pretends that it answers to no one, it realizes
that it depends on the authority of the Nobel Foundation in Stockholm to
continue as executor of Nobel's will. According to the Nobel Peace Prize
Watch, a Scandinavian advocacy group founded by the former president
of the International Peace Bureau IBP Tomas Magnusson and Heffermehl,
the Nobel Committee made a formal request to the Swedish Foundations
Authority in 2012 to become independent from the Nobel Foundation
in Stockholm and "not to take instructions from anyone" in its selection
process.[2] The Swedish Foundations Authority turned it down. The committee then moved for an exemption from the Swedish Foundations Act, which
was rejected in March 2014. This means that the ultimate and final responsibility for Nobel's prize remains in Stockholm, with the members of the
board of the Nobel Foundation.

So far, the foundation has been unwilling to exercise its right to get
involved with the Peace Prize. The Norwegian committee has made it very
clear that it does not welcome interference from its Swedish big brother,
and the foundation has kept its distance. Perhaps the foundation's board

members are afraid of the conflict it could create between the two countries if they got involved. Because the committee consists mostly of politicians, the Swedes wouldn't just be interfering with the five members of the Nobel Committee, but also with the Norwegian political elite and, indirectly, the government.

In the meanwhile, the unsupervised committee—instead of showing willingness to listen to critics and making an attempt to restore trust—is becoming more arrogant. The peace prize executors adamantly fail to show any interest in information about Nobel's actual intention, from Heffermehl or anyone else. The committee members seem determined to keep ignoring the fact that Nobel's will is a legal instrument, and they keep rejecting or ignoring criticism. At the same time, the committee has been unable or unwilling to refute any of the contradictory evidence presented by Heffermehl.

When the committee fails to follow Nobel's instructions, it acts like the bully it frequently condemns in others. An example is the 1996 peace prize to Bishop Carlos Filipe Ximenes Belo and José Ramos-Horta, the leaders in the opposition to the Indonesian occupation of East Timor.

"It has been said that Indonesia's annexation of East Timor is a historical fact," Francis Sejersted said in his 1996 presentation speech. "But history has never established anything as a fact forever. History always moves on."

Perhaps it is time the Nobel Prize also moved on and became what its testator intended. At the heart of the prize as it stands now is hypocrisy. Sometimes the Nobel Committee hands out the medal within the terms of Nobel's will, such as the Tunisian National Dialogue Quartet in 2015, or the International Campaign to Abolish Nuclear Weapons (ICAN) in 2017. Other times, it rewards honorable people whose work falls outside of the scope of the prize, as we have seen multiple examples of throughout this book. And again, sometimes, the committee hands Nobel's prize to power-hungry belligerents such as Yasser Arafat in 1994 and Ellen Johnson Sirleaf in 2011, or to a banker such as Muhammad Yunus in 2006 who has enriched himself to the detriment of the poor and illiterate.

INDEPENDENCE AND TRUST

Peace is not a field for small egos. "To declare someone a champion of peace is a bold act," author Jay Nordlinger wrote. "To declare him the greatest of such champions in the world is an even bolder one." The committee, over-confident in its choices, and sometimes more interested in pointing fingers, has proven that it often lacks the humility and self-awareness to make the best decisions in the name of peace.

Somehow, the Norwegian Nobel Committee—in its Norwegian *exception-alism*, as described in Chapter Three—has become the international judge of what is morally right and wrong in the world. Yet, in its own backyard, Norway is inventing, manufacturing, and distributing weapons that end up in those same conflicts. The state's business shouldn't matter, one might argue. When it comes to the Nobel Peace Prize, however, it does because no one really believes the committee is independent from the Norwegian government. With only one exception—the appointment of Henrik Syse in 2015—committee members are chosen by Parliament as a reward for their political careers, rather than for their interest in peace. Naturally, then, the selections of the committee often reflect the political view of the government.

Some politicians are beginning to realize that this washed out line between the government and the committee discredits the Nobel Peace Prize and its laureates. Former member of parliament Erik Solheim believes that if the government wishes to increase the committee's credibility, parliament must stop selecting old party-liners and refrain from embracing every laureate immediately after the announcement. It would also help, he added, if the committee consisted of members from different countries.[3]

According to the Norwegian newspaper *Verdens Gang* in May 2014, the Conservative Party expressed a wish to replace then Chairman Thorbjørn Jagland with the late former secretary-general to the United Nations, Kofi Annan. Other possible candidates were Hillary Clinton and former Swed-ish prime minister and diplomat Carl Bildt, said parliament member Linda Hofstad Helland.[4]

"I have to say that this is an interesting proposal," former Prime Minister Kåre Willoch said to *Verdens Gang* about opening up the committee to non-Norwegians. He went on to say that "A lot indicates that the leader [of the committee] should not be a former Norwegian politician."

Even during the early days of the peace prize, there was a discussion whether the committee should be made up of Norwegian citizens only, or if it should be international. Parliament can legally appoint anyone it wishes, including other nationals. So far, that has not happened, and the committee is made up solely of Norwegians. Bjørnstjerne Bjørnson, member of the original Nobel Committee from 1901 to 1906, declared that he would refuse to serve on the committee if it went international. Although he was a champion of the oppressed and persecuted everywhere, Bjørnson was also a nationalist. Present-day politicians seem to agree with this nationalistic view.

"It is natural that only Norwegians sit on the Nobel Committee," former Foreign Minister Jonas Gahr Støre said to NRK *Brennpunkt* in 2014, which was the last time the question was up for public discussion. According to him, it is the *Norwegian* Nobel Committee that presents the winner each year, and the committee should remain as such.

"An international Nobel Committee sounds grand. Who would be against it?" former secretary to the committee Geir Lundestad said. In practice, he continued, an international committee would be more complicated. "During the Cold War, should the committee have had one member from the East and one from the West? Another possibility is a committee modeled after the UN Security Council. Heaven forbid, we would only get boring selections."[5] Lundestad raises a valid point.

Perhaps there is another way. Michael Nobel suggested in an interview with me in December 2019 that even if the committee remains Norwegian, it could more actively make use of foreign academics and experts when making its selection. "Nevertheless, an open and transparent process is key to regain credibility," he said.

* * *

RESTORING MEANING TO THE PRIZE

The dynamite king's name may have become synonymous with peace; however, the committee, with its inconsistent and politically expedient choices, has distorted Nobel's vision. *Life* magazine called Nobel's peace prize "A Weird Insult from Norway," referring to the 1962 award to Linus Pauling, the scientist who, according to *Liberation* "is not a pacifist; nor is he a crusader for unilateral disarmament."[6] Instead of being an insult, Nobel's prize should be an inspiration and a beacon of hope.

The committee's betrayal may not always have been intentional. Since Alfred Nobel's death in 1896, our societies have changed and so has warfare. In choosing human rights activists and advocates for the environment, the committee has expressed a wish to widen the scope of Nobel's prize to keep up with the evolution of our societies.

The biggest threat to most of us, at least in Western countries, is not being attacked by another country's army, but a polarized and isolated population. Someone who feels marginalized by society will often struggle with belonging, support, and connection—all of which create emotional isolation. According to a 2018 article by Bruce Y. Lee on Forbes.com, former US Surgeon General Dr. Vivek Murthy claimed that more than 40 percent of American adults suffer from loneliness, making it the fastest growing epidemic on the planet. Loneliness makes people easy targets for fake news and propaganda created to manipulate people into certain political camps, following leaders who make them feel seen, worthy, and important. These often extreme political factions are founded by people who themselves often feel emotionally disconnected and have a need to fight for power to prove their own worth or relevance. Frequently, these leaders—as well as their following—have been ridiculed and made to feel inferior by a political elite, over whom they seek revenge, while being completely disconnected from the people they are supposed to serve. Such humiliated leaders understand that most people crave a sense of belonging and they give it to their followers in return for loyalty and power. This is how terrorist groups such as al-Qaeda or ISIS recruit new members across borders and continents.

The problem is that our current leadership model creates more isolation, because it is based on a false belief of separation. When we believe in separation, we victimize ourselves and dehumanize those who are different from us. Many people turn to extremism; those who don't can become numb and indifferent to suffering and therefore contribute to creating conflicts, riots, and war. Our need for connection and belonging has been underestimated for too long. So has the damaging effects of humiliation.

Nothing is more dangerous than a person who is humiliated over and over again. Hitler would have never been able to sway the German population had they not been deeply denigrated by the Versailles Treaty. President Donald Trump, whose divisive style of communication is widely criticized both within and outside the United States, could not have gotten such wide support during the 2016 US election campaign if Americans did not feel humiliated and stepped on by that country's political elite. The people presidential candidate Hillary Clinton called "deplorables" were never going to vote for her. Young people everywhere, treated as deplorables, would not be attracted to extremist groups—or to violence at all—if they felt included, seen, and valued in our societies.

The Nobel Peace Prize is a symbolic reference as to how we, as a society, are doing. It shows how our leaders are functioning right now. By keeping the selection process a secret, by selecting state leaders who keep up the status quo, by arrogantly justifying winners as a slap in other people's faces, and by staying loyal to political and financial interests instead of Nobel's spirit and intentions, the committee is participating in keeping societal dysfunctions alive.

Trust is the glue that holds people together. Without trust, it doesn't matter if we do everything else right. That is also true for the Nobel Peace Prize Committee. When the Nobel Committee selects winners who maintain power and greed as the underlying values, the divide between the world leaders and their people deepens. Distrust does not unify people. Neither does humiliation. Both are divisive to the brotherhood between people and nations.

THE IMPORTANCE OF VALUES

Leaders' behavior has a ripple effect down to the individual on the street. When trust is low, because we ignore trust issues at the expense of an organization's success, we get a divided society filled with people who don't lean on each other because they're not certain that the person next to them will have their backs.

All humans have a responsibility in that we are contributing to maintaining a vicious cycle of humiliation and distrust in the world. Many of our leaders are not courageous enough to end our overexploitation of the world's natural resources. They also ignore the fact that our use of cheap labor and overconsumption is humiliating to a large part of the world.

To create brotherhood across borders, a peace champion must have the courage to oppose dysfunctional leadership and speak to those feelings of humiliation—as they are the underlying reasons for most conflicts, violence, and war—and make people feel seen and valued.

If the Norwegian Nobel Peace Prize Committee is to restore trust and meaning in the most prestigious prize in the world, it's essential that the committee makes its selection according to established values. The world and conflicts may evolve. Values do not. These must be Nobel's values, of course, not the Norwegian government's or the committee members' personal values.

In Chapter One, we saw that even though Nobel's last will didn't specifically express his values, his life and career do. He wished his peace champions to share his love of humanity, have the courage to stand up to greed and selfish leadership, and do work that unifies people through peaceful means.

Love. Courage. Unity. Leaders who love their people will put the people's needs before their own personal advancement. These leaders' mission is to create a better world for everyone, not just a select few. They will stand up for what's right, even if that means losing an election or risk being unpopular. Such leaders will unify people by empowering them, making sure they know that they matter and are worthy.

The Nobel Peace Prize, through Alfred Nobel's values, should be used to address those underlying reasons for conflict and thus restore dignity and trust through equality, diversity, and cooperation.

DEFINING PEACE

"Peace is an easy word to say in any language," former UN secretary-general Javier Pérez de Cuéllar said in his 1988 Nobel lecture on behalf of the UN peacekeeping forces. "I hear it so frequently from so many different sources that it sometimes seems to me to be a general incantation more or less deprived of practical meaning."

To restore meaning in Nobel's prize, there is a need to define "peace." To accommodate Nobel's vision in contemporary times, a broader interpretation might be necessary. Malala may not be a peace champion in Nobel's original definition of the term. Neither was Mother Teresa or Al Gore. But perhaps the narrow, literal interpretation of Nobel's will is obsolete.

"You can't build peace on empty stomachs," 1949 peace prize recipient John Boyd Orr said. He raises a valid point.

"Peace cannot be maintained unless people are capable of maintaining it," Mukesh Rawat, a New Delhi-based freelance journalist wrote on October 18, 2014, in *The Diplomat*. "And people become capable of maintaining peace when they are liberated from poverty, illiteracy, and repression."

Human dignity is important to sustain peace, which supports humanitarian efforts, poverty elevation, and human rights activism as part of work toward brotherhood between nations. In addition to active and direct disarmament, perhaps the rights to education and prodemocracy movements should also be included. Without resources such as clean air, water, and food, riots would break out, which speaks in favor of environmental campaigns.

No matter the changes or inclusions the committee wishes to make to Nobel's will, they must be done through official channels, and with the agreement of the Nobel Foundation. The manner in which the committee has widened the scope of Nobel's last will, so far, is at best clumsy. At worst, it's hubristic. By not going through proper channels to widen the peace prize scope, the committee has created uncertainty and diminished the impact of the prize. The committee, according to Nordlinger, seems to say, "We admire you, we support you, you are our flavor of the month. Therefore we will reward you. And we'll call it peace."

Who will be deemed peace champions in the future? If the committee is allowed to continue to do as it pleases, what causes will fall under the peace umbrella? In Chapter Two, I wrote about how the Nobel Peace Prize has become a big enterprise and marketing tool for Norway and the committee. Awarding celebrities is part of the committee's, albeit perhaps unconscious, hunger to show its self-importance. Inviting other celebrities, such as Oprah Winfrey, Meryl Streep, and Tom Cruise, to host the peace prize concert in the evening of the ceremony confirms that need. As to the laureates, most state leaders or famous people do not need Nobel's prize to do their jobs. They already have a platform.

"And if the Nobel Peace Prize is boring, rather than flashy? So be it," Nordlinger wrote. "One Oscar ceremony is enough. Hollywood does Hollywood better than Oslo does."

Had Nobel known what would become of his prize, he would probably have been more specific in his last words.

But there is reason for optimism. We can restore trust and credibility in the Nobel Peace Prize, and it can again become a beacon of hope, role-modeling honorable and unifying leadership. To do that, the Nobel Committee has to declare which values it will follow and develop a set of clear guidelines in cooperation with the Nobel Foundation in Stockholm.

In order to maintain its integrity and do the work Nobel intended, the prize:

- Should not be given by political veterans of the governing parties, but by a committee consisting of members who have a proven interest in the peace movement. These members may be of different nationalities or only Norwegians, but they need to be supported by international researchers and experts who can provide information on each nominated candidate.

- Should be focused on the definition of peace according to Nobel's will, or according to a public list of work considered within the scope of Nobel's intention. A new scope of the Nobel Peace Prize must be made through legal channels and approved by the Nobel Foundation in Stockholm, according to the Swedish Foundations Act.

- Should implement a transparent selection process, which should include making the list of nominees and nominators public. The necessary changes in the bylaws must, again, be validated by the Nobel Foundation.

Somewhere between Nobel's vision and the present day, something went wrong. Norway took itself too seriously. Now it is time for the Nobel Foundation in Stockholm to exercise its legal right to restore the meaning, honor, and integrity of the prize. Perhaps then, the prize will mean what it was intended to. Until then, the committee will continue on its many roads toward peace, and ultimately prove Tony Blair right.

"If I win the Nobel Peace Prize," he said while he was attempting to solve the Arab-Israeli conflict, "you will know I have failed."

LIST OF NOBEL PEACE PRIZE LAUREATES

—✄—

1901	Jean Henry Dunant and Frédéric Passy
1902	Élie Ducommun and Charles Albert Gobat
1903	William Randal Cremer
1904	The Institute of International Law
1905	Baroness Bertha Sophie Felicita von Suttner
1906	Theodore Roosevelt
1907	Ernesto Teodoro Moneta and Louis Renault
1908	Klas Pontus Arnoldson and Fredrik Bajer
1909	Auguste Marie François Beernaert and Paul Henri Benjamin Balluet d'Estournelles de Constant
1910	The Permanent International Peace Bureau
1911	Tobias Michael Carel Asser and Alfred Hermann Fried
1912	Elihu Root
1913	Henri La Fontaine
1917	The International Committee of the Red Cross
1919	Thomas Woodrow Wilson
1920	Léon Victor Auguste Bourgeois
1921	Karl Hjalmar Branting and Christian Lous Lange
1922	Fridtjof Nansen
1925	Sir Austen Chamberlain and Charles Gates Dawes
1926	Aristide Briand and Gustav Stresemann
1927	Ferdinand Buisson and Ludwig Quidde
1929	Frank Billings Kellogg

1930   Lars Olof Jonathan (Nathan) Söderblom
1931   Jane Addams and Nicholas Murray Butler
1933   Sir Norman Angell (Ralph Lane)
1934   Arthur Henderson
1935   Carl von Ossietzky
1936   Carlos Saavedra Lamas
1937   Lord Edgar Algernon Robert Gascoyne Cecil
1938   The Nansen International Office for Refugees
1944   The International Committee of the Red Cross
1945   Cordell Hull
1946   Emily Greene Balch and John Raleigh Mott
1947   The Friends Service Council and the American Friends Service
        Committee
1949   Lord John Boyd Orr of Brechin
1950   Ralph Bunche
1951   Léon Jouhaux
1952   Albert Schweitzer
1953   George Catlett Marshall
1954   The Office of the UN High Commissioner for Refugees
1957   Lester Bowles Pearson
1958   Father Dominique Georges Pire
1959   Philip J. Noel-Baker
1960   Albert John Lutuli
1961   Dag Hjalmar Agne Carl Hammarskjöld
1962   Linus Carl Pauling
1963   The International Committee of the Red Cross and the League of
        Red Cross Societies
1964   Martin Luther King, Jr.
1965   The United Nations Children's Fund (known by its original acronym
        UNICEF)
1968   René Cassin
1969   The International Labour Organization

1970   Norman E. Borlaug

1971   Willy Brandt

1973   Henry A. Kissinger and Le Duc Tho

1974   Seán MacBride and Eisaku Sato

1975   Andrei Dmitrievich Sakharov

1976   Betty Williams and Mairead Corrigan

1977   Amnesty International

1978   Mohamed Anwar al-Sadat and Menachem Begin

1979   Mother Teresa

1980   Adolfo Pérez Esquivel

1981   The Office of the UN High Commissioner for Refugees

1982   Alva Myrdal and Alfonso García Robles

1983   Lech Walesa

1984   Desmond Mpilo Tutu

1985   International Physicians for the Prevention of Nuclear War

1986   Elie Wiesel

1987   Óscar Arias Sánchez

1988   The UN Peacekeeping Forces

1989   The 14th Dalai Lama (Tenzin Gyatso)

1990   Mikhail Sergeyevich Gorbachev

1991   Aung San Suu Kyi

1992   Rigoberta Menchú Tum

1993   Nelson Mandela and Frederik Willem de Klerk

1994   Yasser Arafat, Shimon Peres, and Yitzhak Rabin

1995   Joseph Rotblat and the Pugwash Conference on Science and World Affairs

1996   Carlos Filipe Ximenes Belo and José Ramos-Horta

1997   The International Campaign to Ban Landmines and Jody Williams

1998   John Hume and David Trimble

1999   Médecins sans Frontières (Doctors Without Borders)

2000   Kim Dae-jung

2001   The United Nations and Kofi Annan

2002   Jimmy Carter
2003   Shirin Ebadi
2004   Wangari Muta Maathai
2005   The International Atomic Energy Agency and Mohamed ElBaradei
2006   Muhammad Yunus and Grameen Bank
2007   The Intergovernmental Panel on Climate Change and
        Albert Arnold (Al) Gore, Jr.
2008   Martti Ahtisaari
2009   Barack Hussein Obama
2010   Liu Xiaobo
2011   Ellen Johnson Sirleaf, Leymah Gbowee, and Tawakkol Karman
2012   European Union
2013   Organisation for the Prohibition of Chemical Weapons
2014   Kailash Satyarthi and Malala Yousafzai
2015   Tunisian National Dialogue Quartet
2016   Juan Manuel Santos
2017   International Campaign to Abolish Nuclear Weapons (ICAN)
2018   Denis Mukwege and Nadia Murad
2019   Abiy Ahmed Ali

ALFRED NOBEL'S LAST WILL

—⁓—

I, THE UNDERSIGNED, Alfred Bernhard Nobel, after mature delibera-
tion, hereby declare the following to be my last will and testament with
regard to such property as I may leave upon my death:

My nephews, Hjalmar and Ludvig Nobel, sons of my brother Robert Nobel,
will each receive the sum of two hundred thousand crowns;

My nephew Emmanuel Nobel will receive the sum of three hundred thousand, and my niece Mina Nobel one hundred thousand crowns;

My brother Robert Nobel's daughters, Ingeborg and Tyra, will each receive
the sum of one hundred thousand crowns;

Miss Olga Boettger, presently residing with Mrs Brand, 10 Rue St Florentin
in Paris, will receive one hundred thousand francs;

Mrs Sofie Kapy von Kapivar, whose address is known to the Anglo-
Oesterreichische Bank in Vienna, is entitled to an annuity of 6000 florins Ö.W.
which will be paid to her by the aforementioned bank, and to this end I have deposited in this bank the amount of 150 000 florins in Hungarian sovereign bonds.

Mr Alarik Liedbeck, residing at 26 Sturegatan, Stockholm, will receive one
hundred thousand crowns;

Miss Elise Antun, residing at 32 Rue de Lubeck, Paris, is entitled to an annuity of two thousand five hundred francs. In addition, she is entitled to be repaid forty-eight thousand francs of capital that belongs to her and is currently deposited with me;

Mr Alfred Hammond, of Waterford, Texas, United States, will receive ten thousand dollars;

Miss Emmy Winkelmann and Miss Marie Winkelmann, of Potsdamerstrasse 51, Berlin, will each receive fifty thousand marks;

Mrs Gaucher, of 2 bis Boulevard du Viaduc, Nimes, France will receive one hundred thousand francs;

My servants, Auguste Oswald and his wife Alphonse Tournand, employed at my laboratory at San Remo, will each receive an annuity of one thousand francs;

My former servant, Joseph Girardot, of 5 Place St. Laurent, Châlons sur Saône, France, is entitled to an annuity of five hundred francs, and my former gardener, Jean Lecof, residing with Mrs Desoutter, receveur Curaliste, Mesnil, Aubry pour Ecouen, S.& O., France, will receive an annuity of three hundred francs.

Mr Georges Fehrenbach, of 2 Rue Compiègne, Paris, is entitled to collect an annual pension of five thousand francs from 1 January [1896] to 1 January 1899, when it will cease.

My brother's children – Hjalmar, Ludvig, Ingeborg and Tyra – each have a sum of twenty thousand crowns, deposited with me against acknowledgement of receipt, which will be repaid to them;

All of my remaining realizable assets are to be disbursed as follows: the capital, converted to safe securities by my executors, is to constitute a fund, the interest on which is to be distributed annually as prizes to those who, during the preceding year, have conferred the greatest benefit to mankind. The interest is to be divided into five equal parts and distributed as follows: one part to the person who made the most important discovery or invention in the field of physics; one part to the person who made the most important chemical discovery or improvement; one part to the person who made the most important discovery within the domain of physiology or medicine; one part to the person who, in the field of literature, produced the most outstanding work in an idealistic direction; and one part to the person who has done the most or best to advance fellowship among nations, the abolition or reduction of standing armies, and the establishment and promotion of peace congresses. The prizes for physics and chemistry are to be awarded by the Swedish Academy of Sciences; that for physiological or medical achievements by the Karolinska Institute in Stockholm; that for literature by the Academy in Stockholm; and that for champions of peace by a committee of five persons to be selected by the Norwegian Storting. It is my express wish that when awarding the prizes, no consideration be given to nationality, but that the prize be awarded to the worthiest person, whether or not they are Scandinavian.

As executors of my testamentary dispositions, I appoint Mr Ragnar Sohlman, resident in Bofors, Värmland, and Mr Rudolf Liljequist, of 31 Malmskillnadsgatan, Stockholm, and Bengtsfors, close to Uddevalla. As compensation for their attention and efforts, I grant to Mr Ragnar Sohlman, who will probably devote most time to this matter, one hundred thousand crowns, and to Mr Rudolf Liljequist, fifty thousand crowns;

My assets currently consist partly of real estate in Paris and San Remo, and partly of securities deposited with the Union Bank of Scotland Ltd in Glasgow and London, with Crédit Lyonnais, Comptoir National d'Escompte, and with Alphen, Messin & Co. in Paris; with stockbroker M.V. Peter of Banque Transatlantique, also in Paris; with the Direction der Disconto Gesellschaft and with Joseph Goldschmidt & Cie in Berlin; with the Russian Central Bank, and with Mr Emmanuel Nobel in Petersburg; with Skandinaviska Kreditaktiebolaget in Gothenburg and Stockholm, with Enskilda Banken in Stockholm and in my strong box at 59 Avenue Malakoff, Paris; as well as of accounts receivable, patents, patent fees or royalties due to me, etc. about which my executors will find information in my papers and books.

As of now, this will and testament is the only one that is valid, and revokes all my previous testamentary dispositions, should any such be found after my death.

Finally, it is my express wish that following my death, my arteries be severed, and when this has been done and competent doctors have confirmed clear signs of death, my remains be incinerated in a crematorium.

Paris, 27 November, 1895
Alfred Bernhard Nobel

We, the undersigned witnesses, attest that Mr Alfred Bernhard Nobel, being of sound mind and of his own free will, signed this document, which he declared in the presence of us all to be his last will and testament:

Sigurd Ehrenborg
former Lieutenant
Paris: 84 Boulevard Haussmann

R. W. Strehlenert
Civil Engineer
4, Passage Caroline

Thos Nordenfelt
Constructor
8, Rue Auber, Paris

Leonard Hwass
Civil Engineer
4, Passage Caroline

Translated from Swedish by Jeffrey Ganellen 2018, Nobel Peace Prize website.

ACKNOWLEDGMENTS

—◊—

BEHIND ANY PROJECT is a team of people who believed and who contributed. My grateful heart goes out to the following:

A special thanks to Michael Nobel, for generously sharing your knowledge and insights into your great grand-uncle Alfred Nobel's mind and mission. I'm honored to know you, and deeply grateful for your support and foreword to this book.

Bonnie Hearn Hill has been with me on this journey since this book was just an idea in my head. Without you, I would not be a writer, this book would not have happened, and it would certainly not be what it is today. You believed in me before I believed in myself and you gave me the courage to express my truth. You are a true rock star and role model.

A huge thanks to Jessica Case and her team at Pegasus Books for believing in me a second time and for giving me and my books a home. We couldn't be in better hands.

To my agent, Beth Davey, for your enthusiasm and for having my back.

Gratitude also to Karen Lacey and Meg DesCamp for your edits and for helping me formulate my message clearly throughout the book.

Gabi Gleichman, for your friendship, mentorship, and for making me feel okay with living in Norway. Thank you.

To Bo Eason for giving me permission to be the best. Kymberlee Weill for giving me confidence on stage, and Jeffrey Van Dyk for reminding me of who I am and what I'm here on this planet to do.

To my squad: Greg Smith, Eric Hodgdon, John Mattes, Michelle Brady, Candice Michelle—for seeing me, being my family, always having my back. I have yours' too.

Mariette Fourmeaux for taking me to prison and for showing me the true meaning of brilliance inside.

Immense gratitude to the following people for their assistance, encouragements, inspiration, and friendship:

Stuart Barton, Geneva Bray, Nico Klein, Mark Cohen, Mehran Azmoudeh, Harald Ludwig, Mark Minevich, Annika Pergament, Michael O'Looney, Stephanie Clark, George Perry, Mary Darling, Barbet Smith, Derek Shearer, Sue Toigo, Siobhan Darrow, Alexandra Caminer, Cavan Linde, Devin Adair, Trent Huffman, T.R. Pescod, Louise and Max Armour, Nathalie and Alex Neury, Hazel Dixon-Cooper, John Brantingham, Jennifer Bedasci, Christopher Poe, Rune Folkedal, Pål Troye, Sophie Rolfsen, Mara Hank Moret, Mariana Pictet, Lisa McNeill, Fawziyah de Sousa-Azevedo, Britta Carpigo, Natascha Armleder, Anne Lombardini, Christina Swenson, Nina Green-Revelsby, Isabella Krasniqi, Hanne Sagstuen, Janne Eikeland, Anja Nitteberg, Lisa Cooper, Marcelle Askew, Birger Løkeng.

Ellen Willas, Andrea Belck-Olsen and the HER-community—my sisters, my tribe.

The Turrettini-clan who have so graciously received me into their family. Special thanks to Sophie, Jean, Emily, and Vanessa. To the Keller clan, especially Claire-Jeanne and Pierre.

Finally, I express gratitude to my husband, Samuel, and our children Axel and Ella—you are the great loves of my life. Without you none of what I do would make any sense. Sam, thank you for accepting me as I am and for believing in me. For your unwavering support in every aspect of my new career. For your integrity, for being my rock, and the best husband and father to our children I could ask for. If all leaders were like you, our world would be a better place. You are a true peace champion and I love you.

NOTES

—※—

INTRODUCTION PRIZE AND PARADOX

1 "Fredsprisens pris" ("The Price of the Peace Prize"), *NRK Brennpunkt*, October 7, 2014.

2 Michael Nobel, "I strid med Nobels vilje" ("Contrary to the Will of Nobel"), *Aftenposten*, December 10, 2011, https://www.aftenposten.no/meninger/i/wP6y1/i-strid-med-nobels-vilje. Michael Nobel, interview, April 23, 2015.

1: ALFRED AND BERTHA

1 Tore Frängsmyr, "Alfred Nobel, Life and Philosophy," Nobelprize.org, March 26, 1996, https://www.nobelprize.org/alfred-nobel/alfred-nobel-life-and-philosophy/.

2 Michael Nobel, interview, April 23, 2015.

3 Kenne Fant, *Alfred Nobel: A Biography* (New York: Arcade Publishing, 1993).

4 Michael Nobel, interview, April 23, 2015.

5 Fant, *Alfred Nobel*.

6 Jay Nordlinger, *Peace, They Say: A History of the Nobel Peace Prize, the Most Famous and Controversial Prize in the World* (New York: Encounter Books, 2012).

7 Fant, *Alfred Nobel*.

8 *Ibid.*

9 Frängsmyr, "Alfred Nobel, Life and Philosophy."

10 Fant, *Alfred Nobel*.

11 *Ibid.*

12 *Ibid.*

13 *Ibid.*

14 *Ibid.*

15 *Ibid.*

16 *Ibid.*

17 Michael Meyer, "The Richest Vagabond," *New York Review of Books*, January 13, 1994.

18 Michael Nobel, interview, April 23, 2015.

2: COMMITTEE OF SECRECY

1 Fredrik S. Heffermehl, *The Nobel Peace Prize: What Nobel Really Wanted* (Santa Barbara, CA: Praeger, 2010).

2   Frängsmyr, "Alfred Nobel, Life and Philosophy."
3   Michael Nobel, interview, April 23, 2015.
4   Fant, *Alfred Nobel*. Michael Nobel, interview, April 23, 2015.
5   Øyvind Tønnesson, "The Norwegian Nobel Committee," Nobelprize.org, December 1, 1999, https://www.nobelprize.org/prizes/themes/the-norwegian -nobel-institute/.
6   Sheila Rule, "UN Peacekeeping Forces Named Winner of the Nobel Peace Prize," Special to *New York Times*, September 30, 1988.
7   Nordlinger, *Peace, They Say.*
8   Heffermehl, *The Nobel Peace Prize.*
9   Helge Pharo, interview, *New York Times Magazine*, January 11, 2013.
10 Nobel, "I strid med Nobels vilje."
11 Heffermehl, *The Nobel Peace Prize.*
12 *Ibid.*
13 Nobel, "I strid med Nobels vilje."
14 Michael Nobel, interview, April 23, 2015.
15 "Fredsprisens pris," *NRK Brennpunkt.*
16 *Ibid.*
17 Erik Solheim, interview by *NRK Brennpunkt*, "Fredsprisens pris" ("The Price of the Peace Prize"), *NRK Brennpunkt*, October 7, 2014.
18 *Ibid.*
19 "The Nobel Peace Prize 2011," NobelPrize.org, https://www.nobelprize.org/prizes /peace/2011/summary/.
20 Heffermehl, *The Nobel Peace Prize.*
21 *Ibid.*

3: NORWEGIAN EXCEPTIONALISM
1   Nordlinger, *Peace, They Say.*
2   Nobelprize.org.
3   Lisa Miller, "25 Reasons Norway Is The Greatest Place On Earth," *Huffington Post*, January 7, 2014, https://www.huffpost.com/entry/norway-greatest-place-on -earth_n_4550413.
4   Tove Lie and Øystein Mikalsen, *Fredsnasjonens grenseløse våpenhandel* (*The Unlimited Weapons Trade of a Peace-Nation*) (Oslo: Aschehoug, 2012).
5   "SWFI Sovereign Wealth Fund Rankings, 2014 : Norway's Government Pension Fund ranked number one with U.S. $893 billion" (swfinstitute.org).
6   www.newsinenglish.no.
7   The Government Pension Fund, (regjeringen.no).
8   Lie and Mikalsen, *Fredsnasjonens grenseløse våpenhandel.*
9   Heffermehl, *The Nobel Peace Prize.*
10 *Ibid.*

11 Geir Lundestad, interview in *Aftenposten*, October 17, 2007. Heffermehl, *The Nobel Peace Prize*.

12 Geir Lundestad, interview.

4: PEACE PRIZE IN A WORLD OF WAR

1 Asle Sveen, interview by *NRK Brennpunkt*, "Fredsprisens pris" ("The Price of the Peace Prize"), *NRK Brennpunkt*, October 7, 2014.

2 Nordlinger, *Peace, They Say.*

3 "Elihu Root, Biographical," NobelPrize.org, accessed July 30, 2020, https://www.nobelprize.org/prizes/peace/1912/root/biographical/. Frederick W. Haberman, ed., *Nobel Lectures: Peace 1901–1925* (Amsterdam: Elsevier Publishing Company, 1972), 264.

4 Nordlinger, *Peace, They Say.*

5 "Elihu Root, Biographical," NobelPrize.org, accessed July 30, 2020, https://www.nobelprize.org/prizes/peace/1912/root/biographical/. Haberman, *Nobel Lectures*, 264.

6 Nobelprize.org.

7 Nordlinger, *Peace, They Say.*

8 *Ibid.*

5: INCONSISTENT CHOICES

1 Stephen E. Ambrose, *Citizen Soldiers: The U.S. Army from the Normandy Beaches to the Bulge to the Surrender of Germany* (New York: Simon and Schuster, 1997), 271-84. William R. Keast, *Provision of Enlisted Replacements, Army Ground Forces Study No. 7.* Historical Section—Headquarters Army Ground Forces, 314.7 (September 1, 1946). Washington, D.C., GNHIS. September 1, 1945.

2 Andreas Enderlin, "The Marshall Plan and the Cold War," Historyinanhour.com, February 9, 2012.

3 Nordlinger, *Peace, They Say.*

4 Nobelprize.org.

6: PISTOLS AMONG THE OLIVE BRANCHES

1 Heffermehl, *The Nobel Peace Prize.*

2 Associated Press, January 7, 1994. Israel Government Press Office "Palestinian Incitement To Violence Since Oslo: A Four-Year Compendium," Israel Ministry of Foreign Affairs, August 10, 1997, https://mfa.gov.il/mfa/foreignpolicy/peace/mfadocuments/pages/palestinian%20incitement%20to%20violence%20since%20oslo-%20a%20f.aspx.

3 *Haaretz*, November 22, 1994. Israel Government Press Office "Palestinian Incitement To Violence Since Oslo."

4 Nordlinger, *Peace, They Say.*

5 *Ibid.*

6   *Ibid.*

7   *Ibid.*

8   Asle Sveen, interview.

9   Nordlinger, *Peace, They Say.*

7: DEVALUING WOMEN

1   Lov om likestilling mellom kjønnene (likestillingsloven) (Gender Equality Act),
    Norwegian Ministry of Children and Equality, June 21, 2013, https://lovdata.no
    /dokument/LTI/lov/2013-06-21-59.

2   Alice Lee, "Gender Quotas Worked In Norway, Why Not Here?" *New Republic*,
    September 5, 2014.

3   Phyllis Chesler, *Woman's Inhumanity to Woman* (New York: Laurence Hill Books, 2009).

4   Nobelprize.org.

5   David Stoll, *Rigoberta Menchú and the Story of All Poor Guatemalans*, expanded
    edition (Abingdon-on-Thames, UK: Routledge, 2007).

6   Larry Rother, "TARNISHED LAUREATE: A Special Report; Nobel Winner
    Finds Her Story Challenged," *New York Times*, December 15, 1998.

7   Nobelprize.org.

8   "A Worthy Winner," *NRK Brennpunkt*, 2012.

9   *Ibid.*

10 "Cora Weiss Interviewed by GPF's Catherine Defontaine," by Catherine
    Defontaine, *Global Policy Forum*, December 2011, https://www.globalpolicy.org
    /security-council/peacekeeping/analysis-and-articles-on-peacekeeping/51103-cora
    -weiss-interviewed-by-gpfs-catherine-defontaine.html.

11 "Cora Weiss Oral History Project," Columbia Center for Oral History Research,
    accessed July 30, 2020, https://www.ccohr.incite.columbia.edu/cora-weiss-oral
    -history.

8: UNITED NATIONS: A LOVE AFFAIR

1   Nobelprize.org.

2   Max Boot, "Paving the Road to Hell: The Failure of UN Peacekeeping," *Foreign
    Affairs*, March/April 2000, https://www.foreignaffairs.com/reviews/review-essay
    /2000-03-01/paving-road-hell-failure-un-peacekeeping.

3   Nordlinger, *Peace, They Say.*

4   Nobelprize.org.

5   Nordlinger, *Peace, They Say*, p. 273.

6   un.org.

7   *Ibid.*

8   "Where We Operate," United Nations Peacekeeping, https://peacekeeping.un.org
    /en/where-we-operate.

9   David Bosco, "The Price of Peace," *Foreign Policy*, May 30, 2013.

10 Julian Borger and Mark Tran, "UN Votes to Increase Somalia Peacekeeping Force," *Guardian*, February 22, 2012, https://www.theguardian.com/world/2012/feb/22 /somalia-un-peacekeeping-force.

11 Editorial, "Somalia: Chronicle of Failure," *Guardian*, February 22, 2012, https://www .theguardian.com/commentisfree/2012/feb/22/somalia-chronicle-of-failure.

12 CNN, April 17, 1997, (edition.cnn.com).

13 "'May We All Learn and Act on the Lessons of Srebrenica.' Says Secretary-General, in Message to Anniversary Ceremony," United Nations Press Release, July 11, 2005, https://www.un.org/press/en/2005/sgsm9993.doc.htm.

14 "The Fall of Srebrenica and the Failure of UN Peacekeeping," *Human Rights Watch*, October 1995, Volume 7, No. 13.

15 Chris McGreal, "What's the Point of Peacekeepers When They Don't Keep the Peace," *The Guardian*, September 17, 205, accessed July 30, 2020, https://www.the guardian.com/world/2015/sep/17/un-united-nations-peacekeepers-rwanda-bosnia.

16 Sudhir Chella Rajan, "Global Politics and Institutions: A 'Utopistic' View," *Economic and Political Weekly* 42, no. 41 (2007): 4174-182, www.jstor.org/stable/40276552.

17 Dore Gold, *Tower of Babble: How the United Nations Has Fueled Global Chaos* (New York: Crown Forum, 2005).

18 "UN Admits Rwanda Genocide Failure," *BBC News*, April 15, 2000, http://news.bbc .co.uk/2/hi/africa/714025.stm.

19 A. Walter Dorn, Jonathan Matloff, and Jennifer Matthews, "Preventing the Bloodbath: Could the UN have Predicted and Prevented the Rwanda Genocide?" November, 1999, accessed July 30, 2020, https://walterdorn.net/35-preventing-the -bloodbath-could-the-un-have-predicted-and-prevented-the-rwanda-genocide-20.

20 Nordlinger, *Peace, They Say*, p. 274.

21 Max Boot, "Paving the Road to Hell."

22 Sudarsan Raghavan, "Record Number of UN Peacekeepers Fails to Stop African Wars," *Washington Post*, January 3, 2014, https://www.washingtonpost.com/world /record-number-of-un-peacekeepers-fails-to-stop-african-wars/2014/01/03 /17ed0574-7487-11e3-9389-09ef9944065e_story.html.

23 "France Accused on Rwanda Killings," *BBC News*, October 24, 2006, http://news .bbc.co.uk/2/hi/africa/6079428.stm.

24 *New York Times*, August 6, 2008.

25 Michael Barnett, *Eyewitness to a Genocide: The United Nations and Rwanda*, (Ithaca, NY: Cornell University Press, 2003).

26 Nordlinger, *Peace, They Say*, p. 274.

27 Michael J. Jordan, "Sex Charges Haunt UN Forces," *Christian Science Monitor*, November 26, 2004, https://www.csmonitor.com/2004/1126/p06s02-wogi.html.

28 Nisha Lilia Diu, "What the UN Doesn't Want You to Know," *Telegraph*, February 6, 2012, https://www.telegraph.co.uk/culture/9041974/What-the-UN-Doesnt -Want-You-to-Know.html.

29 Nobelprize.org.

30 "Rolling up the Culprits," *The Economist*, March 13, 2008, https://www
    .economist.com/international/2008/03/13/rolling-up-the-culprits.

31 Colum Lynch, "Oil-for-Food Panel Rebukes Annan, Cites Corruption,"
    Washington Post, September 8, 2005, https://www.washingtonpost.com/archive
    /politics/2005/09/08/oil-for-food-panel-rebukes-annan-cites-corruption/08aaeb81
    -9cbc-488a-814d-27a629f51893/.

32 *Ibid.*

33 Nile Gardiner, "The Cotecna Memorandum: End of the Road for Kofi Annan?"
    The Heritage Foundation, June 15, 2005, https://www.heritage.org/report/the
    -cotecna-memorandum-end-the-road-kofi-annan.

34 Nobelprize.org.

35 Nordlinger, *Peace, They Say*, p. 342.

36 *Ibid*, p. 342.

37 *Ibid*, p. 341.

38 Roméo Dallaire, *Shake Hands with the Devil: The Failure of Humanity in Rwanda*
    (London: Arrow Books, 2004).

39 Nordlinger, *Peace, They Say*, p. 341.

40 *Ibid.*

41 Ian Black, "Kofi Annan Resigns as Syria Envoy," *Guardian*, August 2, 2012,
    https://www.theguardian.com/world/2012/aug/02/kofi-annan-resigns-syria-envoy.

9: POLITICAL CURRENCY

1   Heffermehl, *The Nobel Peace Prize*.

2   "Remembering Lyndon Johnson," *Presidential History Geeks* (blog), January 22,
    2020, accessed July 30, 2020, https://potus-geeks.livejournal.com/1170366.html.

3   *The Trials of Henry Kissinger*, a 2002 documentary based on Christopher Hitchens's
    book about the Nobel laureate and famous US diplomat. *The Trials of Henry
    Kissinger*, directed by Eugene Jarecki (2002).

4   *Ibid.*

5   *Ibid.*

6   *Ibid.*

7   *Ibid.*

8   *Ibid.*

9   Christopher Hitchens, *The Trials of Henry Kissinger* (New York: Twelve, 2012).

10 *The Trials of Henry Kissinger*, Jarecki.

11 *BBC News Magazine* article from December 24, 2012.

12 Nordlinger, *Peace, They Say*.

13 *The Trials of Henry Kissinger*, Jarecki.

14 Asle Sveen, interview.

15 Nobelprize.org.

10: ET SPARK I LEGGEN

1 Nordlinger, *Peace, They Say.*
2 *Ibid.*
3 The Carter Center, www.cartercenter.org.
4 Nobelprize.org.
5 Nordlinger, *Peace, They Say.*
6 Gold, *Tower of Babble.*
7 Nordlinger, *Peace, They Say.*
8 *Ibid.*
9 Nobelprize.org.
10 Nordlinger, *Peace, They Say.*
11 Nobelprize.org.
12 Michael Jansen, "'We Understand Each Other': An Irishwoman's Diary on Ireland and the Middle East," *The Irish Times*, October 22, 2018, https://www.irishtimes .com/opinion/we-understand-each-other-an-irishwoman-s-diary-on-ireland-and -the-middle-east-1.3670701.
13 Nordlinger, *Peace, They Say.*
14 Christi Parsons and W. J. Hennigan, "President Obama, who hoped to sow peace, instead lead the nation in war," *LA Times*, January 13, 2017, https://www.latimes .com/projects/la-na-pol-obama-at-war/.
15 John Feffer "The Comparative Politics of Atrocity," *HuffPost*, March 5, 2015, https://www.huffpost.com/entry/the-comparative-politics_b_6808614.
16 Parsons and Hennigan, "President Obama, who hoped to sow peace, instead lead the nation in war."
17 *Ibid.*

11: BANKER TO THE POOR

1 "Muhammad Yunus: Facts" NobelPrize.org, accessed July 30, 2020, https://www .nobelprize.org/prizes/peace/2006/yunus/facts/.
2 *Ibid.*
3 "Fanget i mikrogjeld" ("Caught in Micro Debt"), *NRK Brennpunkt*, November 2010.
4 Milford Bateman, *Why Doesn't Microfinance Work? The Destructive Rise of Local Neoliberalism* (London: Zed Books, 2012).
5 Dean Mitchell Jolliffe and Divyanshi Wadhwa, "Nearly 1 in 2 in the World Lives Under $5.50 a day," *World Bank Blogs* (blog), October 24, 2018, https://blogs .worldbank.org/opendata/nearly-1-2-world-lives-under-550-day.
6 "Fanget i mikrogjeld," *NRK Brennpunkt.*
7 David Roodman, "Quick: What's the Grameen Bank's Interest Rate?" Center for Global Development, September 24, 2010, https://www.cgdev.org/blog/quick -whats-grameen-banks-interest-rate.

8 "Hundreds of Suicides in India Linked to Microfinance Organizations," *Business Insider*, February 24, 2012, https://www.businessinsider.com/hundreds-of-suicides-in-india-linked-to-microfinance-organizations-2012-2.

9 *NRK Brennpunkt.*

10 Nordlinger, *Peace, They Say.*

11 "Fanget i mikrogjeld," *NRK Brennpunkt.*

12: GANDHI: OVERLOOKED AND DISREGARDED

1 Heffermehl, *The Nobel Peace Prize.*

2 Nobelprize.org

3 *Ibid.*

4 Øyvind Tønnesson, "Mahatma Gandhi, the Missing Laureate," Nobelprize.org, December 1, 1999, https://www.nobelprize.org/prizes/themes/mahatma-gandhi-the-missing-laureate/.

5 Eknath Easwaran, *Gandhi the Man: How One Man Changed Himself to Change the World*, 4th ed. (Tomales, CA: Nilgiri Press, 2011).

6 Mahatma Gandhi and Louis Fischer, *The Essential Gandhi: An Anthology of His Writings on His Life, Work, and Ideas* (1962; repr., New York: Vintage, 2012).

7 M. K. Gandhi, *An Autobiography* (New York: Penguin Modern Classics, 2001), Kindle ebook.

8 B. R. Nanda, "Mahatma Gandhi: Indian leader," *Encyclopaedia Britannica*, accessed July 26, 2020, https://www.britannica.com/biography/Mahatma-Gandhi/Place-in-history.

9 *Ibid.*

10 *Ibid.*

11 *Ibid.*

12 *Ibid.*

13 "46. The Gandhi-Smuts compromise explained," South African History Online, January 13, 2012, Updated June 18, 2019, https://www.sahistory.org.za/archive/46-gandhi-smuts-compromise-explained.

14 Nanda, "Mahatma Gandhi."

15 Encyclopedia Britannica.

16 "'The Stain of Indigo' and Gandhi's Satyagraha in Champaran," IndianCulture.gov, accessed July 30, 2020, https://indianculture.gov.in/stories/gandhis-satyagraha-champaran.

17 Akrita Reyar, "Kheda Satyagraha: How Gandhi Made the Journey from Mohandas to Mahatma," *TimesNowNews.com*, September 20, 2019, accessed July 30, 2020, https://www.timesnownews.com/india/article/kheda-satyagraha-how-gandhi-made-the-journey-from-mohandas-to-mahatma/210282.

18 Vedika Kant, *If I Die Here, Who Will Remember Me: India and the First World War* (New Delhi: Roli Books, 2015).

19 Therlee Gipson, *India's Struggle: Justice and Compassion* (New Delhi: Lulu, 2019).

20 Nanda, "Mahatma Gandhi."
21 "Mohandas Karamchand Gandhi," *Incredible India*, accessed July 30, 2020, https://sites.google.com/site/increedibleindia/m-k-gandhi.
22 "Returning His Medals," Gandhian Institutions: Bombay Sarvodaya Mandal and Gandhi Research Foundation, accessed July 30, 2020, https://www.mkgandhi.org/short/ev6.htm.
23 The Editors of Encyclopedia Britannica, "Khilafat Movement," Encyclopedia Britannica, Inc., February 24, 2014, accessed July 30, 2020, https://www.britannica.com/event/Khilafat-movement.
24 Nanda, "Mahatma Gandhi."
25 Sujay Biswas, "Gandhi Denounced Caste and Untouchability," *National Herald India*, accessed July 30, 2020, https://www.nationalheraldindia.com/opinion/gandhi-denounced-caste-and-untouchability#:~:text=Gandhi%20declared%20that%20the%20.
26 Nanda, "Mahatma Gandhi."
27 *Ibid.*
28 *Ibid.*
29 *Ibid.*
30 *Ibid.*
31 *Ibid.*
32 Frank R. Moraes, "Jawaharla Nehru," Encyclopedia Britannica, Inc., May 23, 2020, accessed July 30, 2020, https://www.britannica.com/biography/Jawaharlal-Nehru.
33 Nanda, "Mahatma Gandhi."
34 *Ibid.*
35 *Ibid.*
36 *Ibid.*

13: OVERLOOKED PEACE CHAMPIONS

1 Heffermehl, *The Nobel Peace Prize.*
2 Michael Nobel, interview, April 23, 2015.
3 "Soka Gakkai Internatonal—USA: About Us," Soka Gakkai International—USA, accessed August 11, 2020, https://www.sgi-usa.org/about-us/.
4 *Ibid.*
5 "Daisaku Ikeda," Soka Gakkai International, accessed August 11, 2020, https://www.daisakuikeda.org/.
6 *Ibid.*
7 *Ibid.*
8 Sari Nusseibeh, *Once Upon a Country: A Palestinian Life* (2007; repr. London: Picador, 2008).
9 Sari Nusseibeh, *What Is a Palestinian State Worth?* (Cambridge, MA: Harvard University Press, 2011).

10 Jonathan Wittenberg, "Double Vision," review of *Once Upon a Country*, by Sari
    Nusseibeh, *The Gaurdian*, March 15, 2008, https://www.theguardian.com/book
    /2008/mar/15/politics.

11 "U Thant's Gamble," WalterDorn.net, http://walterdorn.net/151-unsung
    -mediator-u-thant-and-the-cuban-missile-crisis-u-thants-gamble.

12 Nobelprize.org.

13 Marlise Simons, "Pope in Haiti, Assails Inequality, Hunger and Fear," *New York
    Times*, March 10, 1983, https://www.nytimes.com/1983/03/10/world/pope-in
    -haiti-assails-inequality-hunger-and-fear.html.

14 Georgi Gotev, "Church Leader: John Paul II Left a Legacy in Kazakhstan,"
    EURACTIV, October 15, 2018, https://www.euractiv.com/section/central-asia
    /news/church-leader-john-paul-ii-left-a-legacy-in-kazakhstan/.

15 "John Paul II", BBC, April 27, 2011, https://www.bbc.co.uk/religion/religions
    /christianity/pope/johnpaulii_1.shtml#h5.

16 Richard Bernstein, "Pope Helped Bring Poland Its Freedom," *New York Times,*
    April 6, 2005, https://www.nytimes.com/2005/04/06/world/europe/pope-helped
    -bring-poland-its-freedom.html.

17 *Ibid.*

18 Rachel Sanderson, "The Scandal at the Vatican Bank," *FT Magazine*, December 6,
    2013.

19 *Ibid.*

20 Timothy Garton Ash, "The First World Leader," *Guardian*, April 3, 2005, https://www
    .theguardian.com/world/2005/apr/04/catholicism.religion13.

21 Bernstein, "Pope Helped Bring Poland Its Freedom."

22 *Ibid.*

23 Ryan Chilcote, "Gorbachev: Pope was 'example to all of us,'" *CNN.com*, April 4,
    2005, https://www.cnn.com/2005/WORLD/europe/04/03/pope.gorbachev/.

24 Johan Galtung, *Norge sett utenfra* (*Norway Seen from the Outside*) (Oslo: Kagge
    Forlag, 2008).

14: THE FASCIST, THE DICTATOR, THE ASSASSIN & THE HEIR APPARENT

1 Nobelprize.org.

2 *Ibid.*

3 *Ibid.*

4 Christopher Hibbert and John Foot, "Benito Mussolini," Encyclopedia Britannica,
   Inc., July 25, 2020, accessed August 11, 2020, https://www.britannica.com
   /biography/Benito-Mussolini.

5 *Ibid.*

6 *Ibid.*

7 *Ibid.*

8 *Ibid.*

9 *Ibid.*

10 *Ibid.*

11 *Ibid.*

12 Nobelprize.org; Nordlinger, *Peace, They Say*, p. 146.

13 Nobelprize.org.

14 Ronadl Francis Hingley, "Joseph Stalin," Encyclopedia Britannica, Inc., March 27, 2020, accessed August 11, 2020, https://www.britannica.com/biography/Joseph-Stalin.

15 Dan Stone, "How Vladimir Putin became a Nobel Peace Prize Nominee," *National Geographic*, March 6, 2014, https://www.nationalgeographic.com/news /2014/3/140307-putin-nobel-peace-prize-politics-syria/.

16 Pamela Engel, "How Vladimir Putin became one of the most feared leaders in the world," *Business Insider*, February 14, 2017, https://www.businessinsider.com/how -vladimir-putin-rose-to-power-2017-2.

17 International Monetary Fund, imf.org.

18 Sergei Guriev and Aleh Tsyvinski, "Challenges Facing the Russian Economy After the Crisis," in *Russia After the Global Economic Crisis*, eds. Anders Aslund, Sergei Guriev, and Andrew Kuchins (Washington, DC: Peter G. Peterson Institute for International Economics and Center for Strategic and International Studies, 2010).

19 Sarah Rainsford, "Putin strong backed in controversial Russian reform vote," *BBC News*, July 2, 2020, accessed August 11, 2020, https://www.bbc.com/news /world-europe-53255964.

20 Bruno Waterfield, Peter Dominiczak, and David Blair, "Russia Suspended From G8 Club of Rich Countries," *Daily Telegraph*, March 24, 2014.

21 Yulia Gorbunova and Konstantin Baranov, "Laws of Attrition: Crackdown on Russia's Civil Society after Putin's Return to the Presidency," *Human Rights Watch*, April 24, 2013, https://www.hrw.org/report/2013/04/24/laws-attrition /crackdown-russias-civil-society-after-putins-return-presidency.

22 *Ibid.*

23 Abigail Abrams, "Here's What We Know So Far About Russia's 2016 Meddling," *Time* Magazine, April 18, 2019, https://time.com/5565991/russia-influence -2016-election/.

24 Associated Press in Stavanger, "Edward Snowden Nominated for Nobel Peace Prize," *Guardian*, January 29, 2014, https://www.theguardian.com/world/2014 /jan/29/edward-snowden-nominated-nobel-peace-prize.

25 Geoffrey Ingersoll, "Edward Snowden Nominated For Peace Prize," *Business Insider*, January 29, 2014, https://www.businessinsider.com/edward-snowden -nominated-for-peace-prize-2014-1.

15: LIFE AFTER THE PRIZE

1   Marshall Kilduff, "Last Word: A Nobel Peace prize winner disappoints," *San Francisco Chronicle*, December 13, 2019, https://www.sfchronicle.com/opinion /lastword/article/Last-Word-A-Nobel-Peace-prize-winner-disappoints-14905839 .php.

2   *Ibid.*
3   Nobelprize.org; "Kim Dae-jung: Dedicated to reconciliation," CNN, June 14, 2001, https://www.cnn.com/2001/WORLD/asiapcf/east/06/12/bio.kim.daejung/.
4   Nordlinger, *Peace, They Say*, p. 328.
5   Jason Strother, "North Korea threats loom over tension between the US and South Korea," *The World*, December 18, 2019, https://www.pri.org/stories/2019-12-18/north-korea-threats-loom-over-tension-between-us-and-south-korea.

16: THE OTHER SIDE OF THE MEDAL
1   Michael Nobel, "I strid med Nobels vilje" ("Contrary to the Will of Nobel"), *Aftenposten*, December 10, 2011, https://www.aftenposten.no/meninger/i/wP6y1/i-strid-med-nobels-vilje.
2   The Nobel Peace Prize Watch, www.nobelwill.org.
3   "Fredsprisens pris," *NRK Brennpunkt.*
4   Verdens Gang, May 10, 2014, (Vg.no).
5   "Fredsprisens pris," *NRK Brennpunkt.*
6   "The Road to Oslo: the Media Passes Judgement," *Pauling Blog* (blog), November 6, 2013, https://paulingblog.wordpress.com/tag/new-york-times/.

INDEX

—·—

A

Aarvik, Egil, 116, 178
Abbas, Mahmoud, 91, 92
Abdel-Rahman, Omar, 96
abortion, 100–101, 207, 224
Adebajo, Adekeye, 109
Afghanistan, 43, 147, 156, 158, 159
Against Martyrdom Attacks, 199
Ahlsell, Andriette, 3
Ahmad, Q. K., 167
Ahmed, Abiy, 233
Ahtisaari, Martti, 34
Alexander II, 5
Al Gaaeem, Khaled, 43
All-India Muslim Conference, 186
Alterman, Jon, 160
Amano, Yukiya, 153
Amazon, xiv
American Dream, 163
Americans For Peace Now, 76
Amirav, Moshe, 198
Amnesty International, 199, 234, 235
Amristar massacre, 185
Angell, Norman, 38–39
Annan, Kofi, 120, 123, 126–131, 146, 150, 246
anti-Semitism, 69, 82, 134, 215
al-Aqsa Mosque, 91–92
Arafat, Yasser, x, 30, 32, 33, 79–88, 90, 149, 198, 245
Aristide, Jean-Bertrand, 149
arms industry: Nobel and, 2; in Norway, 39–40, 44
Arusha Accords, 122
Ash, Timothy Garton, 207, 208
Ashrawi, Hanan, 199
al-Assad, Bashar, 221, 224

Astrup, Nicolai, 26
atomic bomb, 2, 73
"Atoms for Peace" speech, 150
Aung San Suu Kyi, xi
Ayalon, Ami, 199
Azango, Mae, 111

B

Bangladesh, 162–164, 167, 170, 173–175
Bangura, Zainab Hawa, 126
Banker to the Poor (Yunnus), 163
Barnett, Michael, 123, 124, 125
Bateman, Milford, 165–166, 169
Battle of San Juan Hill, 53
Becker, Elisabeth, 137
Begin, Menachem, 32–33, 93–96, 147, 233
Begum, Narunnahar, 164
Begum, Sufiya, 164
Belo, Carlos Filipe Ximenes, 245
Beloff, Max, 90, 96
Berge, Gunnar, 128, 146, 148, 149–150, 240
Berglund, Nina, 43
Berlin Wall, 208, 209
Berner, Carl Christian, 95
Bezos, Jeff, xiv
Bildt, Carl, 246
bin Laden, Osama, 96
birth control, 207
Bjørnson, Bjørnstjerne, 20, 23, 247
Black September, 84
Blair, Tony, 253
Blix, Hans, 151
blue berets. *See* UN Peacekeeping Forces
Bøås, Morten, 112
Boer War, 181–182, 184, 186
Bojaxhiu, Agnes Gonxha. *See* Mother Teresa

Bolkovac, Kathryn, 126
Bonner, Yelena, 90
Boot, Max, 116
Bosco, David, 118
Bose, Subhas Chandra, 189
Bosnia, 120–121, 126
Bosnian War, 60, 120–121
Boston Research Center for the 21st Century, 194–195
Boulding, Elise, 195
Brandt, E. G. C., 218
Brende, Børge, 29
Brennpunkt, 163–164, 168, 170, 171, 174, 175, 176
Briand, Aristide, 61, 62, 64
British Empire, 180, 181, 184, 189, 190
British Raj, 185, 186, 188–189
Brown, Gordon, 238
Brundtland, Gro Harlem, 30
Bryce, James, 56
Buller, Redvers, 182
Bunche, Ralph, 203
Burgos-Debray, Elisabeth, 104
Burma. *See* Myanmar
Bush, George H. W., 116
Bush, George W., 128, 145–148, 150–151, 153–157, 209

C
California, 53–54
Cambodia, 137–139, 142, 144
Cambridge Analytica, xiv
Camp David Accords, 32–33, 93–96, 147, 149
Carl (prince), 54
Carter, Jimmy, 33, 75, 93, 147–150, 157
Carter Center, 149
Cassin, René, 130
caste system, of India, 187
Castro, Fidel, 149, 202
Catholic Church, 204–205
Cédras, Raoul, 148
celebrities, 252
Centesimus Annus, 208–209
Central American Court of Justice, 55
Central American Peace Conference, 55
Central Pacific Railroad, 6
Chamberlain, Austen, 60, 61, 62
Chamberlain, Joseph, 181
Chamberlain, Neville, 218
Chang, Ha-Joon, 169, 176

Chazov, Yevgeny I., 75
Chénard, Geneviève, 101
Chesler, Phyllis, 98
China, xv, 28–29, 157–158, 160
Christmas Bombing, 138–139
Churchill, Winston, 38, 39, 71
Clark, Bronson P., 142–143
climate change, 154–155
Clinton, Bill, 87, 116, 154, 173
Clinton, Hillary, 164–165, 172, 225–226, 246, 249
Cold War, 24, 26, 73, 75, 116, 117, 131, 140, 144, 209, 220
Colombia, 43
Colton, Timothy J., 223
Committee of the Peasant Union (CUC), 103, 104
Communism, 73, 207–208
Communist Party, 219
conflicts of interest, 25, 26, 27, 130–131
Congress of Leaders of World and Traditional Religions, 206
Congress Party, 189
Conquest, Robert, 221
Conservative Party (Norway), 26, 42, 246
Coolidge, Calvin, 62–63
Corinth Canal, 6
Cotecna, 127–128
Counts, Alex, 166–167
courage, 53
COVID-19 pandemic, xv
Cox, Michael, 73
Crimea, 224, 226
Cuba, 52, 55
Cuban Missile Crisis, 202–203
Czechoslovakia, 60, 218, 220

D
Dae-jung, Kim, x
Dahlan, Mohammed, 86
Dalai Lama, 28–29, 30
Dalen, Erik, 42
Dallaire, Roméo, 130
Dallek, Robert, 134, 136
Daoud, Abu, 84
Darfur, 130
Davidson, Daniel, 135–136
Dawes, Charles G., 60–63
Dawes Plan, 60–61
de Gaulle, Charles, 131

demilitarization, 74
democracy, 109, 113, 149, 163, 212, 225, 234
Democratic Republic of the Congo, 118
Denmark, 20, 38
Desai, Mahadev Haribhai, 185
deterrent effect of arms, 2, 15, 19, 24, 46, 53,
    71, 74, 134
Dichter, Thomas, 163, 170, 172
disarmament, 14, 19, 40, 46, 48, 116, 159, 243
distrust, xiv, 249–250
Doe, Samuel, 107, 109
drones, 158, 159, 195
Dunant, Henry, 178
du Pont, Henry, 6
Du Pont de Nemours, 6
Durant, Henri, 68
Duvalier, Jean-Claude, 101–102, 205, 207
dynamite, 177; intended uses of, 6, 40;
    invention of, 1–5; violence and, 5–6

E
East Timor, 245
Ebadi, Shirin, 209
Edward VII, 54
Egypt, 93–94, 147, 148, 206
Einstein, Albert, 2, 192
Eisenhower, Dwight, 150
ElBaradei, Mohamed, 150–153
election process, 30–33
Elizabeth II, 205
Ellick, Adam B., 237
Ellis, Stephen, 108
El Salvador, 118
environment, 47, 67, 154–156, 248, 251
Erekay, Saeb, 198
Ethiopia, 214–215, 216, 233
Europe: Marshall Plan and, 41, 73–74; united,
    208
European Council, 27
extremist groups, 201, 249

F
Facebook, xiv
Facta, Luigi, 214
FARC (Revolutionary Armed Forces of
    Colombia), 43
Fascism, 211
Feffer, John, 159
female recipients, 97–114
female role models, 98, 100, 112, 114, 165

Fernando, Jude, 165
Finkelstein, Norman, 76–77
First Gulf War, 198, 199
Ford, Gerald, 144
Fourteen Points, 57–58
France, xv, 64
Frängsmyr, Tore, 1, 6

G
Gaddhafi, Mu'ammar, 131, 152–153
Galtung, Johan, 209
Gandhi, Mahatma, xv, 177–192, 193
Gaza Strip, 82, 84, 85, 87, 92, 157, 199
Gbowee, Leymah, 33
gender inequality, 97–98
Geneva Accords, 140
genocides, 76–77, 120–125, 130, 233
Gentlemen's Agreement, 55
Geremek, Bronislaw, 207
Gerhardsen, Einar, 41–42
Germany: Dawes Plan and, 60–61; Nazi,
    25, 28, 68, 71, 215, 217–218, 220; Soviet
    Union and, 73; Versailles Treaty and,
    58–60, 249; World War I and, 57; World
    War II and, 65
girls' education, 237, 239
global warming, 154–156
Gokhale, Gopal Krishna, 183–184
Gold, Dore, 123
good-neighbor policy, 70
Gorbachev, Mikhail, 195, 208
Gore, Al, x, 47, 154–156, 226
Government Pension Fund Global, 41, 44
Grameen Bank, 161–176
Grameen Kalyan, 174–175
greedy leadership, xiv
Greenwald, Glenn, 228
Griffith, Courtenay, 109, 110
Guantánamo Bay prison, 157, 158
Gulf of Tonkin Resolution, 135
gunpowder, 5, 6

H
Habyarimana, Juvénal, 122
Haig, Alexander, 138
Haiti, 149, 205, 207
Haldeman, H. R., 134
Hale, Henry E., 223
Hamas, 80, 90, 92
Hambro, C. J., 71

Hamilton, Adrian, 90
Hammarskjöld, Dag, 33, 76, 192, 201
Hanson, Jessica, 111
Hansson, Rasmus, 40
Harper, Malcom, 172
Heffermehl, Fredrik, xi, 18, 24–25, 34, 46, 49,
    210, 243, 244
Heineman, Tom, 163
Helland, Linda Hofstad, 246
Hellevik, Ottar, 42, 45
Herzegovina, 120–121
Hess, Sofie, 11–12, 19, 241–242
Hezbollah, 91, 129
Hillary Village, 164–165
Hiroshima, 2, 73
Hitchens, Christopher, 101, 102, 139
Hitler, Adolf, xi, 59, 73, 155, 215–218, 220,
    224, 249
Holocaust, 68, 74–77, 81
Holy Land, 81–82. See also Israel; Jerusalem
Hong Kong, xv
Houston, Anjelica, 172
Howar, Barbara, 136
Hugo, Victor, 7
Hull, Cordell, 24, 69–71, 78, 115
human dignity, 251–252
humanitarian work, 47, 67–69, 99–102, 123,
    193, 250, 251
human rights, 67, 75, 103, 248, 251
humiliation, 249
Humphrey, Hubert, 134
Hussein, Saddam, 127, 147, 151, 153
Husseini, Faisal, 198
Hutus, 121–125

I
I, Rigoberta Menchú (Menchú), 104–105
idealism, 2, 210
Ikeda, Daisaku, 194–196
immigration, 225
An Inconvenient Truth, 155
India, 240; caste system in, 187; Gandhi and,
    177–192; microfinance and, 171–172;
    partition of, 190–191; World War II and,
    190–191
Indian National Congress, 184, 188, 189, 190
Indochina War, 140
Indonesia, 166–167, 245
Institute of Oriental Philosophy, 195
interest rates, on microloans, 169

Intergovernmental Panel on Climate Change,
    47, 154–156
International Academy of Spiritual Unity and
    Cooperation of Peoples of the World, 222,
    226
International Association of Lawyers against
    Nuclear Arms, 47
International Atomic Energy Agency (IAEA),
    150–153
International Campaign to Abolish Nuclear
    Weapons (ICAN), 245
International Committee of the Red Cross
    (ICRC), 68–69
International Court of Arbitration, 53
International Court of Justice, 233
International Parliamentary Union, 115
International Peace Bureau, 47
International Physicians for the Prevention of
    Nuclear War, 47, 75–76
Intifada, 81, 85, 86, 89–90, 197, 199
Iran, 131, 150, 152, 158
Iraq, 127, 147, 150, 151, 159, 198
Iraq War, 209
Irgun Zvai Leumi, 94
Islam, 173
Islamic State, 201, 224, 249
isolation, 248–249
Israel, 42, 76, 82, 85–88, 91, 95–96, 129, 147,
    148, 153, 157
Israeli-Hezbollah War, 91
Israeli-Palestinian conflict, 76, 77, 80–96, 148,
    157, 196–201
Italy, 211–216
"It's All in the Game" (Dawes), 63

J
Jagland, Thorbjørn, 27, 34, 108, 156–157, 159,
    246
Jahn, Gunnar, 48, 49, 70, 73, 203
Jallianwala Bagh massacre, 185
Japan, 41, 55, 64, 65, 73
Jaruzelski, Wojciech, 208
Jerusalem, 76, 91–92, 206
Jewish refugees, 69–70
Jews, 70–71, 82, 83, 87, 91, 94, 134, 200, 215,
    217. See also anti-Semitism; Israel
Jinnah, Muhammad Ali, 190, 191
John Paul II, 204–210, 235
Johnson, Lyndon, 135–136
Judt, Tony, 208

K

Kabir, Khushi, 168, 170
Kamara, Abdullai, 109
Kanafani, Ghassan, 84
Kanoe, Musa, 111
Karman, Tawakkul, 33
Karolinska Institute, ix, 19
Kazakhstan, 206
Keating, Charles, 102
Kellogg, Frank B., 63–65
Kellogg-Briand Pact, 64–65
Kennedy, John F., 201–202
Kennedy-Pipe, Caroline, 73
Kerry, John, 91
Khilafat movement, 186
Khmer Rouge, 139
Khrushchev, Nikita, 202
kibbutz, 197
Kilduff, Marshall, 233–234
Kim Dae-jung, 234–237
Kim Il-sung, 149
Kim Jong-il, 236
King, Martin Luther, Jr., 192
Kinsky, Bertha. *See* von Suttner, Bertha
Kirkpatrick, Jean, 131
Kissinger, Henry, x, 24, 32, 75, 133–144, 233
Kjenseth, Ketil, 30
Klein, Joe, 158
Kohl, Helmut, 77
Koht, Halvdan, 25, 218, 220
Korean War, 74
Kristiansen, Kare, 32, 80, 81, 89
Kuwait, 123, 127, 151
Kwasniewski, Aleksander, 208

L

Labor Party (Norway), 26, 41–42, 85
Laghi, Pio, 209
Laos, 138, 142
Law of Gender Equality, 97
Law of Jante, 160
Lay Down Your Arms (von Suttner), 10, 13–14
leadership: current model of, 249–250; greedy, xiv; lack of trust in, xiv; values and, 250–251
League of Nations, 56, 57–58, 60, 61, 69, 115
Lebanon, 95–96
Le Duc Tho, 32, 133, 139, 140–143, 144, 233
Lee, Bruce Y., 248
Lehne, Hans Frederik, 174

Lenin, Vladimir, 219, 221
Liberia, 106–112
Libya, 43, 131, 152–153, 159
Lie, Tove, 39
Liedbeck, Alarik, 9
Limited Test Ban Treaty, 112
Lionaes, Aase, 140, 141, 143
Lithuania, 59
Litvinenko, Alexander, 225
Locarno Treaties, 60, 61–62
Lomberg, Bjøn, 155
loneliness, 248
Løvland, Jørgen, 54
lower-class citizens, rage of, xv
Lunde, Leiv, 43
Lundestad, Geir, xiii, xiv, 22–23, 29, 48, 49, 105–106, 147, 179, 192, 209, 247

M

Maathai, Wangari, x, 47
MacArthur, Douglas, 74
Machel, Graça, 125
Macron, Emmanuel, xv
madman theory, 137
Magnusson, Tomas, 244
Mahajan, Vijay, 171
Maidan, Gowalia Tank, 190
Malraux, André, 195
Mandela, Nelson, 192, 235
Marcus, Ruth, 158–159
marriage, 9
Marshall, George C., 41, 71–74
Marshall Plan, 41, 73–74, 78, 140
Marx, Karl, 211, 219
Massey, Elie-Georges, 128
Mazowiecki, Tadeusz, 121
McCarthy, Colman, 117
McKinley, William, 54–55
Medvedev, Dmitry, 223
"Melody in A Major" (Dawes), 63
Menchù, Rigoberta, x, 102–106, 126, 233
Merkel, Angela, 239
Meuse-Argonne Offensive, 72
Mexico, 53–54
microcredit, 161–176
middle class, rage of, xv
Middle East conflict, 42–43, 76, 77, 80–96, 148, 158, 196–201
military intervention, 47
Min-On Concert Association, 195

Mjøs, Ole Danbolt, 34, 150, 153, 154, 173
Mladic, Ratko, 120
mobile phones, 166–167
Moe, Ragnvald, 55
Molotov-Ribbentrop Pact, 220
Moneta, Ernesto Teodoro, 38
Monroe Doctrine, 65
Morduch, Jonathan, 171, 174
Morgenthau, Henry, Jr., 70
Morris, Roger, 136, 139, 140
Morrow, Lance, 149
Mother Teresa, 99–102, 178, 207
Mountbatten Plan, 191
Mowinckel, Johan Ludwig, 25, 58
Mozambique, 118
Mueller, Robert, 226
Mugabe, Robert, 131
Munich Agreement, 218
Municipal Act, 97
Murray, Gilbert, 183
Murthy, Vivek, 248
Muslim Brotherhood, 80, 83
Muslim League, 190–191
Muslims, 76, 91, 120, 121, 180, 186, 188,
    205–206
Mussolini, Benito, 64, 212–216
Myanmar, xiv, 232–234

N
Nagasaki, 2, 73
Naidoo, Kumi, 234
Narayana, K. Venkat, 172
Natal Indian Congress, 181
National League for Democracy (NLD), 232
National Patriotic Front of Liberia (NPFL),
    109, 110
National Security Agency (NSA), 227, 228
Nazabayev, Nursultan, 206
Nazi Germany, 25, 28, 68, 71, 215, 217–218,
    220
Nehru, Jawaharlal, 188, 189
Nemesis (Nobel), 144, 241
Nemtsov, Boris, 225
Netanyahu, Benjamin, 91
Night (Wiesel), 74–75
nitroglycerine, 3, 4
Nixon, Richard, 131, 134–138, 142, 143–144
Njølstad, Olav, 23
Nobel, Alfred, 17, 145, 231; Bertha and,
    9–11, 13–15, 98; business success of, 6–7;

conditions of peace prize set by, x–xi; death
    of, 15; early life of, 3–4; generosity of,
    12–13, 241–242; on guns, 67; on honesty,
    133; on hope, 79; intentions of, xv, 1–3,
    19, 34–35, 45–46, 48–49, 51–52, 68, 161,
    178, 242–243, 249; invention of dynamite
    by, 1–5, 40, 177; on justice, 193; on
    nationality of candidates, 97; Nemesis, 144,
    241; in Paris, 7–11; personal life of, 7–12,
    14–15; public image of, 6–7; values of, 106,
    250–251; on war, 51, 211; will of, 15, 17–19,
    20, 34, 48, 193–194, 242, 245, 259–262;
    women and, 98
Nobel, Emil, 4
Nobel, Immanuel, 3
Nobel, Ludvig, xiv, 2
Nobel, Michael, xiv, 2; on Alfred, 15; on
    dynamite, 3; on Lundestad, 23; on Nobel
    Committee, 25, 27, 34–35, 48–49, 247; on
    Peace Prize, 20, 243–244
Nobel Assembly, ix
Nobel Family Society, ix
Nobel Foundation, 18, 21, 22, 30, 34, 48–49,
    244–245, 253
Nobel Institute, 21–22, 194
Nobel Memorial Prize in Economic Sciences, ix
Nobel Peace Center, 22
Nobel Peace Prize: awarding of, ix–xi, 19,
    30–33; controversial choices for, x, xi,
    xiii–xiv, 25–26, 28–30, 32, 52–65, 80–86,
    89–93; as corrupt, xiii; criteria for, 45–46,
    161; erosion of trust in, 80; legally binding
    basis for, 243–245; Nobel's intention for,
    xv, 1–3, 19, 34–35, 45–46, 48–49, 51–52,
    68, 161, 178, 242–243, 249; nominations
    for, 30–32, 211–230; Norway and, 20–21,
    38–39, 41, 44; overlooked peace champions
    and, 193–210; prestige of, xiii; purpose
    of, 161–162, 193; reasons for creation of,
    1–3, 14; as reprimand, 145–160; restoring
    meaning to, 248–250, 252–253; selection
    process for, 37, 194; United Nations and,
    115–131; widening of, 251–252. See also
    Nobel Peace Prize recipients
Nobel Peace Prize Committee, x, 15; choices
    by, xiii–xiv; composition of, 21–24,
    26–27, 247; conflicts of interest and, 25,
    26, 27; director/secretary, 22–23; divisive
    leadership by, xv–xvi; election of members
    to, 24–25, 26, 246; evaluation of, 3;

ignoring of Nobel's intentions by, 51–52,
   178, 193–194, 243–245, 252; inconsistent
   choices by, 67–78; independence of, 22–23,
   25, 27, 29–30, 32, 40, 45, 246–247;
   nomination process of, 30–32; Norwegian
   government and, 38–39, 41, 44, 246–247;
   peace champions overlooked by, 193–210;
   political considerations of, 133–144,
   209–210; prize criteria and, 45–46, 48–49;
   secrecy of decisions of, 17–35, 49, 108, 194,
   195; UN and, 146–147; U.S. government
   and, 63, 146–147, 151, 153
Nobel Peace Prize recipients: controversial,
   x, xi, xiii–xiv, 25–26, 28–30, 32, 52–65,
   80–86, 89–93; election process of, 30–33,
   253; female, 97–114; life after prize for,
   231–240; list of, 255–258; politically
   motivated, 24, 54, 56, 65, 79–96, 133–144.
   See also specific recipients
Nobel Peace Prize Watch, 244
Nobel Prizes: awarding of, ix–x, 19–20;
   establishment of, 18–19. See also Nobel
   Peace Prize
nominations, 30–32, 211–212, 229–230
nonviolence, 182, 185, 187, 189, 200
Nordlinger, Jay, 34, 43, 81, 86, 125, 146–147,
   151, 156, 221, 246, 252
North Korea, 74, 131, 153, 234–235, 236
North Vietnam, 133, 135–141
Norway, 20–21, 24, 28–30, 35; China and,
   157–158; economy of, 41–42; foreign
   policy of, 52, 54, 78, 144, 209, 210; group
   culture in, 44–45, 49; Israeli-Palestinian
   conflict and, 85; liberation of, 220;
   Nobel Peace Prize and, 38–39, 41, 44,
   246–247; peace negotiations by, 42–43;
   post-war reconstruction of, 41–42, 45, 140;
   promotion of women by, 97–98; society of,
   44–45; United Nations and, 116; United
   States and, 54, 56, 60, 63, 65, 78, 140, 146;
   weapons industry in, 39–40, 44
Norwegian Agency for Development
   Cooperation (NORAD), 174–175
Norwegian Dream, 163
Norwegian exceptionalism, 37–49, 246
Norwegian Nobel Committee. See Nobel Peace
   Prize Committee
Norwegian Parliament, 21, 24–26
Norwegian Storting (Parliament), 19, 28–30,
   38, 40, 48, 243, 246–247

Ntaryamira, Cyprien, 122
nuclear weapons, 41, 47, 73, 75, 131, 134,
   150–153, 157, 226, 245
Nusseibeh, Sari, 196–201
Nybakk, Marit, 108

O
Obama, Barack, x, 29, 32, 34, 47, 91, 156–160,
   173
Oil-for-Food Program, 127–128
Oil Fund. See Government Pension Fund
   Global
ØKOKRIM, 244
Oman, 40
open door policy, 55
Orr, John Boyd, 251
Oscar II, 18, 20
Oslo Accords, 32
Oslo Peace Accord, 33, 42–43, 79, 81, 85,
   87–93
Ossietzky, Carl von, 25–26, 28, 32, 216
Ottoman Empire, 186
Oudeh, Mohammed, 84

P
Pachauri, Rajendra, 154–155
Pact of Paris, 64–65
Pakistan, 159, 191, 237–240
Palestine, 42
Palestinian Liberation Organization (PLO),
   80–86, 87, 90
Palestinians, 157. See also Israeli-Palestinian
   conflict
Paris, France, 7–9
Paris Accords, 139–143
Passy, Frédéric, 115
Patel, Vallabhbhai, 184
Pauling, Linus, 248
peace, defining, 251–253
peace champions: Norway as, 40; overlooked,
   193–210; selection of, xiii–xiv. See also
   Nobel Peace Prize recipients
Peace Congress, 14
peace congresses, 46–47
peace education, 113
Peace Women Across the Globe (PWAG), 112
Pelouze, Théophile-Jules, 3–4
The People's Voice campaign, 199–200
Peres, Shimon, 30, 32, 33, 79, 88–89
Peres Center for Peace, 89

Pérez de Cuéllar, Javier, 251
Permanent American-Canadian Joint High
    Commission, 56
Pershing, John J., 72
Persian Gulf War, 87, 151, 208
Pharo, Helge, 22–23
Pillalamarri, Akhilesh, 239–240
Pious Fund, 53–54
Poitras, Laura, 228
Poland, 60, 65, 207, 208, 209, 220
politicians, 24–27, 133
Pol Pot, 139
Portsmouth Treaty, 52, 53
poverty, 162, 163, 166, 167, 170, 172, 173,
    175–176, 251
presidential election, xiv, 154, 225–226, 249
Progressive Party (Norway), 26
Proliferation Security Initiative, 153
protest movements, xv
Putin, Vladimir, 221–226

Q
al-Qaeda, 96, 128, 145–146, 209, 249
Quanza, 70
Quit India protest, 190

R
Rabin, Yitzhak, 30, 32, 33, 79–80, 86–88, 90
Rajan, Sudhir Chella, 123
Ramos-Horta, José, 245
rape, 110–111, 131
Rawat, Mukesh, 251
Reagan, Ronald, 75, 77
realism, 210
Reardon, Betty, 113
Red Cross, 68–69
religion, 186, 204–205, 206
remorse, as motivator for peace prize, 2
Resolution 1325 on Women, Peace and
    Security, 113
Rieger, Wladyslaw, 220–221
Robinson, Mary, 157
robot-warfare, 47
Rockefeller, Nelson, 134
Roodman, David, 169, 170–171, 175–176
Roosevelt, Eleanor, 70, 130
Roosevelt, Franklin D., 69, 70, 72
Roosevelt, Theodore, 24, 52–54, 55
Root, Elihu, 54–56
Rosove, John, 198

Rotblat, Joseph, 195
Rough Riders, 53
Rowlatt Acts, 185
Rubio, Marco, 225
Ruch, Phillip, 130
Rudbeck, Olof, 3
Rummel, Rudolph J., 221
Russia, 146, 160, 221–226
Russian Revolution, 218, 219
Russo-Japanese War, 52
Rwanda, 121–125, 129, 130

S
Sadat, Anwar, 32–33, 93–96, 147
Sahgal, Gita, 125–126
Saint Gotthard Tunnel, 6
Sakharov, Andrei, 90
Salam, Abdus, 164
Salt March, 189
Santos, Juan Manual, 43
Sarkozy, Nicolas, 156
Satyarthi, Kailash, 239
Schwartz, Berthold, 5
Second Boer War, 181–182
secrecy, in selection process, 17–35, 37, 49, 108,
    194, 195
Segev, Tom, 77
Sejersted, Francis, 80, 89, 245
self-defense, 65
September 11, 2001, 145, 146, 173, 206, 209,
    236
Serbs, 120–121
Sevan, Benon, 128
sexual violence, 125–126
Sharansky, Nathan, 158
Simon, John, 188–189
Sirleaf, Ellen Johnson, 33, 106–112, 226, 245
Sitton, Ray, 138
Smuts, Jan Christian, 182–183
Snowden, Edward, 226–229
Snyder, Timothy, 220
Sobrero, Ascanio, 4
social protests, xv
Sohlman, Michael, ix
Sohlman, Ragnar, 18
Soka Gakkai, 194
Solberg, Erna, 29
Solheim, Erik, 29, 30, 246
Solhjell, Baard Vegar, 228
Solidarity, 207–208

Somalia, 118, 119, 125, 130, 159
South Africa, 180–183
South Korea, 74, 234–237
South Vietnam, 135, 137–139, 141, 142, 143
Soviet Union, 24, 73, 116, 140, 144, 202,
    218–221
Spanish-American War, 52, 53, 54–55
SS *St. Louis*, 69–70
Stalin, Joseph, xi, 65, 218–221, 224
Stang, Fredrik, 28
Stanghelle, Harald, 28, 30
Stevenson, Adlai, 202
Stimson, Henry L., 55
Stoll, David, 104
Stoltenberg, Jens, 174
Stone, Sharon, 172
Støre, Jonas Gahr, 247
Strand, Tove, 175
Stresemann, Gustav, 62
Strindberg, August, 2, 5
subprime mortgage crisis, 171–172
Sudan, 130–131
Sudetenland, 60
suicide, microdebt and, 170–172
Sunshine Policy, 234–235, 236, 237
Suu Kyi, Aung San, 232–234, 240
Swaraj Party, 188
Sweden, 20, 21, 38, 54
Swedish Academy, 19–20
Swedish Academy of Science, ix, 19
Swedish Central Bank, ix
Swedish Foundations Act, 48, 244, 253
Swedish Law of Foundations, 243
Syria, 131, 153, 159, 221, 222, 224
Syse, Henrik, 26, 27, 246

T
Taliban, 43, 237–238
tandemocracy, 223
Taylor, Charles, 107, 108, 109–110
terrorism, 5, 84, 86, 90–91, 94, 123, 128, 129,
    145, 146, 209
testaments, 47–48
Thune, Henrik, 43
Thuy, Xuan, 135–136
Tito, Josip, 149
Toda Institute for Global Peace and Policy
    Research, 195
Tokyo Fuji Art Museum, 195
Tonnesson, Oyvind, 20–21

Treaty of Paris, 52
Trotsky, Leon, 219
Truman, Harry S., 73
Trump, Donald, 91, 160, 225–226, 230, 249
trust, 249–250; lack of, xiv
Truth and Reconciliation Commission
    (Liberia), 107, 111–112
Tunisian National Dialogue Quartet, 245
Tutsis, 121–125
Tutu, Desmond, xiii, 76, 126, 130, 238
Twatzinze, Jean-Pierre, 123

U
Ukraine, 224, 226
Umayyad Mosque, 206
UN Charter, 69
UN Commission on the Status of Women, 131
UN Disarmament Commission, 131
UN High Commissioner for Refugees, 115
UN Human Rights Council, 130–131
United Nations, 69–71, 115–131; conflicting
    interest of, 130–131; criticism of, 131;
    Department of Peacekeeping Operations,
    123; IAEA and, 150–153; Kofi Annan and,
    126–131; moral relativism of, 123; Nobel
    Committee and, 146–147
United Nations Children's Fund (UNICEF),
    115, 203
United States, 24, 41, 43; climate change and,
    155; Cold War and, 75, 116, 140; Cuban
    Missile Crisis, 202–203; foreign policy of,
    55–56, 70; IPCC and, 154–156; Iraq War
    and, 209; Israeli-Palestinian conflict and,
    91; Jewish refugees and, 69–70; Monroe
    Doctrine, 65; Nobel Committee and, 151,
    153; Norway and, 54, 56, 60, 63, 65, 78;
    peace prize as reprimand to, 145–160;
    Spanish-American War, 52, 53, 54–55;
    subprime mortgage crisis in, 171–172;
    United Nations and, 128, 146; Vietnam
    War and, 112–113, 135, 137–139, 141–143;
    War on Terror and, 146, 147, 151, 236;
    during World War II, 72–74
UN Peacekeeping Forces, 116–126; in Bosnia,
    120–121; cost of, 117–118; role of, 117; in
    Rwanda, 121–125; sexual violence and,
    125–126; in Somalia, 119, 125; successes
    of, 118
UN Security Council, 113, 117, 123, 131, 152
U Thant, 201–204

V

Valen, Snorre, 228
values, 250–251
Varagur, Krithika, 101
Versailles Treaty, 25, 57–60, 61, 217, 249
Victor Emmanuel III, 214, 216
Viet Minh, 140
Vietnam War, 112–113, 135, 137–139,
    141–143
Volcker, Paul, 127, 128
von Suttner, Arthur, 9, 11
von Suttner, Bertha, 3, 242; Alfred and, 9–11,
    13–15, 98; establishment of Peace Prize
    and, 19; Peace Prize awarded to, 15, 98;
    peace work of, 13–14, 46

W

Wachsman, Nachshon, 80
Walesa, Lech, 76, 207, 209
war: causes of, 56; outlawing of, 64–65;
    prevention of, 2
war economy, 47
War on Terror, 146, 147, 151, 236
Watergate scandal, 134, 143–144
weapons: deterrent effect of, 2, 24, 46, 53, 71,
    74, 134; nuclear, 41, 47, 53, 75, 131, 134,
    150–153, 157, 226, 245
weapons industry, in Norway, 39–40, 44
Weiss, Cora, 112–113
Wergeland, Henrik, 37
West Bank, 82, 84, 85, 87, 91, 199
Western Wall, 206
whistleblowers, 47

Wiesel, Elie, 74–77
Wiesenthal, Simon, 77
Williams, Jody, 126–127
Willoch, Kåre, 247
Wilson, Woodrow, 56, 57–60, 61, 115
Woewiyu, Tom, 110
Wojtyla, Karol. See John Paul II
Wolpert, Stanley, 191
women: Gandhi's support for, 187; in Iran,
    131; microfinance and, 172, 174; Peace
    Prize recipients, 97–114; promotion of, by
    Norwegian government, 97–98
Women Strike for Peace, 112
World Economic Forum, xv, 155
World War I, 25, 33, 56–57, 62, 64, 184, 186
World War II, 24, 33, 61, 65, 71–74, 190–191,
    215, 217, 219–220

X

Xiaobo, Liu, x, 28, 29, 30, 158

Y

Yellow Vest protests, xv
Yeltsin, Boris, 222
Yemen, 159
Yousafzai, Malala, x, 47, 226, 237–240
Yugoslavia, 60, 118, 120
Yunus, Muhammad, 160, 161–176, 226, 245

Z

al-Zawahiri, Ayman, 96
Zuckerberg, Mark, xiv
Zumach, Andreas, 124